Blue Prints

Tiso

Fundamentals of Financial Management
Concise
Fourth Edition

Eugene F. Brigham

University of Florida

Joel F. Houston

University of Florida

THOMSON

SOUTH-WESTERN

Australia · Canada · Mexico · Singapore · Spain · United Kingdom · United States

THOMSON
✶
™
SOUTH-WESTERN

Blue Prints for **Fundamentals of Financial Management, Concise, 4e**

Eugene F. Brigham and Joel F. Houston

Editorial Director:
Jack W. Calhoun

Editor-in-Chief:
Michael P. Roche

Executive Editor:
Michael R. Reynolds

Developmental Editor:
Elizabeth R. Thomson

Senior Marketing Manager:
Charlie Stutesman

Senior Production Editor:
Kara ZumBahlen

Manufacturing Coordinator:
Sandee Milewski

Printer:
Edwards Brothers, Ann Arbor, MI

For more information
contact South-Western,
5191 Natorp Boulevard,
Mason, Ohio 45040.
Or you can visit our Internet site at:
http://www.swlearning.com

ISBN: 0-324-26984-6

PREFACE

Blueprints has become an integral part of the material we provide to students. At the University of Florida, we teach a large class, with upwards of 1,000 students each semester. This large class size forces us to lecture, even though we prefer discussion-oriented classes. To get the students more involved, we have developed a set of integrated cases which cover the key points in each chapter and which we use as the basis for our lectures. For our classes, we use the computer slide show to present the material that is summarized in each integrated case. Early on, students began asking us to make copies of the slides available to them. We did so, and that improved the class considerably. With paper copies of the slides, students could focus on what was being said in the lecture without having to copy things down for later review. *Blueprints* includes a copy of each integrated case, copies of the slides, space to write down additional notes, and extra exam-type problems for each chapter.

We consider the current version quite complete. However, the <u>optimal</u> product varies from instructor to instructor, depending on how the class is conducted. Therefore, instructors are encouraged to modify *Blueprints* to suit their own styles and interests. For example, if one covers chapters in a different order, or does not cover certain chapters, or covers only part of some chapters, or has additional materials not covered in the text, or anything else, the *Blueprints* chapters can be rearranged, added to or subtracted from, or modified in any other way.

Students always want copies of old exams. Also, we have review sessions, conducted by TAs, and those sessions are devoted to working exam-type problems. So, we have included a number of exam-type problems at the end of each *Blueprints* chapter. Students work them on their own or else go to review sessions where the TAs work them. The solutions for these exam-type problems are provided at the end of the last *Blueprints* chapter.

Instructors can use *Blueprints* in conjunction with the computer slide show, which is based on the integrated cases. Also, we frequently use the blackboard, both to explain the calculations that lie behind some of the numbers and to provide different examples. Our students end up with lots of marginal notes that clarify various points.

One thing has become crystal clear over the years—the best lecture notes, and materials related thereto, are instructor-specific. It is difficult to use someone else's notes verbatim. However, there is no point in reinventing the wheel, and if the *Blueprints* wheel fits a particular instructor's wagon, he or she might do well to use it, spending time adapting it to his or her own style and coverage rather than taking the time to develop lecture notes de novo. Therefore, you are encouraged to look over the *Blueprints* package, decide if and how you might use it, and then go to it. If you are like us, you will change things from semester to semester—there is no such thing as static optimality!

If you do use the package, and find some modifications that work well for you, we would very much appreciate hearing from you—your modifications might well help us and others.

Eugene F. Brigham
Joel F. Houston

Houston & Associates
4723 N.W. 53rd Ave., Suite A
Gainesville, FL 32606
e-mail address: concise@joelhouston.com

February 2003

SUGGESTIONS FOR STUDENTS USING BLUEPRINTS

1.   Read the textbook chapter first, going through the entire chapter rapidly. Don't expect to understand everything on this first reading, but do try to get a good idea of what the chapter covers, the key terms, and the like. <u>It is useful to read the chapter before the first lecture on it.</u>

2.   You could also read the *Blueprints* chapter material before class, but that is not necessary.

3.   *Blueprints* was designed as the basis for a lecture—the most important material in each chapter is covered, and the material most likely to give you trouble is emphasized. As your instructor goes through *Blueprints*, you should (1) see what we regard as the most important material and (2) get a better feel for how to think about issues and work relevant problems.

4.   You could read *Blueprints*, in connection with the text, and get a reasonably good idea of what is going on in the course. However, the real value of *Blueprints* is as a vehicle to help the class lecture make more sense and to help you get a good set of notes. In class, your instructor will discuss various points raised in *Blueprints* and elaborate on different issues. Also, he or she will explain how formulas are used, where data in tables come from, and the like. <u>You will end up with lots of marginal notes on your copy if you use *Blueprints* as it is supposed to be used.</u> Indeed, these marginal notes will constitute your class notes.

BLUEPRINTS

Table of Contents

1-1   Kato Summers opened Take a Dive 17 years ago; the store is located in Malibu, California, and sells surfing-related equipment. Today, Take a Dive has 50 employees including Kato and his daughter Amber, who works part time in the store to help pay for her college education.

Kato's business has boomed in recent years, and he is looking for new ways to take advantage of his increasing business opportunities. Although Kato's formal business training is limited, Amber will soon graduate with a degree in finance. Kato has offered her the opportunity to join the business as a full-fledged partner. Amber is interested, but she is also considering other career opportunities in finance.

Right now, Amber is leaning toward staying with the family business, partly because she thinks it faces a number of interesting challenges and opportunities. Amber is particularly interested in further expanding the business and then incorporating it. Kato is intrigued by her ideas, but he is also concerned that her plans might change the way in which he does business. In particular, Kato has a strong commitment to social activism, and he has always tried to strike a balance between work and pleasure. He is worried that these goals will be compromised if the company incorporates and brings in outside shareholders.

Amber and Kato plan to take a long weekend off to sit down and think about all of these issues. Amber, who is highly organized, has outlined a series of questions for them to address:

a. What kinds of career opportunities are open to finance majors?

b. What are the primary responsibilities of a corporate financial staff?

c. What are the most important financial management issues today?

d. (1) What are the alternative forms of business organization?

(2) What are their advantages and disadvantages?

e. What is the primary goal of the corporation?

(1) Do firms have any responsibilities to society at large?

(2) Is stock price maximization good or bad for society?

(3) Should firms behave ethically?

f. What is an agency relationship?

   (1) What agency relationships exist within a corporation?

   (2) What mechanisms exist to influence managers to act in shareholders' best interests?

   (3) Should shareholders (through managers) take actions that are detrimental to bondholders?

g. Is maximizing stock price the same thing as maximizing profit?

h. What factors affect stock prices?

i. What factors affect the level and riskiness of cash flows?

CHAPTER 1
An Overview of Financial Management

- Career Opportunities
- Issues of the New Millennium
- Forms of Businesses
- Goals of the Corporation
- Agency Relationships

1-1

Career Opportunities in Finance

- Money and capital markets
- Investments
- Financial management

1-2

Responsibility of the Financial Staff

- Maximize stock value by:
  - Forecasting and planning
  - Investment and financing decisions
  - Coordination and control
  - Transactions in the financial markets
  - Managing risk

1-3

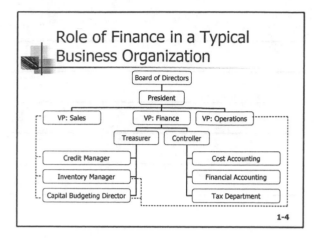

Role of Finance in a Typical Business Organization

```
                        Board of Directors
                             |
                         President
                             |
        +--------------------+--------------------+
     VP: Sales          VP: Finance          VP: Operations
                     +-------+-------+
                  Treasurer   Controller
        +---------+              +----------+
   Credit Manager            Cost Accounting
   Inventory Manager         Financial Accounting
   Capital Budgeting Director   Tax Department
```

1-4

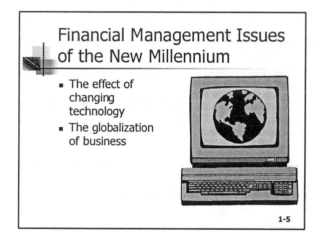

Financial Management Issues of the New Millennium

- The effect of changing technology
- The globalization of business

1-5

Percentage of Revenue and Net Income from Overseas Operations for 10 Well-Known Corporations, 2001

Company	% of Revenue from overseas	% of Net Income from overseas
Coca-Cola	60.8	35.9
Exxon Mobil	69.4	60.2
General Electric	32.6	25.2
General Motors	26.1	60.6
IBM	57.9	48.4
JP Morgan Chase & Co.	35.5	51.7
McDonald's	63.1	61.7
Merck	18.3	58.1
3M	52.9	47.0
Sears, Roebuck	10.5	7.8

1-6

Alternative Forms of Business Organization

- Sole proprietorship
- Partnership
- Corporation

1-7

Sole proprietorships & Partnerships

- Advantages
  - Ease of formation
  - Subject to few regulations
  - No corporate income taxes
- Disadvantages
  - Difficult to raise capital
  - Unlimited liability
  - Limited life

1-8

Corporation

- Advantages
  - Unlimited life
  - Easy transfer of ownership
  - Limited liability
  - Ease of raising capital
- Disadvantages
  - Double taxation
  - Cost of set-up and report filing

1-9

Financial Goals of the Corporation

- The primary financial goal is shareholder wealth maximization, which translates to maximizing stock price.
    - Do firms have any responsibilities to society at large?
    - Is stock price maximization good or bad for society?
    - Should firms behave ethically?

1-10

Is stock price maximization the same as profit maximization?

- No, despite a generally high correlation amongst stock price, EPS, and cash flow.
- Current stock price relies upon current earnings, as well as future earnings and cash flow.
- Some actions may cause an increase in earnings, yet cause the stock price to decrease (and vice versa).

1-11

Agency relationships

- An agency relationship exists whenever a principal hires an agent to act on their behalf.
- Within a corporation, agency relationships exist between:
    - Shareholders and managers
    - Shareholders and creditors

1-12

Shareholders versus Managers

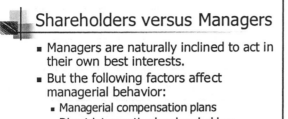

- Managers are naturally inclined to act in their own best interests.
- But the following factors affect managerial behavior:
  - Managerial compensation plans
  - Direct intervention by shareholders
  - The threat of firing
  - The threat of takeover

1-13

Shareholders versus Creditors

- Shareholders (through managers) could take actions to maximize stock price that are detrimental to creditors.
- In the long run, such actions will raise the cost of debt and ultimately lower stock price.

1-14

Factors that affect stock price

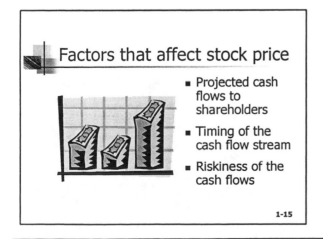

- Projected cash flows to shareholders
- Timing of the cash flow stream
- Riskiness of the cash flows

1-15

Basic Valuation Model

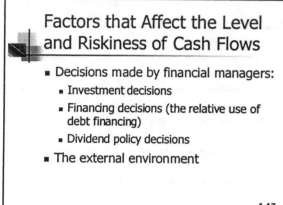

$$\text{Value} = \frac{CF_1}{(1+k)^1} + \frac{CF_2}{(1+k)^2} + \cdots + \frac{CF_n}{(1+k)^n}$$

$$= \sum_{t=1}^{n} \frac{CF_t}{(1+k)^t}.$$

- To estimate an asset's value, one estimates the cash flow for each period t (CF_t), the life of the asset (n), and the appropriate discount rate (k)
- Throughout the course, we discuss how to estimate the inputs and how financial management is used to improve them and thus maximize a firm's value.

1-16

Factors that Affect the Level and Riskiness of Cash Flows

- Decisions made by financial managers:
  - Investment decisions
  - Financing decisions (the relative use of debt financing)
  - Dividend policy decisions
- The external environment

1-17

EXAM-TYPE PROBLEMS

1-1.   Which of the following statements is most correct?

   a. A proxy fight is the main method of transferring ownership interest in a corporation.

   b. The corporation is a legal entity created by the state and is a direct extension of the legal status of its owners and managers, that is, the owners and managers are the corporation.

   c. Unlimited liability and limited life are two key advantages of the corporate form over other forms of business organization.

   d. Due in large part to limited liability and ease of ownership transfer, corporations have less trouble raising money in financial markets than other organizational forms.

   e. The stockholders of the corporation are insulated by limited legal liability, and the legal status of the corporation protects the firm's managers from civil and criminal charges arising from business operations.

1-2.   Which of the following statements is most correct?

   a. The proper goal of the financial manager should be to maximize the firm's expected cash flow, because this will add the most wealth to each of the individual shareholders (owners) of the firm.

   b. One way to state the decision framework most useful for carrying out the firm's objective is as follows: "The financial manager should seek that combination of assets, liabilities, and capital which will generate the largest expected projected after-tax income over the relevant time horizon."

   c. The riskiness inherent in a firm's earnings per share (EPS) depends on the characteristics of the projects the firm selects, which means it depends upon the firm's assets, but EPS does not depend on the manner in which those assets are financed.

   d. Since large, publicly-owned firms are controlled by their management teams, and typically, ownership is widely dispersed, managers have great freedom in managing the firm. Managers may operate in stockholders' best interests, but they may also operate in their own personal best interests. As long as managers stay within the law, there simply aren't any effective controls over managerial decisions in such situations.

   e. Agency problems exist between stockholders and managers, and between stockholders (through managers) and creditors.

2-19 Donna Jamison, a 1997 graduate of the University of Florida with four years of banking experience, was recently brought in as assistant to the chairman of the board of D'Leon Inc., a small food producer that operates in north Florida and whose specialty is high-quality pecan and other nut products sold in the snack-foods market. D'Leon's president, Al Watkins, decided in 2001 to undertake a major expansion and to "go national" in competition with Frito-Lay, Eagle, and other major snack-food companies. Watkins felt that D'Leon's products were of a higher quality than the competition's, that this quality differential would enable it to charge a premium price, and that the end result would be greatly increased sales, profits, and stock price.

The company doubled its plant capacity, opened new sales offices outside its home territory, and launched an expensive advertising campaign. D'Leon's results were not satisfactory, to put it mildly. Its board of directors, which consisted of its president and vice-president plus its major stockholders (who were all local business people), was most upset when directors learned how the expansion was going. Suppliers were being paid late and were unhappy, and the bank was complaining about the deteriorating situation and threatening to cut off credit. As a result, Watkins was informed that changes would have to be made, and quickly, or he would be fired. Also, at the board's insistence Donna Jamison was brought in and given the job of assistant to Fred Campo, a retired banker who was D'Leon's chairman and largest stockholder. Campo agreed to give up a few of his golfing days and to help nurse the company back to health, with Jamison's help.

Jamison began by gathering the financial statements and other data given in Tables IC2-1, IC2-2, IC2-3, and IC2-4. Assume that you are Jamison's assistant, and you must help her answer the following questions for Campo. (Note: We will continue with this case in Chapter 3, and you will feel more comfortable with the analysis there, but answering these questions will help prepare you for Chapter 3. Provide clear explanations, not just yes or no answers!)

TABLE IC2-1. Balance Sheets

	2002	2001
Assets:		
Cash	$ 7,282	$ 57,600
Accounts receivable	632,160	351,200
Inventories	1,287,360	715,200
Total current assets	$1,926,802	$1,124,000
Gross fixed assets	1,202,950	491,000
Less accumulated depreciation	263,160	146,200
Net fixed assets	$ 939,790	$ 344,800
Total assets	$2,866,592	$1,468,800
Liabilities and Equity:		
Accounts payable	$ 524,160	$ 145,600
Notes payable	636,808	200,000
Accruals	489,600	136,000
Total current liabilities	$1,650,568	$ 481,600
Long-term debt	723,432	323,432
Common stock (100,000 shares)	460,000	460,000
Retained earnings	32,592	203,768
Total equity	$ 492,592	$ 663,768
Total liabilities and equity	$2,866,592	$1,468,800

TABLE IC2-2. Income Statements

	2002	2001
Sales	$6,034,000	$3,432,000
Cost of goods sold	5,528,000	2,864,000
Other expenses	519,988	358,672
Total operating costs excluding Depreciation and amortization	$6,047,988	$3,222,672
EBITDA	($ 13,988)	$ 209,328
Depreciation and amortization	116,960	18,900
EBIT	($ 130,948)	$ 190,428
Interest expense	136,012	43,828
EBT	($ 266,960)	$ 146,600
Taxes (40%)	(106,784)[a]	58,640
Net income	($ 160,176)	$ 87,960
EPS	($1.602)	$0.880
DPS	$0.110	$0.220
Book value per share	$4.926	$6.638
Stock price	$2.25	$8.500
Shares outstanding	100,000	100,000
Tax rate	40.00%	40.00%
Lease payments	40,000	40,000
Sinking fund payments	0	0

Note:
[a] The firm had sufficient taxable income in 2000 and 2001 to obtain its full tax refund in 2002.

TABLE IC2-3. Statement of Retained Earnings, 2002

Balance of retained earnings, 12/31/01	$203,768
Add: Net income, 2002	(160,176)
Less: Dividends paid	(11,000)
Balance of retained earnings, 12/31/02	$ 32,592

TABLE IC2-4. Statement of Cash Flows, 2002

OPERATING ACTIVITIES

Net income	($ 160,176)
Additions (Sources of Cash):	
Depreciation and amortization	116,960
Increase in accounts payable	378,560
Increase in accruals	353,600
Subtractions (Uses of Cash):	
Increase in accounts receivable	(280,960)
Increase in inventories	(572,160)
Net cash provided by operating activities	($ 164,176)

LONG-TERM INVESTING ACTIVITIES

Cash used to acquire fixed assets	($ 711,950)

FINANCING ACTIVITIES

Increase in notes payable	436,808
Increase in long-term debt	400,000
Payment of cash dividends	(11,000)
Net cash provided by financing activities	$ 825,808

Sum: Net decrease in cash	($ 50,318)
Plus: Cash at beginning of year	57,600
Cash at end of year	$ 7,282

a. What effect did the expansion have on sales, net operating profit after taxes (NOPAT), net operating working capital (NOWC), total investor-supplied operating capital, and net income?

b. What effect did the company's expansion have on its net cash flow, operating cash flow, and free cash flow?

c. Jamison also has asked you to estimate D'Leon's EVA. She estimates that the after-tax cost of capital was 10 percent in 2001 and 13 percent in 2002.

d. Looking at D'Leon's stock price today, would you conclude that the expansion increased or decreased MVA?

e. D'Leon purchases materials on 30-day terms, meaning that it is supposed to pay for purchases within 30 days of receipt. Judging from its 2002 balance sheet, do you think D'Leon pays suppliers on time? Explain. If not, what problems might this lead to?

f. D'Leon spends money for labor, materials, and fixed assets (depreciation) to make products, and still more money to sell those products. Then, it makes sales that result in receivables, which eventually result in cash inflows. Does it appear that D'Leon's sales price exceeds its costs per unit sold? How does this affect the cash balance?

g. Suppose D'Leon's sales manager told the sales staff to start offering 60-day credit terms rather than the 30-day terms now being offered. D'Leon's competitors react by offering similar terms, so sales remain constant. What effect would this have on the cash account? How would the cash account be affected if sales doubled as a result of the credit policy change?

h. Can you imagine a situation in which the sales price exceeds the cost of producing and selling a unit of output, yet a dramatic increase in sales volume causes the cash balance to decline?

i. Did D'Leon finance its expansion program with internally generated funds (additions to retained earnings plus depreciation) or with external capital? How does the choice of financing affect the company's financial strength?

j. Refer to Tables IC2-2 and IC2-4. Suppose D'Leon broke even in 2002 in the sense that sales revenues equaled total operating costs plus interest charges. Would the asset expansion have caused the company to experience a cash shortage that required it to raise external capital?

k. If D'Leon started depreciating fixed assets over 7 years rather than 10 years, would that affect (1) the physical stock of assets, (2) the balance sheet account for fixed assets, (3) the company's reported net income, and (4) its cash position? Assume the same depreciation method is used for stockholder reporting and for tax calculations, and the accounting change has no effect on assets' physical lives.

l. Explain how earnings per share, dividends per share, and book value per share are calculated, and what they mean. Why does the market price per share *not* equal the book value per share?

m. Explain briefly the tax treatment of (1) interest and dividends paid, (2) interest earned and dividends received, (3) capital gains, and (4) tax loss carry-back and carry-forward. How might each of these items impact D'Leon's taxes?

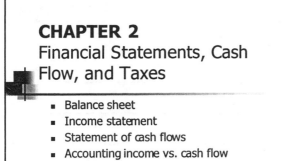

CHAPTER 2
Financial Statements, Cash Flow, and Taxes

- Balance sheet
- Income statement
- Statement of cash flows
- Accounting income vs. cash flow
- MVA and EVA
- Federal tax system

2-1

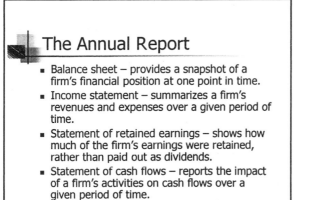

The Annual Report

- Balance sheet – provides a snapshot of a firm's financial position at one point in time.
- Income statement – summarizes a firm's revenues and expenses over a given period of time.
- Statement of retained earnings – shows how much of the firm's earnings were retained, rather than paid out as dividends.
- Statement of cash flows – reports the impact of a firm's activities on cash flows over a given period of time.

2-2

Balance Sheet: Assets

	2002	2001
Cash	7,282	57,600
A/R	632,160	351,200
Inventories	1,287,360	715,200
Total CA	1,926,802	1,124,000
Gross FA	1,202,950	491,000
Less: Dep.	263,160	146,200
Net FA	939,790	344,800
Total Assets	2,866,592	1,468,800

2-3

Balance sheet: Liabilities and Equity

	2002	2001
Accts payable	524,160	145,600
Notes payable	636,808	200,000
Accruals	489,600	136,000
Total CL	1,650,568	481,600
Long-term debt	723,432	323,432
Common stock	460,000	460,000
Retained earnings	32,592	203,768
Total Equity	492,592	663,768
Total L & E	2,866,592	1,468,800

2-4

Income statement

	2002	2001
Sales	6,034,000	3,432,000
COGS	5,528,000	2,864,000
Other expenses	519,988	358,672
EBITDA	(13,988)	209,328
Depr. & Amort.	116,960	18,900
EBIT	(130,948)	190,428
Interest Exp.	136,012	43,828
EBT	(266,960)	146,600
Taxes	(106,784)	58,640
Net income	(160,176)	87,960

2-5

Other data

	2002	2001
No. of shares	100,000	100,000
EPS	-$1.602	$0.88
DPS	$0.11	$0.22
Stock price	$2.25	$8.50
Lease pmts	$40,000	$40,000

2-6

Statement of Retained Earnings (2002)

Balance of retained earnings, 12/31/01	$203,768
Add: Net income, 2002	(160,176)
Less: Dividends paid	(11,000)
Balance of retained earnings, 12/31/02	$32,592

2-7

Statement of Cash Flows (2002)

OPERATING ACTIVITIES

Net income	(160,176)
Add (Sources of cash):	
Depreciation	116,960
Increase in A/P	378,560
Increase in accruals	353,600
Subtract (Uses of cash):	
Increase in A/R	(280,960)
Increase in inventories	(572,160)
Net cash provided by ops.	(164,176)

2-8

Statement of Cash Flows (2002)

L-T INVESTING ACTIVITIES

Investment in fixed assets	(711,950)
FINANCING ACTIVITIES	
Increase in notes payable	436,808
Increase in long-term debt	400,000
Payment of cash dividend	(11,000)
Net cash from financing	825,808
NET CHANGE IN CASH	(50,318)
Plus: Cash at beginning of year	57,600
Cash at end of year	7,282

2-9

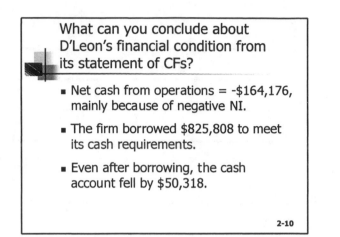

What can you conclude about D'Leon's financial condition from its statement of CFs?

- Net cash from operations = -$164,176, mainly because of negative NI.
- The firm borrowed $825,808 to meet its cash requirements.
- Even after borrowing, the cash account fell by $50,318.

2-10

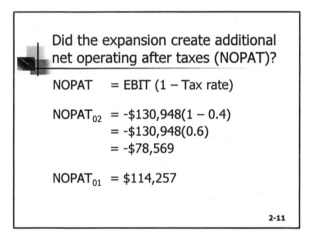

Did the expansion create additional net operating after taxes (NOPAT)?

$$NOPAT = EBIT (1 - \text{Tax rate})$$

$$NOPAT_{02} = -\$130,948(1 - 0.4)$$
$$= -\$130,948(0.6)$$
$$= -\$78,569$$

$$NOPAT_{01} = \$114,257$$

2-11

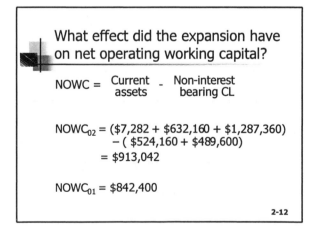

What effect did the expansion have on net operating working capital?

$$NOWC = \frac{Current}{assets} - \frac{Non\text{-}interest}{bearing\ CL}$$

$$NOWC_{02} = (\$7,282 + \$632,160 + \$1,287,360)$$
$$- (\$524,160 + \$489,600)$$
$$= \$913,042$$

$$NOWC_{01} = \$842,400$$

2-12

What effect did the expansion have on operating capital?

Operating capital = NOWC + Net Fixed Assets

$$\text{Operating Capital}_{02} = \$913{,}042 + \$939{,}790$$
$$= \$1{,}852{,}832$$

$$\text{Operating Capital}_{01} = \$1{,}187{,}200$$

2-13

What is your assessment of the expansion's effect on operations?

	2002	2001
Sales	$6,034,000	$3,432,000
NOPAT	-$78,569	$114,257
NOWC	$913,042	$842,400
Operating capital	$1,852,832	$1,187,200
Net Income	-$160,176	$87,960

2-14

What effect did the expansion have on net cash flow and operating cash flow?

$$NCF_{02} = NI + Dep = (\$160{,}176) + \$116{,}960$$
$$= -\$43{,}216$$
$$NCF_{01} = \$87{,}960 + \$18{,}900 = \$106{,}860$$
$$OCF_{02} = NOPAT + Dep$$
$$= (\$78{,}569) + \$116{,}960$$
$$= \$38{,}391$$
$$OCF_{01} = \$114{,}257 + \$18{,}900$$
$$= \$133{,}157$$

2-15

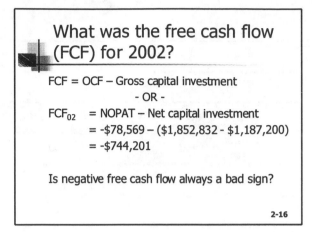

What was the free cash flow (FCF) for 2002?

FCF = OCF – Gross capital investment

- OR -

FCF_{02} = NOPAT – Net capital investment

= -$78,569 – ($1,852,832 - $1,187,200)

= -$744,201

Is negative free cash flow always a bad sign?

2-16

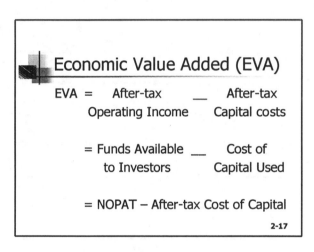

Economic Value Added (EVA)

EVA = After-tax __ After-tax
Operating Income   Capital costs

= Funds Available __ Cost of
to Investors   Capital Used

= NOPAT – After-tax Cost of Capital

2-17

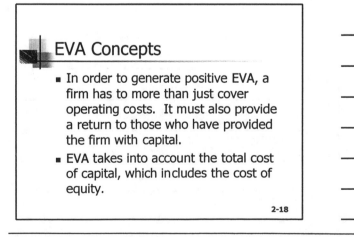

EVA Concepts

- In order to generate positive EVA, a firm has to more than just cover operating costs. It must also provide a return to those who have provided the firm with capital.
- EVA takes into account the total cost of capital, which includes the cost of equity.

2-18

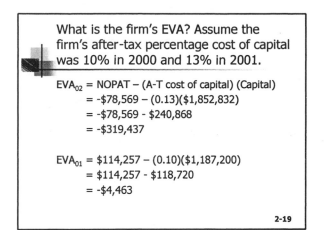

What is the firm's EVA? Assume the firm's after-tax percentage cost of capital was 10% in 2000 and 13% in 2001.

EVA_{02} = NOPAT − (A-T cost of capital) (Capital)
= −$78,569 − (0.13)($1,852,832)
= −$78,569 - $240,868
= −$319,437

EVA_{01} = $114,257 − (0.10)($1,187,200)
= $114,257 - $118,720
= −$4,463

2-19

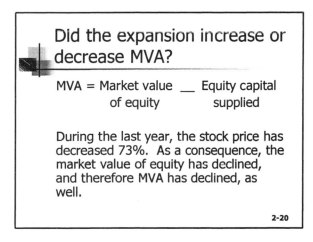

Did the expansion increase or decrease MVA?

MVA = Market value __ Equity capital
     of equity   supplied

During the last year, the stock price has decreased 73%. As a consequence, the market value of equity has declined, and therefore MVA has declined, as well.

2-20

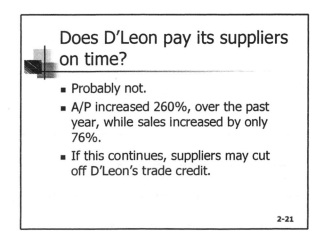

Does D'Leon pay its suppliers on time?

- Probably not.
- A/P increased 260%, over the past year, while sales increased by only 76%.
- If this continues, suppliers may cut off D'Leon's trade credit.

2-21

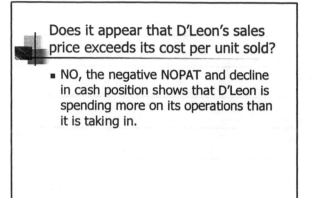

Does it appear that D'Leon's sales price exceeds its cost per unit sold?

- NO, the negative NOPAT and decline in cash position shows that D'Leon is spending more on its operations than it is taking in.

2-22

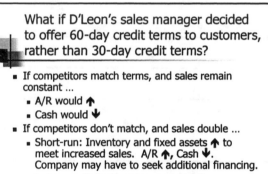

What if D'Leon's sales manager decided to offer 60-day credit terms to customers, rather than 30-day credit terms?

- If competitors match terms, and sales remain constant ...
  - A/R would ↑
  - Cash would ↓
- If competitors don't match, and sales double ...
  - Short-run: Inventory and fixed assets ↑ to meet increased sales. A/R ↑, Cash ↓. Company may have to seek additional financing.
  - Long-run: Collections increase and the company's cash position would improve.

2-23

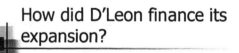

How did D'Leon finance its expansion?

- D'Leon financed its expansion with external capital.
- D'Leon issued long-term debt which reduced its financial strength and flexibility.

2-24

Would D'Leon have required external capital if they had broken even in 2001 (Net Income = 0)?

- YES, the company would still have to finance its increase in assets. Looking to the Statement of Cash Flows, we see that the firm made an investment of $711,950 in net fixed assets. Therefore, they would have needed to raise additional funds.

2-25

What happens if D'Leon depreciates fixed assets over 7 years (as opposed to the current 10 years)?

- No effect on physical assets.
- Fixed assets on the balance sheet would decline.
- Net income would decline.
- Tax payments would decline.
- Cash position would improve.

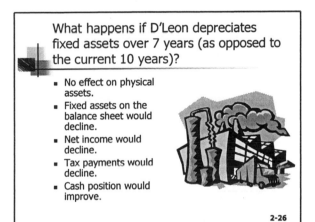

2-26

Federal Income Tax System

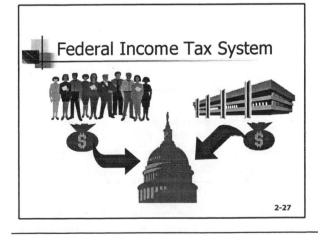

2-27

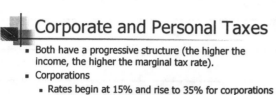

Corporate and Personal Taxes

- Both have a progressive structure (the higher the income, the higher the marginal tax rate).
- Corporations
  - Rates begin at 15% and rise to 35% for corporations with income over $10 million.
  - Also subject to state tax (around 5%).
- Individuals
  - Rates begin at 10% and rise to 38.6% for individuals with income over $307,050.
  - May be subject to state tax.

2-28

Tax treatment of various uses and sources of funds

- Interest paid – tax deductible for corporations (paid out of pre-tax income), but usually not for individuals (interest on home loans being the exception).
- Interest earned – usually fully taxable (an exception being interest from a (muni").
- Dividends paid – paid out of after-tax income.
- Dividends received – taxed as ordinary income for individuals ("double taxation"). A portion of dividends received by corporations is tax excludable, in order to avoid "triple taxation".

2-29

More tax issues

- Tax Loss Carry-Back and Carry-Forward – since corporate incomes can fluctuate widely, the tax code allows firms to carry losses back to offset profits in previous years or forward to offset profits in the future.
- Capital gains – defined as the profits from the sale of assets not normally transacted in the normal course of business, capital gains for individuals are generally taxed as ordinary income if held for less than a year, and at the capital gains rate if held for more than a year. Corporations face somewhat different rules.

2-30

EXAM-TYPE PROBLEMS

2-1.   Purcell Corporation has operating income (EBIT) of $1,250,000. The company's depreciation expense is $300,000. Purcell is 100 percent equity financed, and it faces a 40 percent tax rate. In addition, the firm's net investment in operating capital is $500,000.

   a. What is the company's net income? ($750,000)

   b. What is its net cash flow? ($1,050,000)

   c. What is its operating cash flow? ($1,050,000)

   d. What is its net operating profit after taxes (NOPAT)? ($750,000)

   e. What is its free cash flow (FCF)? ($250,000)

3-26 Part I of this case, presented in Chapter 2, discussed the situation that D'Leon Inc., a regional snack-foods producer, was in after an expansion program. D'Leon had increased plant capacity and undertaken a major marketing campaign in an attempt to "go national." Thus far, sales have not been up to the forecasted level, costs have been higher than were projected, and a large loss occurred in 2002 rather than the expected profit. As a result, its managers, directors, and investors are concerned about the firm's survival.

Donna Jamison was brought in as assistant to Fred Campo, D'Leon's chairman, who had the task of getting the company back into a sound financial position. D'Leon's 2001 and 2002 balance sheets and income statements, together with projections for 2003, are given in Tables IC3-1 and IC3-2. In addition, Table IC3-3 gives the company's 2001 and 2002 financial ratios, together with industry average data. The 2003 projected financial statement data represent Jamison's and Campo's best guess for 2003 results, assuming that some new financing is arranged to get the company "over the hump."

Jamison examined monthly data for 2002 (not given in the case), and she detected an improving pattern during the year. Monthly sales were rising, costs were falling, and large losses in the early months had turned to a small profit by December. Thus, the annual data look somewhat worse than final monthly data. Also, it appears to be taking longer for the advertising program to get the message across, for the new sales offices to generate sales, and for the new manufacturing facilities to operate efficiently. In other words, the lags between spending money and deriving benefits were longer than D'Leon's managers had anticipated. For these reasons, Jamison and Campo see hope for the company—provided it can survive in the short run.

Jamison must prepare an analysis of where the company is now, what it must do to regain its financial health, and what actions should be taken. Your assignment is to help her answer the following questions. Provide clear explanations, not yes or no answers.

TABLE IC3-1. Balance Sheets

	2003E	2002	2001
Assets			
Cash	$ 85,632	$ 7,282	$ 57,600
Accounts receivable	878,000	632,160	351,200
Inventories	1,716,480	1,287,360	715,200
Total current assets	$2,680,112	$1,926,802	$1,124,000
Gross fixed assets	1,197,160	1,202,950	491,000
Less accumulated depreciation	380,120	263,160	146,200
Net fixed assets	$ 817,040	$ 939,790	$ 344,800
Total assets	$3,497,152	$2,866,592	$1,468,800
Liabilities and Equity			
Accounts payable	$ 436,800	$ 524,160	$ 145,600
Notes payable	300,000	636,808	200,000
Accruals	408,000	489,600	136,000
Total current liabilities	$1,144,800	$1,650,568	$ 481,600
Long-term debt	400,000	723,432	323,432
Common stock	1,721,176	460,000	460,000
Retained earnings	231,176	32,592	203,768
Total equity	$1,952,352	$ 492,592	$ 663,768
Total liabilities and equity	$3,497,152	$2,866,592	$1,468,800

Note: "E" indicates estimated. The 2003 data are forecasts.

TABLE IC3-2. Income Statements

	2003E	2002	2001
Sales	$7,035,600	$6,034,000	$3,432,000
Cost of goods sold	5,875,992	5,528,000	2,864,000
Other expenses	550,000	519,988	358,672
Total operating costs excluding depreciation	$6,425,992	$6,047,988	$3,222,672
EBITDA	$ 609,608	($ 13,988)	$ 209,328
Depreciation	116,960	116,960	18,900
EBIT	$ 492,648	($ 130,948)	$ 190,428
Interest expense	70,008	136,012	43,828
EBT	$ 422,640	($ 266,960)	$ 146,600
Taxes (40%)	169,056	(106,784)[a]	58,640
Net income	$ 253,584	($ 160,176)	$ 87,960
EPS	$1.014	($1.602)	$0.880
DPS	$0.220	$0.110	$0.220
Book value per share	$7.809	$4.926	$6.638
Stock price	$12.17	$2.25	$8.50
Shares outstanding	250,000	100,000	100,000
Tax rate	40.00%	40.00%	40.00%
Lease payments	40,000	40,000	40,000
Sinking fund payments	0	0	0

Note: "E" indicates estimated. The 2003 data are forecasts.

[a]The firm had sufficient taxable income in 2000 and 2001 to obtain its full tax refund in 2002.

TABLE IC3-3. Ratio Analysis

	2003E	2002	2001	Industry Average
Current		1.2×	2.3×	2.7×
Inventory turnover		4.7×	4.8×	6.1×
Days sales outstanding (DSO)[a]		38.2	37.4	32.0
Fixed assets turnover		6.4×	10.0×	7.0×
Total assets turnover		2.1×	2.3×	2.6×
Debt ratio		82.8%	54.8%	50.0%
TIE		-1.0×	4.3×	6.2×
EBITDA coverage		0.1×	3.0×	8.0×
Profit margin		-2.7%	2.6%	3.5%
Basic earning power		-4.6%	13.0%	19.1%
ROA		-5.6%	6.0%	9.1%
ROE		-32.5%	13.3%	18.2%
Price/earnings		-1.4×	9.7×	14.2×
Price/cash flow		-5.2×	8.0×	11.0×
Market/book		0.5×	1.3×	2.4×
Book value per share		$4.93	$6.64	n.a.

Note: "E" indicates estimated. The 2003 data are forecasts.
[a] Calculation is based on a 365-day year.

a. Why are ratios useful? What are the five major categories of ratios?

b. Calculate D'Leon's 2003 current ratio based on the projected balance sheet and income statement data. What can you say about the company's liquidity position in 2001, 2002, and as projected for 2003? We often think of ratios as being useful (1) to managers to help run the business, (2) to bankers for credit analysis, and (3) to stockholders for stock valuation. Would these different types of analysts have an equal interest in the liquidity ratio?

c. Calculate the 2003 inventory turnover, days sales outstanding (DSO), fixed assets turnover, and total assets turnover. How does D'Leon's utilization of assets stack up against other firms in its industry?

d. Calculate the 2003 debt, times-interest-earned, and EBITDA coverage ratios. How does D'Leon compare with the industry with respect to financial leverage? What can you conclude from these ratios?

e. Calculate the 2003 profit margin, basic earning power (BEP), return on assets (ROA), and return on equity (ROE). What can you say about these ratios?

f. Calculate the 2003 price/earnings ratio, price/cash flow ratio, and market/book ratio. Do these ratios indicate that investors are expected to have a high or low opinion of the company?

g. Use the extended Du Pont equation to provide a summary and overview of D'Leon's financial condition as projected for 2003. What are the firm's major strengths and weaknesses?

h. Use the following simplified 2003 balance sheet to show, in general terms, how an improvement in the DSO would tend to affect the stock price. For example, if the company could improve its collection procedures and thereby lower its DSO from 45.6 days to the 32-day industry average without affecting sales, how would that change "ripple through" the financial statements (shown in thousands below) and influence the stock price?

Accounts receivable	$ 878	Debt	$1,545
Other current assets	1,802		
Net fixed assets	817	Equity	1,952
Total assets	$3,497	Liabilities plus equity	$3,497

i. Does it appear that inventories could be adjusted, and, if so, how should that adjustment affect D'Leon's profitability and stock price?

j. In 2002, the company paid its suppliers much later than the due dates, and it was not maintaining financial ratios at levels called for in its bank loan agreements. Therefore, suppliers could cut the company off, and its bank could refuse to renew the loan when it comes due in 90 days. On the basis of data provided, would you, as a credit manager, continue to sell to D'Leon on credit? (You could demand cash on delivery, that is, sell on terms of COD, but that might cause D'Leon to stop buying from your company.) Similarly, if you were the bank loan officer, would you recommend renewing the loan or demand its repayment? Would your actions be influenced if, in early 2003, D'Leon showed you its 2003 projections plus proof that it was going to raise over $1.2 million of new equity capital?

k. In hindsight, what should D'Leon have done back in 2001?

l. What are some potential problems and limitations of financial ratio analysis?

m. What are some qualitative factors analysts should consider when evaluating a company's likely future financial performance?

CHAPTER 3
Analysis of Financial Statements

- Ratio Analysis
- Du Pont system
- Effects of improving ratios
- Limitations of ratio analysis
- Qualitative factors

3-1

Balance Sheet: Assets

	2003E	2002
Cash	85,632	7,282
A/R	878,000	632,160
Inventories	1,716,480	1,287,360
Total CA	2,680,112	1,926,802
Gross FA	1,197,160	1,202,950
Less: Dep.	380,120	263,160
Net FA	817,040	939,790
Total Assets	3,497,152	2,866,592

3-2

Balance sheet:
Liabilities and Equity

	2003E	2002
Accts payable	436,800	524,160
Notes payable	300,000	636,808
Accruals	408,000	489,600
Total CL	1,144,800	1,650,568
Long-term debt	400,000	723,432
Common stock	1,721,176	460,000
Retained earnings	231,176	32,592
Total Equity	1,952,352	492,592
Total L & E	3,497,152	2,866,592

3-3

Income statement

	2003E	2002
Sales	7,035,600	6,034,000
COGS	5,875,992	5,528,000
Other expenses	550,000	519,988
EBITDA	609,608	(13,988)
Depr. & Amort.	116,960	116,960
EBIT	492,648	(130,948)
Interest Exp.	70,008	136,012
EBT	422,640	(266,960)
Taxes	169,056	(106,784)
Net income	253,584	(160,176)

3-4

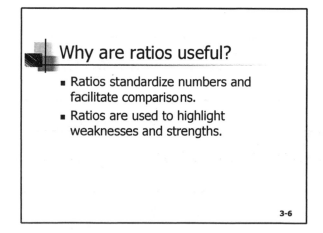

Other data

	2003E	2002
No. of shares	250,000	100,000
EPS	$1.014	-$1.602
DPS	$0.220	$0.110
Stock price	$12.17	$2.25
Lease pmts	$40,000	$40,000

3-5

Why are ratios useful?

- Ratios standardize numbers and facilitate comparisons.
- Ratios are used to highlight weaknesses and strengths.

3-6

What are the five major categories of ratios, and what questions do they answer?

- Liquidity: Can we make required payments?
- Asset management: right amount of assets vs. sales?
- Debt management: Right mix of debt and equity?
- Profitability: Do sales prices exceed unit costs, and are sales high enough as reflected in PM, ROE, and ROA?
- Market value: Do investors like what they see as reflected in P/E and M/B ratios?

3-7

Calculate D'Leon's forecasted current ratio for 2003.

Current ratio = Current assets / Current liabilities

= $2,680 / $1,145

= 2.34x

3-8

Comments on current ratio

	2003	2002	2001	Ind.
Current ratio	2.34x	1.20x	2.30x	2.70x

- Expected to improve but still below the industry average.
- Liquidity position is weak.

3-9

What is the inventory turnover vs. the industry average?

Inv. turnover = Sales / Inventories
= $7,036 / $1,716
= 4.10x

	2003	2002	2001	Ind.
Inventory Turnover	4.1x	4.70x	4.8x	6.1x

3-10

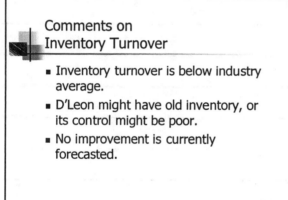

Comments on Inventory Turnover

- Inventory turnover is below industry average.
- D'Leon might have old inventory, or its control might be poor.
- No improvement is currently forecasted.

3-11

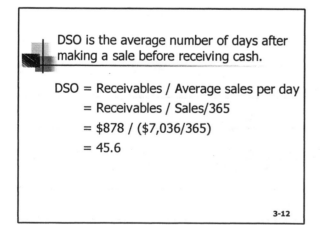

DSO is the average number of days after making a sale before receiving cash.

DSO = Receivables / Average sales per day
= Receivables / Sales/365
= $878 / ($7,036/365)
= 45.6

3-12

Appraisal of DSO

	2003	2002	2001	Ind.
DSO	45.6	38.2	37.4	32.0

- D'Leon collects on sales too slowly, and is getting worse.
- D'Leon has a poor credit policy.

3-13

Fixed asset and total asset turnover ratios vs. the industry average

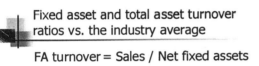

FA turnover = Sales / Net fixed assets
= $7,036 / $817 = 8.61x

TA turnover = Sales / Total assets
= $7,036 / $3,497 = 2.01x

3-14

Evaluating the FA turnover and TA turnover ratios

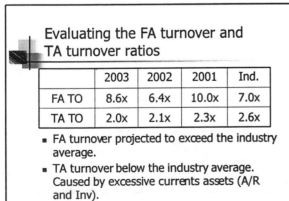

	2003	2002	2001	Ind.
FA TO	8.6x	6.4x	10.0x	7.0x
TA TO	2.0x	2.1x	2.3x	2.6x

- FA turnover projected to exceed the industry average.
- TA turnover below the industry average. Caused by excessive currents assets (A/R and Inv).

3-15

Calculate the debt ratio, TIE, and EBITDA coverage ratios.

Debt ratio = Total debt / Total assets
= ($1,145 + $400) / $3,497 = 44.2%

TIE = EBIT / Interest expense
= $492.6 / $70 = 7.0x

3-16

Calculate the debt ratio, TIE, and EBITDA coverage ratios.

$$\frac{\text{EBITDA}}{\text{coverage}} = \frac{(\text{EBITDA+Lease pmts})}{\text{Int exp + Lease pmts + Principal pmts}}$$

$$= \frac{\$609.6 + \$40}{\$70 + \$40 + \$0}$$

$$= 5.9x$$

3-17

How do the debt management ratios compare with industry averages?

	2003	2002	2001	Ind.
D/A	44.2%	82.8%	54.8%	50.0%
TIE	7.0x	-1.0x	4.3x	6.2x
EBITDA coverage	5.9x	0.1x	3.0x	8.0x

- D/A and TIE are better than the industry average, but EBITDA coverage still trails the industry.

3-18

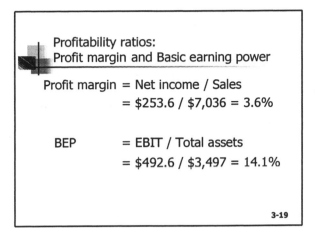

Profitability ratios:
Profit margin and Basic earning power

Profit margin = Net income / Sales
$$= \$253.6 / \$7,036 = 3.6\%$$

BEP = EBIT / Total assets
$$= \$492.6 / \$3,497 = 14.1\%$$

3-19

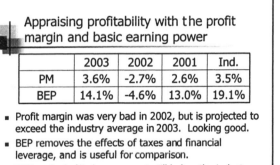

Appraising profitability with the profit margin and basic earning power

	2003	2002	2001	Ind.
PM	3.6%	-2.7%	2.6%	3.5%
BEP	14.1%	-4.6%	13.0%	19.1%

- Profit margin was very bad in 2002, but is projected to exceed the industry average in 2003. Looking good.
- BEP removes the effects of taxes and financial leverage, and is useful for comparison.
- BEP projected to improve, yet still below the industry average. There is definitely room for improvement.

3-20

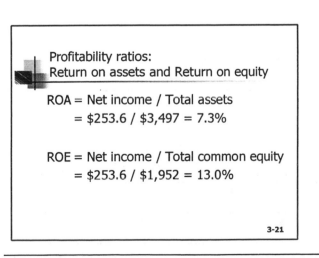

Profitability ratios:
Return on assets and Return on equity

ROA = Net income / Total assets
$$= \$253.6 / \$3,497 = 7.3\%$$

ROE = Net income / Total common equity
$$= \$253.6 / \$1,952 = 13.0\%$$

3-21

Appraising profitability with the return on assets and return on equity

	2003	2002	2001	Ind.
ROA	7.3%	-5.6%	6.0%	9.1%
ROE	13.0%	-32.5%	13.3%	18.2%

- Both ratios rebounded from the previous year, but are still below the industry average. More improvement is needed.
- Wide variations in ROE illustrate the effect that leverage can have on profitabilty.

3-22

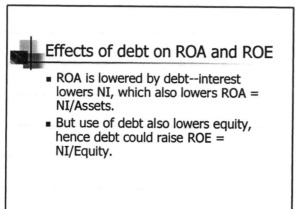

Effects of debt on ROA and ROE

- ROA is lowered by debt--interest lowers NI, which also lowers ROA = NI/Assets.
- But use of debt also lowers equity, hence debt could raise ROE = NI/Equity.

3-23

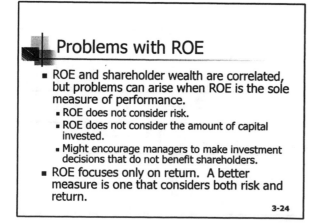

Problems with ROE

- ROE and shareholder wealth are correlated, but problems can arise when ROE is the sole measure of performance.
  - ROE does not consider risk.
  - ROE does not consider the amount of capital invested.
  - Might encourage managers to make investment decisions that do not benefit shareholders.
- ROE focuses only on return. A better measure is one that considers both risk and return.

3-24

Calculate the Price/Earnings, Price/Cash flow, and Market/Book ratios.

P/E = Price / Earnings per share
= $12.17 / $1.014 = 12.0x

P/CF = Price / Cash flow per share
= $12.17 / [($253.6 + $117.0) ÷ 250]
= 8.21x

3-25

Calculate the Price/Earnings, Price/Cash flow, and Market/Book ratios.

M/B = Mkt price per share / Book value per share
= $12.17 / ($1,952 / 250) = 1.56x

	2003	2002	2001	Ind.
P/E	12.0x	-1.4x	9.7x	14.2x
P/CF	8.21x	-5.2x	8.0x	11.0x
M/B	1.56x	0.5x	1.3x	2.4x

3-26

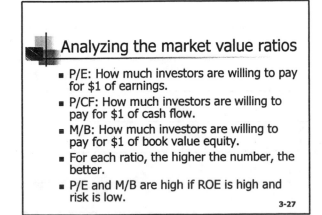

Analyzing the market value ratios

- P/E: How much investors are willing to pay for $1 of earnings.
- P/CF: How much investors are willing to pay for $1 of cash flow.
- M/B: How much investors are willing to pay for $1 of book value equity.
- For each ratio, the higher the number, the better.
- P/E and M/B are high if ROE is high and risk is low.

3-27

Extended DuPont equation:
Breaking down Return on equity

ROE = (Profit margin) x (TA turnover) x (Equity multiplier)
   =   3.6%   x   2   x   1.8
   =   13.0%

	PM	TA TO	EM	ROE
2001	2.6%	2.3	2.2	13.3%
2002	-2.7%	2.1	5.8	-32.5%
2003E	3.6%	2.0	1.8	13.0%
Ind.	3.5%	2.6	2.0	18.2%

3-28

The Du Pont system

Also can be expressed as:

ROE = (NI/Sales) x (Sales/TA) x (TA/Equity)

- Focuses on:
    - Expense control (PM)
    - Asset utilization (TATO)
    - Debt utilization (Eq. Mult.)
- Shows how these factors combine to determine ROE.

3-29

Trend analysis

- Analyzes a firm's financial ratios over time
- Can be used to estimate the likelihood of improvement or deterioration in financial condition.

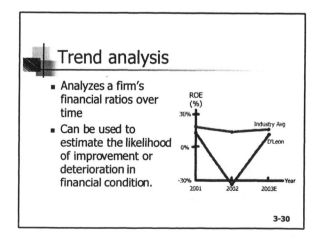

3-30

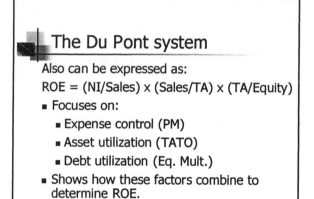

An example:
The effects of improving ratios

A/R	878	Debt	1,545
Other CA	1,802	Equity	1,952
Net FA	817		
TA	3,497	Total L&E	3,497

Sales / day = $7,035,600 / 365 = $19,275.62

How would reducing the firm's DSO to 32 days affect the company?

3-31

Reducing accounts receivable and the days sales outstanding

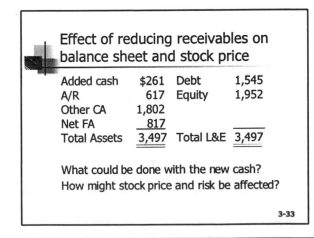

- Reducing A/R will have no effect on sales

Old A/R = $19,275.62 x 45.6 = $878,000
New A/R = $19,275.62 x 32.0 = $616,820
              Cash freed up: $261,180

Initially shows up as addition to cash.

3-32

Effect of reducing receivables on balance sheet and stock price

Added cash	$261	Debt	1,545
A/R	617	Equity	1,952
Other CA	1,802		
Net FA	817		
Total Assets	3,497	Total L&E	3,497

What could be done with the new cash?
How might stock price and risk be affected?

3-33

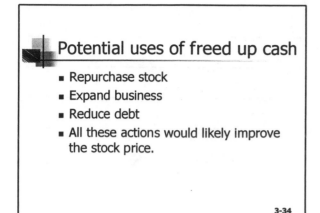

Potential uses of freed up cash

- Repurchase stock
- Expand business
- Reduce debt
- All these actions would likely improve the stock price.

3-34

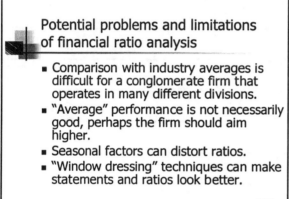

Potential problems and limitations of financial ratio analysis

- Comparison with industry averages is difficult for a conglomerate firm that operates in many different divisions.
- "Average" performance is not necessarily good, perhaps the firm should aim higher.
- Seasonal factors can distort ratios.
- "Window dressing" techniques can make statements and ratios look better.

3-35

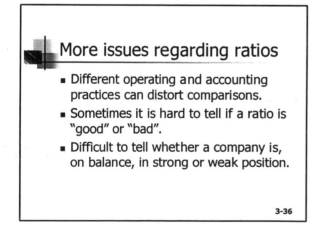

More issues regarding ratios

- Different operating and accounting practices can distort comparisons.
- Sometimes it is hard to tell if a ratio is "good" or "bad".
- Difficult to tell whether a company is, on balance, in strong or weak position.

3-36

Qualitative factors to be considered when evaluating a company's future financial performance

- Are the firm's revenues tied to 1 key customer, product, or supplier?
- What percentage of the firm's business is generated overseas?
- Competition
- Future prospects
- Legal and regulatory environment

3-37

EXAM-TYPE PROBLEMS

3-1. Automotive Supply's ROE last year was only 2 percent, but its new owner has developed an operating plan designed to improve things. The new plan calls for a total debt ratio of 70 percent, which will result in interest charges of $500 per year. Management projects an EBIT of $2,000 on sales of $20,000, and it expects to have a total assets turnover ratio of 2.5. Under these conditions, the average tax rate will be 30 percent. If the changes are made, what return on equity will Automotive earn? (43.75%)

3-2. Capital Garden Supply (CGS) recently hired a new chief financial officer, Louise Johnston, who was brought in and charged with raising the firm's profitability. CGS has sales of $5 million, a profit margin of 5 percent, and the following balance sheet:

Cash	$ 250,000	A/P	$ 750,000
Receivables	2,250,000	Other C.L.	500,000
Inventories	1,750,000	Long-term debt	2,250,000
Net fixed assets	3,250,000	Common equity	4,000,000
Total assets	$7,500,000	Total L/E	$7,500,000

a. Ms. Johnston thinks that receivables are too high, and that they can be lowered to the point where the firm's DSO is equal to the industry average, 60 days, without affecting either sales or net income. If receivables are reduced so as to lower the DSO to 60 days (365-day basis), and if the funds generated are used to reduce common equity (stock can be repurchased at book value), and if no other changes occur, by how much will the ROE change? (+3.47%)

b. Suppose we wanted to modify this problem and use it on an exam, i.e., to create a new problem that you have not seen to test your knowledge of this general type of problem. How would your answer change under each of the following conditions:

(1) Double all dollar amounts. (+3.47%)

(2) Set the target DSO at 70 days. (+2.98%)

(3) State that the target is to achieve a receivables turnover (Sales/Receivables) of 6×. (+3.43%)

(4) State that the company has 250,000 shares of stock outstanding, and ask how much the original change would increase EPS. (+$0.56)

(5) Change part 4 to state that the stock was selling for twice book value, so common equity would not be reduced on a dollar-for-dollar basis. (+$0.22)

c. Now explain how we could have set the problem up to have you focus on changing inventory or fixed assets, or using the funds generated to retire debt, or how the original problem could have stated that the company needed *more* inventory and would finance them with new common equity, or with new debt.

3-3.   Which of the following statements is most correct?

    a.   If two firms pay the same interest rate on their debt and have the same rate of return on assets, and if that ROA is positive, the firm with the *higher* debt ratio will also have a higher rate of return on common equity.

    b.   One of the problems of ratio analysis is that the relationships are subject to manipulation. For example, we know that if we use some of our cash to pay off some of our current liabilities, the current ratio will always increase, especially if the current ratio is weak initially.

    c.   Generally, firms with high profit margins have high asset turnover ratios, and firms with low profit margins have low turnover ratios; this result is exactly as predicted by the extended Du Pont equation.

    d.   Firms A and B have identical earnings and identical dividend payout ratios. If Firm A's growth rate is higher than that of Firm B, Firm A's P/E ratio must be greater than Firm B's P/E ratio.

    e.   None of the above statements is correct.

3-4.   Alumbat Corporation has $800,000 of debt outstanding, and it pays an interest rate of 10 percent annually on its bank loan. Alumbat's annual sales are $3,200,000; its average tax rate is 40 percent; and its net profit margin on sales is 6 percent. If the company does not maintain a TIE ratio of at least 4 times, its bank will refuse to renew its loan, and bankruptcy will result. What is Alumbat's current TIE ratio? (5×)

3-5.   Austin & Company has a debt ratio of 0.5, a total assets turnover ratio of 0.25, and a profit margin of 10 percent. The Board of Directors is unhappy with the current return on equity (ROE), and they think it could be doubled. This could be accomplished (1) by increasing the profit margin to 12 percent, and (2) by increasing debt utilization. Total assets turnover will not change. What new debt ratio, along with the new 12 percent profit margin, would be required to double the ROE? (70%)

3-6.   Jecko Enterprises has an ROA of 12.5 percent, a 3 percent profit margin, and a return on equity equal to 16 percent.

    a.   What is the company's total assets turnover? (4.167×)

    b.   What is the firm's equity multiplier? (1.28)

    c.   What is the firm's debt ratio? Assume the firm has no preferred stock. (22%)

4-17 Assume that you recently graduated with a degree in finance and have just reported to work as an investment advisor at the brokerage firm of Smyth Barry & Co. Your first assignment is to explain the nature of the U.S. financial markets to Michelle Varga, a professional tennis player who has just come to the United States from Mexico. Varga is a highly ranked tennis player who expects to invest substantial amounts of money through Smyth Barry. She is also very bright, and, therefore, she would like to understand in general terms what will happen to her money. Your boss has developed the following set of questions that you must ask and answer to explain the U.S. financial system to Varga.

   a. What is a market? Differentiate between the following types of markets: physical asset vs. financial markets, spot vs. futures markets, money vs. capital markets, primary vs. secondary markets, and public vs. private markets.

   b. What is an initial public offering (IPO) market?

   c. If Apple Computer decided to issue additional common stock, and Varga purchased 100 shares of this stock from Merrill Lynch, the underwriter, would this transaction be a primary market transaction or a secondary market transaction? Would it make a difference if Varga purchased previously outstanding Apple stock in the dealer market?

   d. Describe the three primary ways in which capital is transferred between savers and borrowers.

   e. What are the two leading stock markets? Describe the two basic types of stock markets.

   f. What do we call the price that a borrower must pay for debt capital? What is the price of equity capital? What are the four most fundamental factors that affect the cost of money, or the general level of interest rates, in the economy?

   g. What is the real risk-free rate of interest (k^*) and the nominal risk-free rate (k_{RF})? How are these two rates measured?

   h. Define the terms inflation premium (IP), default risk premium (DRP), liquidity premium (LP), and maturity risk premium (MRP). Which of these premiums is included when determining the interest rate on (1) short-term U.S. Treasury securities, (2) long-term U.S. Treasury securities, (3) short-term corporate securities, and (4) long-term corporate securities? Explain how the premiums would vary over time and among the different securities listed above.

i.   What is the term structure of interest rates? What is a yield curve?

j.   Suppose most investors expect the inflation rate to be 5 percent next year, 6 percent the following year, and 8 percent thereafter. The real risk-free rate is 3 percent. The maturity risk premium is zero for bonds that mature in 1 year or less, 0.1 percent for 2-year bonds, and then the MRP increases by 0.1 percent per year thereafter for 20 years, after which it is stable. What is the interest rate on 1-year, 10-year, and 20-year Treasury bonds? Draw a yield curve with these data. What factors can explain why this constructed yield curve is upward sloping?

k.   At any given time, how would the yield curve facing an AAA-rated company compare with the yield curve for U.S. Treasury securities? At any given time, how would the yield curve facing a BB-rated company compare with the yield curve for U.S. Treasury securities? Draw a graph to illustrate your answer.

l.   What is the pure expectations theory? What does the pure expectations theory imply about the term structure of interest rates?

m. Suppose that you observe the following term structure for Treasury securities:

Maturity	Yield
1 year	6.0%
2 years	6.2
3 years	6.4
4 years	6.5
5 years	6.5

Assume that the pure expectations theory of the term structure is correct. (This implies that you can use the yield curve given above to "back out" the market's expectations about future interest rates.) What does the market expect will be the interest rate on 1-year securities one year from now? What does the market expect will be the interest rate on 3-year securities two years from now?

n.   Finally, Varga is also interested in investing in countries other than the United States. Describe the various types of risks that arise when investing overseas.

CHAPTER 4
The Financial Environment:
Markets, Institutions, and Interest Rates

- Financial markets
- Types of financial institutions
- Determinants of interest rates
- Yield curves

4-1

What is a market?

- A market is a venue where goods and services are exchanged.
- A financial market is a place where individuals and organizations wanting to borrow funds are brought together with those having a surplus of funds.

4-2

Types of financial markets

- Physical assets vs. Financial assets
- Money vs. Capital
- Primary vs. Secondary
- Spot vs. Futures
- Public vs. Private

4-3

How is capital transferred between savers and borrowers?

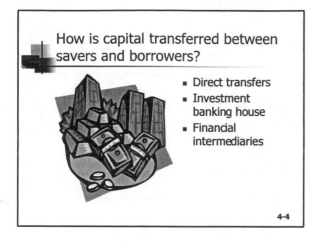

- Direct transfers
- Investment banking house
- Financial intermediaries

4-4

Types of financial intermediaries

- Commercial banks
- Savings and loan associations
- Mutual savings banks
- Credit unions
- Pension funds
- Life insurance companies
- Mutual funds

4-5

Physical location stock exchanges vs. Electronic dealer-based markets

- Auction market vs. Dealer market (Exchanges vs. OTC)
- NYSE vs. Nasdaq
- Differences are narrowing

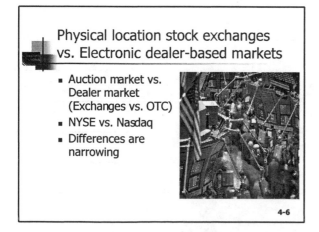

4-6

The cost of money

- The price, or cost, of debt capital is the interest rate.
- The price, or cost, of equity capital is the required return. The required return investors expect is composed of compensation in the form of dividends and capital gains.

4-7

What four factors affect the cost of money?

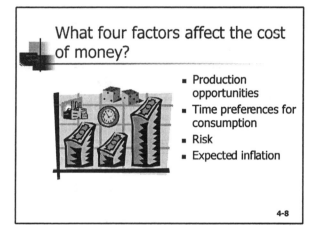

- Production opportunities
- Time preferences for consumption
- Risk
- Expected inflation

4-8

"Nominal" vs. "Real" rates

k = represents any nominal rate

k^* = represents the "real" risk-free rate of interest. Like a T-bill rate, if there was no inflation. Typically ranges from 1% to 4% per year.

k_{RF} = represents the rate of interest on Treasury securities.

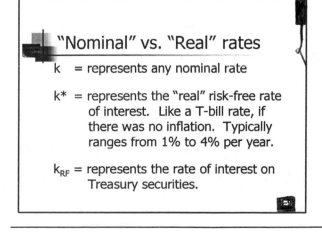

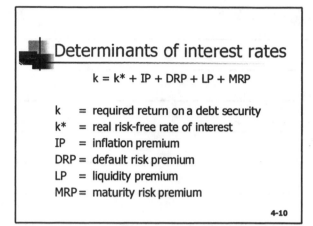

Determinants of interest rates

$$k = k^* + IP + DRP + LP + MRP$$

k   = required return on a debt security
k* = real risk-free rate of interest
IP = inflation premium
DRP = default risk premium
LP = liquidity premium
MRP= maturity risk premium

4-10

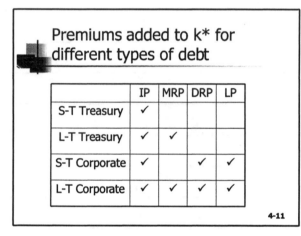

Premiums added to k* for different types of debt

	IP	MRP	DRP	LP
S-T Treasury	✓			
L-T Treasury	✓	✓		
S-T Corporate	✓		✓	✓
L-T Corporate	✓	✓	✓	✓

4-11

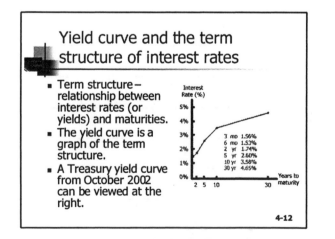

Yield curve and the term structure of interest rates

- Term structure – relationship between interest rates (or yields) and maturities.
- The yield curve is a graph of the term structure.
- A Treasury yield curve from October 2002 can be viewed at the right.

4-12

Constructing the yield curve: Inflation

- Step 1 – Find the average expected inflation rate over years 1 to n:

$$IP_n = \frac{\sum_{t=1}^{n} INFL_t}{n}$$

Constructing the yield curve: Inflation

Suppose, that inflation is expected to be 5% next year, 6% the following year, and 8% thereafter.

$IP_1 = 5\% / 1 = 5.00\%$

$IP_{10} = [5\% + 6\% + 8\%(8)] / 10 = 7.50\%$

$IP_{20} = [5\% + 6\% + 8\%(18)] / 20 = 7.75\%$

Must earn these IPs to break even vs. inflation; these IPs would permit you to earn k* (before taxes).

Constructing the yield curve: Inflation

- Step 2 – Find the appropriate maturity risk premium (MRP). For this example, the following equation will be used find a security's appropriate maturity risk premium.

$$MRP_t = 0.1\% \, (\, t - 1 \,)$$

Constructing the yield curve: Maturity Risk

Using the given equation:

$MRP_1 = 0.1\% \times (1-1) = 0.0\%$

$MRP_{10} = 0.1\% \times (10-1) = 0.9\%$

$MRP_{20} = 0.1\% \times (20-1) = 1.9\%$

Notice that since the equation is linear, the maturity risk premium is increasing in the time to maturity, as it should be.

4-16

Add the IPs and MRPs to k* to find the appropriate nominal rates

Step 3 – Adding the premiums to k*.

$k_{RF, t} = k^* + IP_t + MRP_t$

Assume k* = 3%,

$k_{RF, 1} = 3\% + 5.0\% + 0.0\% = 8.0\%$

$k_{RF, 10} = 3\% + 7.5\% + 0.9\% = 11.4\%$

$k_{RF, 20} = 3\% + 7.75\% + 1.9\% = 12.65\%$

4-17

Hypothetical yield curve

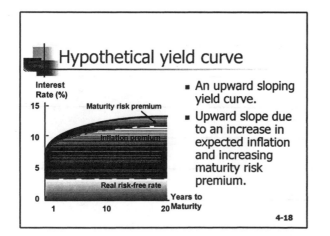

- An upward sloping yield curve.
- Upward slope due to an increase in expected inflation and increasing maturity risk premium.

4-18

What is the relationship between the Treasury yield curve and the yield curves for corporate issues?

- Corporate yield curves are higher than that of Treasury securities, though not necessarily parallel to the Treasury curve.
- The spread between corporate and Treasury yield curves widens as the corporate bond rating decreases.

4-19

Illustrating the relationship between corporate and Treasury yield curves

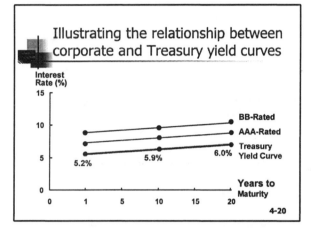

4-20

Pure Expectations Hypothesis

- The PEH contends that the shape of the yield curve depends on investor's expectations about future interest rates.
- If interest rates are expected to increase, L-T rates will be higher than S-T rates, and vice-versa. Thus, the yield curve can slope up, down, or even bow.

4-21

If ST rates are expected to increase LT rates will be higher than ST rates.

Assumptions of the PEH

- Assumes that the maturity risk premium for Treasury securities is zero.
- Long-term rates are an average of current and future short-term rates.
- If PEH is correct, you can use the yield curve to "back out" expected future interest rates.

4-22

An example:
Observed Treasury rates and the PEH

Maturity	Yield
1 year	6.0%
2 years	6.2%
3 years	6.4%
4 years	6.5%
5 years	6.5%

If PEH holds, what does the market expect will be the interest rate on one-year securities, one year from now? Three-year securities, two years from now?

4-23

One-year forward rate

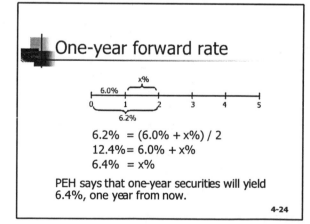

$6.2\% = (6.0\% + x\%) / 2$

$12.4\% = 6.0\% + x\%$

$6.4\% = x\%$

PEH says that one-year securities will yield 6.4%, one year from now.

4-24

Three-year security, two years from now

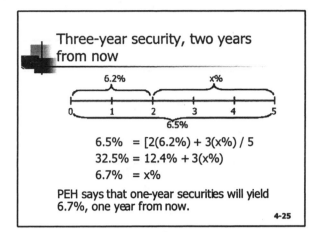

$$6.5\% = [2(6.2\%) + 3(x\%)] / 5$$
$$32.5\% = 12.4\% + 3(x\%)$$
$$6.7\% = x\%$$

PEH says that one-year securities will yield 6.7%, one year from now.

4-25

Conclusions about PEH

- Some would argue that the MRP ≠ 0, and hence the PEH is incorrect.
- Most evidence supports the general view that lenders prefer S-T securities, and view L-T securities as riskier.
- Thus, investors demand a MRP to get them to hold L-T securities (i.e., MRP > 0).

4-26

Other factors that influence interest rate levels

- Federal reserve policy
- Federal budget surplus or deficit
- Level of business activity
- International factors

4-27

Risks associated with investing overseas

- Exchange rate risk – If an investment is denominated in a currency other than U.S. dollars, the investment's value will depend on what happens to exchange rates.
- Country risk – Arises from investing or doing business in a particular country and depends on the country's economic, political, and social environment.

4-28

Factors that cause exchange rates to fluctuate

- Changes in relative inflation
- Changes in country risk

4-29

EXAM-TYPE PROBLEMS

4-1. Which of the following statements is most correct?

a. Since the default risk premium (DRP) and the liquidity premium (LP) are both essentially zero for U.S. Treasury securities, the Treasury yield curve is influenced more heavily by expected inflation than corporate bonds' yield curves, i.e., we can be sure that a given amount of expected inflation will have more effect on the slope of the Treasury yield curve than on the corporate yield curve.

b. Yield curves for government and corporate bonds can be constructed from data that exist in the marketplace. If the yield curves for several companies were plotted on a graph, along with the yield curve for U.S. Treasury securities, the company with the largest total of DRP plus LP would have the highest yield curve.

c. An upward-sloping yield curve is the normal situation, because long-term securities have less interest rate risk than shorter-term securities, hence smaller MRPs. Therefore, long-term rates are normally lower than short-term rates.

d. All of the statements above are true.

e. All of the above statements are false.

4-2. Assume that the real risk-free rate, k*, is 4 percent, and inflation is expected to be 9 percent in Year 1, 6 percent in Year 2, and 4 percent thereafter. Assume also that all Treasury bonds are highly liquid and free of default risk. If 2-year and 5-year Treasury bonds both yield 12 percent, what is the difference in the maturity risk premiums (MRPs) on the two bonds, i.e., what is $MRP_5 - MRP_2$? (+2.1%)

4-3. A Treasury bond that matures in 8 years has a yield of 6.6 percent. An 8-year corporate bond has a yield of 9.3 percent. Assume that the liquidity premium on the corporate bond is 0.6 percent. What is the default risk premium on the corporate bond? (2.1%)

5-23 Assume that you recently graduated with a major in finance, and you just landed a job as a financial planner with Merrill Finch Inc., a large financial services corporation. Your first assignment is to invest $100,000 for a client. Because the funds are to be invested in a business at the end of 1 year, you have been instructed to plan for a 1-year holding period. Further, your boss has restricted you to the following investment alternatives in the table below, shown with their probabilities and associated outcomes. (Disregard for now the items at the bottom of the data; you will fill in the blanks later.)

			Returns on Alternative Investments				
					Estimated Rate of Return		
State of the Economy	Prob.	T-Bills	High Tech	Collec-tions	U.S. Rubber	Market Portfolio	2-stock Portfolio
Recession	0.1	8.0%	(22.0%)	28.0%	10.0%*	(13.0%)	3.0%
Below avg	0.2	8.0	(2.0)	14.7	-10.0	1.0	
Average	0.4	8.0	20.0	0.0	7.0	15.0	10.0
Above avg	0.2	8.0	35.0	(10.0)	45.0	29.0	
Boom	0.1	8.0	50.0	(20.0)	30.0	43.0	15.0
$\hat{k}$				1.7%	13.8%	15.0%	
σ		0.0		13.4	18.8	15.3	3.3
CV				7.9	1.4	1.0	0.3
b				-0.87	0.89		

* Note that the estimated returns of U.S. Rubber do not always move in the same direction as the overall economy. For example, when the economy is below average, consumers purchase fewer tires than they would if the economy was stronger. However, if the economy is in a flat-out recession, a large number of consumers who were planning to purchase a new car may choose to wait and instead purchase new tires for the car they currently own. Under these circumstances, we would expect U.S. Rubber's stock price to be higher if there is a recession than if the economy was just below average.

Merrill Finch's economic forecasting staff has developed probability estimates for the state of the economy, and its security analysts have developed a sophisticated computer program, which was used to estimate the rate of return on each alternative under each state of the economy. High Tech Inc. is an electronics firm; Collections Inc. collects past-due debts; and U.S. Rubber manufactures tires and various other rubber and plastics products. Merrill Finch also maintains a "market portfolio" that owns a market-weighted fraction of all publicly traded stocks; you can invest in that portfolio, and thus obtain average stock market results. Given the situation as described, answer the following questions.

a. (1) Why is the T-bill's return independent of the state of the economy? Do T-bills promise a completely risk-free return?

(2) Why are High Tech's returns expected to move with the economy whereas Collections' are expected to move counter to the economy?

b. Calculate the expected rate of return on each alternative and fill in the blanks on the row for $\hat{k}$ in the table above.

c. You should recognize that basing a decision solely on expected returns is only appropriate for risk-neutral individuals. Since your client, like virtually everyone, is risk averse, the riskiness of each alternative is an important aspect of the decision. One possible measure of risk is the standard deviation of returns.

    (1) Calculate this value for each alternative, and fill in the blank on the row for σ in the table above.

    (2) What type of risk is measured by the standard deviation?

    (3) Draw a graph that shows *roughly* the shape of the probability distributions for High Tech, U.S. Rubber, and T-bills.

d. Suppose you suddenly remembered that the coefficient of variation (CV) is generally regarded as being a better measure of stand-alone risk than the standard deviation when the alternatives being considered have widely differing expected returns. Calculate the missing CVs, and fill in the blanks on the row for CV in the table above. Does the CV produce the same risk rankings as the standard deviation?

e. Suppose you created a 2-stock portfolio by investing $50,000 in High Tech and $50,000 in Collections.

    (1) Calculate the expected return ($\hat{k}_p$), the standard deviation (σ_p), and the coefficient of variation (CV_p) for this portfolio and fill in the appropriate blanks in the table above.

    (2) How does the riskiness of this 2-stock portfolio compare with the riskiness of the individual stocks if they were held in isolation?

f. Suppose an investor starts with a portfolio consisting of one randomly selected stock. What would happen (1) to the riskiness and (2) to the expected return of the portfolio as more and more randomly selected stocks were added to the portfolio? What is the implication for investors? Draw a graph of the two portfolios to illustrate your answer.

g. (1) Should portfolio effects impact the way investors think about the riskiness of individual stocks?

    (2) If you decided to hold a 1-stock portfolio, and consequently were exposed to more risk than diversified investors, could you expect to be compensated for

all of your risk; that is, could you earn a risk premium on that part of your risk that you could have eliminated by diversifying?

h. The expected rates of return and the beta coefficients of the alternatives as supplied by Merrill Finch's computer program are as follows:

Security	Return($\hat{k}$)	Risk (Beta)
High Tech	17.4%	1.30
Market	15.0	1.00
U.S. Rubber	13.8	0.89
T-bills	8.0	0.00
Collections	1.7	-0.87

(1) What is a beta coefficient, and how are betas used in risk analysis?

(2) Do the expected returns appear to be related to each alternative's market risk?

(3) Is it possible to choose among the alternatives on the basis of the information developed thus far? Use the data given at the start of the problem to construct a graph that shows how the T-bill's, High Tech's, and the market's beta coefficients are calculated. Then discuss what betas measure and how they are used in risk analysis.

i. The yield curve is currently flat, that is, long-term Treasury bonds also have an 8 percent yield. Consequently, Merrill Finch assumes that the risk-free rate is 8 percent.

(1) Write out the Security Market Line (SML) equation, use it to calculate the required rate of return on each alternative, and then graph the relationship between the expected and required rates of return.

(2) How do the expected rates of return compare with the required rates of return?

(3) Does the fact that Collections has an expected return that is less than the T-bill rate make any sense?

(4) What would be the market risk and the required return of a 50-50 portfolio of High Tech and Collections? Of High Tech and U.S. Rubber?

j. (1) Suppose investors raised their inflation expectations by 3 percentage points over current estimates as reflected in the 8 percent risk-free rate. What effect would higher inflation have on the SML and on the returns required on high- and low-risk securities?

(2) Suppose instead that investors' risk aversion increased enough to cause the market risk premium to increase by 3 percentage points. (Inflation remains constant.) What effect would this have on the SML and on returns of high- and low-risk securities?

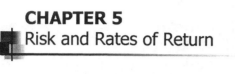

CHAPTER 5
Risk and Rates of Return

- Stand-alone risk
- Portfolio risk
- Risk & return: CAPM / SML

5-1

Investment returns

The rate of return on an investment can be calculated as follows:

$$\text{Return} = \frac{(\text{Amount received} - \text{Amount invested})}{\text{Amount invested}}$$

For example, if $1,000 is invested and $1,100 is returned after one year, the rate of return for this investment is:

($1,100 - $1,000) / $1,000 = 10%.

5-2

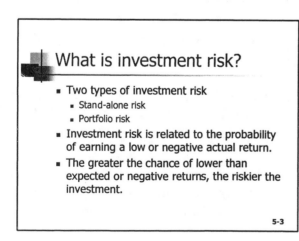

What is investment risk?

- Two types of investment risk
  - Stand-alone risk
  - Portfolio risk
- Investment risk is related to the probability of earning a low or negative actual return.
- The greater the chance of lower than expected or negative returns, the riskier the investment.

5-3

Probability distributions

- A listing of all possible outcomes, and the probability of each occurrence.
- Can be shown graphically.

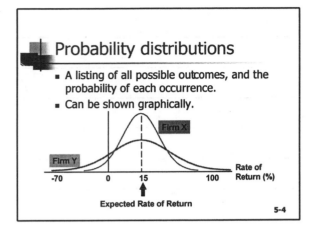

5-4

Selected Realized Returns, 1926 – 2001

	Average Return	Standard Deviation
Small-company stocks	17.3%	33.2%
Large-company stocks	12.7	20.2
L-T corporate bonds	6.1	8.6
L-T government bonds	5.7	9.4
U.S. Treasury bills	3.9	3.2

Source: Based on *Stocks, Bonds, Bills, and Inflation: (Valuation Edition) 2002 Yearbook* (Chicago: Ibbotson Associates, 2002), 28.

5-5

Investment alternatives

Economy	Prob.	T-Bill	HT	Coll	USR	MP
Recession	0.1	8.0%	-22.0%	28.0%	10.0%	-13.0%
Below avg	0.2	8.0%	-2.0%	14.7%	-10.0%	1.0%
Average	0.4	8.0%	20.0%	0.0%	7.0%	15.0%
Above avg	0.2	8.0%	35.0%	-10.0%	45.0%	29.0%
Boom	0.1	8.0%	50.0%	-20.0%	30.0%	43.0%

5-6

Why is the T-bill return independent of the economy? Do T-bills promise a completely risk-free return?

- T-bills will return the promised 8%, regardless of the economy.
- No, T-bills do not provide a risk-free return, as they are still exposed to inflation. Although, very little unexpected inflation is likely to occur over such a short period of time.
- T-bills are also risky in terms of reinvestment rate risk.
- T-bills are risk-free in the default sense of the word.

5-7

How do the returns of HT and Coll. behave in relation to the market?

- HT – Moves with the economy, and has a positive correlation. This is typical.
- Coll. – Is countercyclical with the economy, and has a negative correlation. This is unusual.

5-8

Return: Calculating the expected return for each alternative

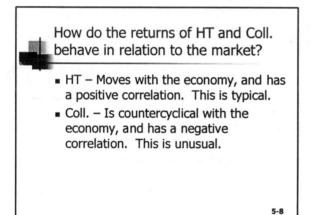

$\hat{k}$ = expected rate of return

$$\hat{k} = \sum_{i=1}^{n} k_i P_i$$

$\hat{k}_{HT} = (-22.\%)(0.1) + (-2\%)(0.2)$
$+ (20\%)(0.4) + (35\%)(0.2)$
$+ (50\%)(0.1) = 17.4\%$

5-9

Summary of expected returns for all alternatives

	Exp return
HT	17.4%
Market	15.0%
USR	13.8%
T-bill	8.0%
Coll.	1.7%

HT has the highest expected return, and appears to be the best investment alternative, but is it really? Have we failed to account for risk?

5-10

_____

_____

_____

_____

_____

_____

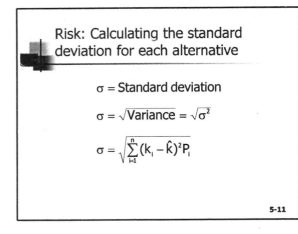

Risk: Calculating the standard deviation for each alternative

σ = Standard deviation

$\sigma = \sqrt{\text{Variance}} = \sqrt{\sigma^2}$

$\sigma = \sqrt{\sum_{i=1}^{n}(k_i - \hat{k})^2 P_i}$

5-11

_____

_____

_____

_____

_____

_____

_____

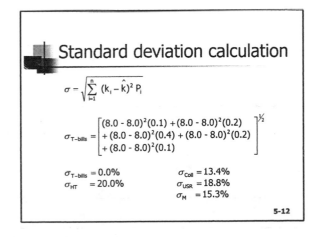

Standard deviation calculation

$\sigma = \sqrt{\sum_{i=1}^{n}(k_i - \hat{k})^2 P_i}$

$$\sigma_{T-bills} = \left[\begin{array}{l} (8.0 - 8.0)^2(0.1) + (8.0 - 8.0)^2(0.2) \\ + (8.0 - 8.0)^2(0.4) + (8.0 - 8.0)^2(0.2) \\ + (8.0 - 8.0)^2(0.1) \end{array} \right]^{1/2}$$

$\sigma_{T-bills} = 0.0\%$ $\sigma_{Coll} = 13.4\%$

$\sigma_{HT} = 20.0\%$ $\sigma_{USR} = 18.8\%$

$\sigma_M = 15.3\%$

5-12

_____

_____

_____

_____

_____

_____

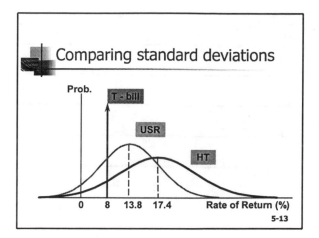

Comparing standard deviations

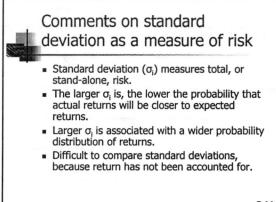

Comments on standard deviation as a measure of risk

- Standard deviation (σ_i) measures total, or stand-alone, risk.
- The larger σ_i is, the lower the probability that actual returns will be closer to expected returns.
- Larger σ_i is associated with a wider probability distribution of returns.
- Difficult to compare standard deviations, because return has not been accounted for.

5-14

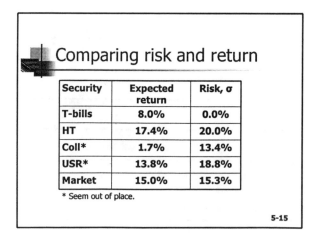

Comparing risk and return

Security	Expected return	Risk, σ
T-bills	8.0%	0.0%
HT	17.4%	20.0%
Coll*	1.7%	13.4%
USR*	13.8%	18.8%
Market	15.0%	15.3%

* Seem out of place.

5-15

Coefficient of Variation (CV)

A standardized measure of dispersion about the expected value, that shows the risk per unit of return.

$$CV = \frac{\text{Std dev}}{\text{Mean}} = \frac{\sigma}{\hat{k}}$$

5-16

Risk rankings, by coefficient of variation

	CV
T-bill	0.000
HT	1.149
Coll.	7.882
USR	1.362
Market	1.020

- Collections has the highest degree of risk per unit of return.
- HT, despite having the highest standard deviation of returns, has a relatively average CV.

5-17

Illustrating the CV as a measure of relative risk

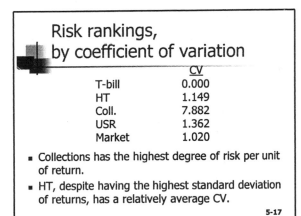

$\sigma_A = \sigma_B$, but A is riskier because of a larger probability of losses. In other words, the same amount of risk (as measured by σ) for less returns.

5-18

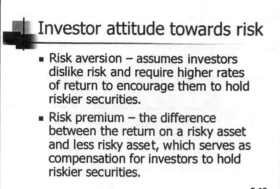

Investor attitude towards risk

- Risk aversion – assumes investors dislike risk and require higher rates of return to encourage them to hold riskier securities.
- Risk premium – the difference between the return on a risky asset and less risky asset, which serves as compensation for investors to hold riskier securities.

5-19

Portfolio construction: Risk and return

Assume a two-stock portfolio is created with $50,000 invested in both HT and Collections.

- Expected return of a portfolio is a weighted average of each of the component assets of the portfolio.
- Standard deviation is a little more tricky and requires that a new probability distribution for the portfolio returns be devised.

5-20

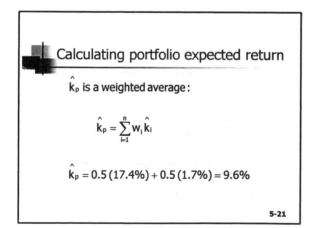

Calculating portfolio expected return

$\hat{k}_p$ is a weighted average:

$$\hat{k}_p = \sum_{i=1}^{n} w_i \hat{k}_i$$

$$\hat{k}_p = 0.5\,(17.4\%) + 0.5\,(1.7\%) = 9.6\%$$

5-21

An alternative method for determining portfolio expected return

Economy	Prob.	HT	Coll	Port.
Recession	0.1	-22.0%	28.0%	**3.0%**
Below avg	0.2	-2.0%	14.7%	**6.4%**
Average	0.4	20.0%	0.0%	**10.0%**
Above avg	0.2	35.0%	-10.0%	**12.5%**
Boom	0.1	50.0%	-20.0%	**15.0%**

$$\hat{k}_P = 0.10\,(3.0\%) + 0.20\,(6.4\%) + 0.40\,(10.0\%)$$
$$+ 0.20\,(12.5\%) + 0.10\,(15.0\%) = 9.6\%$$

5-22

Calculating portfolio standard deviation and CV

$$\sigma_p = \left[\begin{array}{l} 0.10\,(3.0 - 9.6)^2 \\ + 0.20\,(6.4 - 9.6)^2 \\ + 0.40\,(10.0 - 9.6)^2 \\ + 0.20\,(12.5 - 9.6)^2 \\ + 0.10\,(15.0 - 9.6)^2 \end{array} \right]^{\frac{1}{2}} = 3.3\%$$

$$CV_p = \frac{3.3\%}{9.6\%} = 0.34$$

5-23

Comments on portfolio risk measures

- σ_p = 3.3% is much lower than the σ_i of either stock (σ_{HT} = 20.0%; $\sigma_{Coll.}$ = 13.4%).
- σ_p = 3.3% is lower than the weighted average of HT and Coll.'s σ (16.7%).
- ∴ Portfolio provides average return of component stocks, but lower than average risk.
- Why? Negative correlation between stocks.

5-24

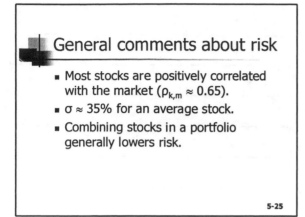

General comments about risk

- Most stocks are positively correlated with the market ($\rho_{k,m} \approx 0.65$).
- $\sigma \approx 35\%$ for an average stock.
- Combining stocks in a portfolio generally lowers risk.

5-25

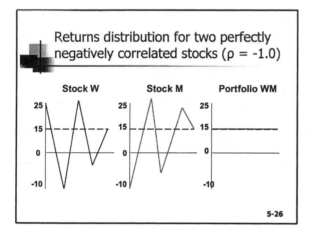

Returns distribution for two perfectly negatively correlated stocks ($\rho = -1.0$)

Stock W   Stock M   Portfolio WM

5-26

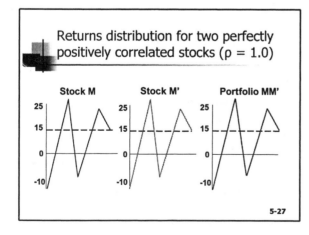

Returns distribution for two perfectly positively correlated stocks ($\rho = 1.0$)

Stock M   Stock M'   Portfolio MM'

5-27

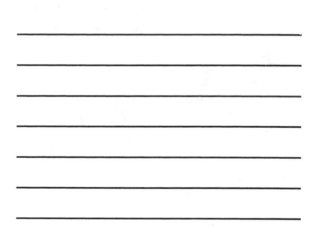

Creating a portfolio:
Beginning with one stock and adding randomly selected stocks to portfolio

- σ_p decreases as stocks added, because they would not be perfectly correlated with the existing portfolio.
- Expected return of the portfolio would remain relatively constant.
- Eventually the diversification benefits of adding more stocks dissipates (after about 10 stocks), and for large stock portfolios, σ_p tends to converge to $\approx$ 20%.

5-28

Illustrating diversification effects of a stock portfolio

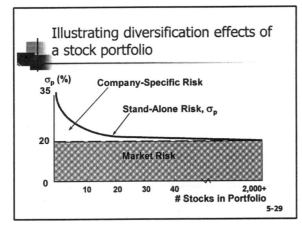

5-29

Breaking down sources of risk

Stand-alone risk = Market risk + Firm-specific risk

- Market risk – portion of a security's stand-alone risk that cannot be eliminated through diversification. Measured by beta.
- Firm-specific risk – portion of a security's stand-alone risk that can be eliminated through proper diversification.

5-30

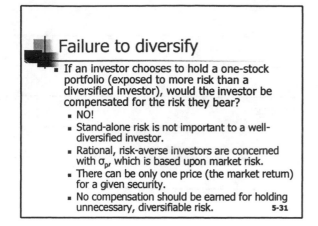

Failure to diversify

- If an investor chooses to hold a one-stock portfolio (exposed to more risk than a diversified investor), would the investor be compensated for the risk they bear?
  - NO!
  - Stand-alone risk is not important to a well-diversified investor.
  - Rational, risk-averse investors are concerned with σ_p, which is based upon market risk.
  - There can be only one price (the market return) for a given security.
  - No compensation should be earned for holding unnecessary, diversifiable risk.

5-31

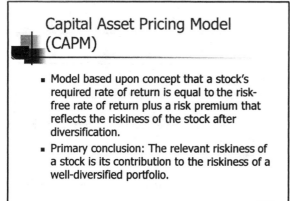

Capital Asset Pricing Model (CAPM)

- Model based upon concept that a stock's required rate of return is equal to the risk-free rate of return plus a risk premium that reflects the riskiness of the stock after diversification.
- Primary conclusion: The relevant riskiness of a stock is its contribution to the riskiness of a well-diversified portfolio.

5-32

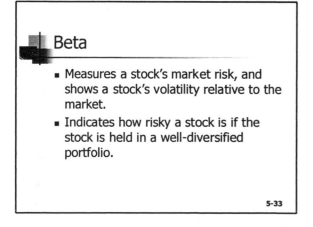

Beta

- Measures a stock's market risk, and shows a stock's volatility relative to the market.
- Indicates how risky a stock is if the stock is held in a well-diversified portfolio.

5-33

Calculating betas

- Run a regression of past returns of a security against past returns on the market.
- The slope of the regression line (sometimes called the security's characteristic line) is defined as the beta coefficient for the security.

5-34

Illustrating the calculation of beta

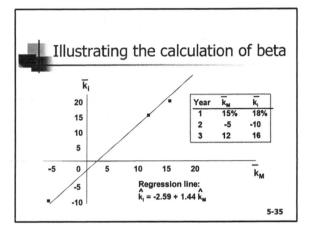

Year	$\overline{k}_M$	$\overline{k}_i$
1	15%	18%
2	-5	-10
3	12	16

Regression line:
$$\hat{k}_i = -2.59 + 1.44\,\hat{k}_M$$

5-35

Comments on beta

- If beta = 1.0, the security is just as risky as the average stock.
- If beta > 1.0, the security is riskier than average.
- If beta < 1.0, the security is less risky than average.
- Most stocks have betas in the range of 0.5 to 1.5.

5-36

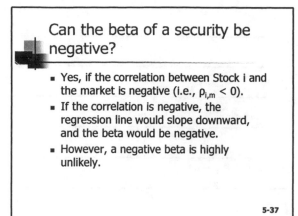

Can the beta of a security be negative?

- Yes, if the correlation between Stock i and the market is negative (i.e., $\rho_{i,m} < 0$).
- If the correlation is negative, the regression line would slope downward, and the beta would be negative.
- However, a negative beta is highly unlikely.

5-37

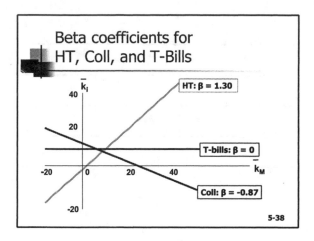

Beta coefficients for HT, Coll, and T-Bills

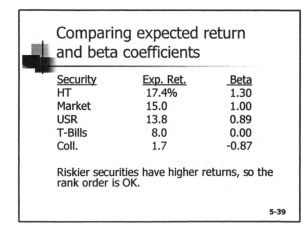

5-38

Comparing expected return and beta coefficients

Security	Exp. Ret.	Beta
HT	17.4%	1.30
Market	15.0	1.00
USR	13.8	0.89
T-Bills	8.0	0.00
Coll.	1.7	-0.87

Riskier securities have higher returns, so the rank order is OK.

5-39

The Security Market Line (SML): Calculating required rates of return

$$\text{SML: } k_i = k_{RF} + (k_M - k_{RF})\,\beta_i$$

- Assume $k_{RF} = 8\%$ and $k_M = 15\%$.
- The market (or equity) risk premium is $RP_M = k_M - k_{RF} = 15\% - 8\% = 7\%$.

5-40

What is the market risk premium?

- Additional return over the risk-free rate needed to compensate investors for assuming an average amount of risk.
- Its size depends on the perceived risk of the stock market and investors' degree of risk aversion.
- Varies from year to year, but most estimates suggest that it ranges between 4% and 8% per year.

5-41

Calculating required rates of return

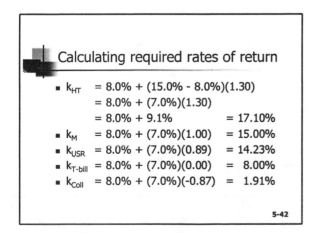

- k_{HT} = 8.0% + (15.0% - 8.0%)(1.30)
  = 8.0% + (7.0%)(1.30)
  = 8.0% + 9.1%   = 17.10%
- k_M = 8.0% + (7.0%)(1.00) = 15.00%
- k_{USR} = 8.0% + (7.0%)(0.89) = 14.23%
- $k_{T\text{-bill}}$ = 8.0% + (7.0%)(0.00) = 8.00%
- k_{Coll} = 8.0% + (7.0%)(-0.87) = 1.91%

5-42

Expected vs. Required returns

	$\hat{k}$	k	
HT	17.4%	17.1%	Undervalued ($\hat{k} > k$)
Market	15.0	15.0	Fairly valued ($\hat{k} = k$)
USR	13.8	14.2	Overvalued ($\hat{k} < k$)
T - bills	8.0	8.0	Fairly valued ($\hat{k} = k$)
Coll.	1.7	1.9	Overvalued ($\hat{k} < k$)

5-43

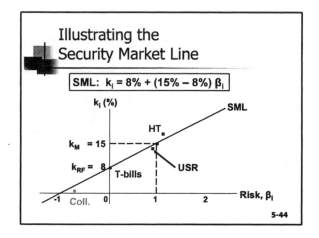

Illustrating the Security Market Line

SML: $k_i = 8\% + (15\% - 8\%)\beta_i$

5-44

An example: Equally-weighted two-stock portfolio

- Create a portfolio with 50% invested in HT and 50% invested in Collections.
- The beta of a portfolio is the weighted average of each of the stock's betas.

$$\beta_P = w_{HT}\,\beta_{HT} + w_{Coll}\,\beta_{Coll}$$
$$\beta_P = 0.5\,(1.30) + 0.5\,(-0.87)$$
$$\beta_P = 0.215$$

5-45

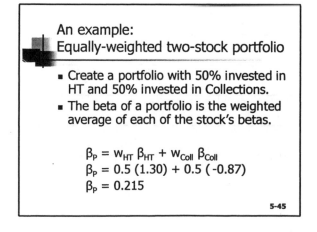

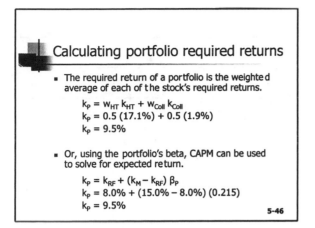

Calculating portfolio required returns

- The required return of a portfolio is the weighted average of each of the stock's required returns.

$$k_P = w_{HT} k_{HT} + w_{Coll} k_{Coll}$$
$$k_P = 0.5 (17.1\%) + 0.5 (1.9\%)$$
$$k_P = 9.5\%$$

- Or, using the portfolio's beta, CAPM can be used to solve for expected return.

$$k_P = k_{RF} + (k_M - k_{RF}) \beta_P$$
$$k_P = 8.0\% + (15.0\% - 8.0\%) (0.215)$$
$$k_P = 9.5\%$$

5-46

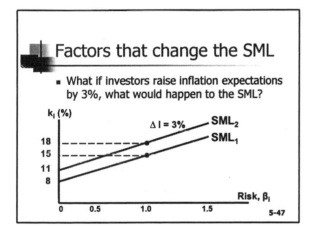

Factors that change the SML

- What if investors raise inflation expectations by 3%, what would happen to the SML?

5-47

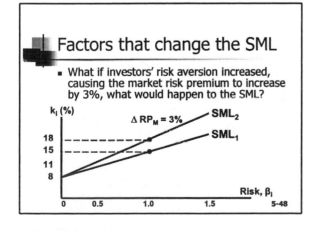

Factors that change the SML

- What if investors' risk aversion increased, causing the market risk premium to increase by 3%, what would happen to the SML?

5-48

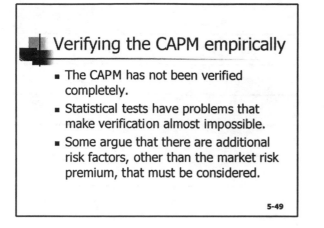

Verifying the CAPM empirically

- The CAPM has not been verified completely.
- Statistical tests have problems that make verification almost impossible.
- Some argue that there are additional risk factors, other than the market risk premium, that must be considered.

5-49

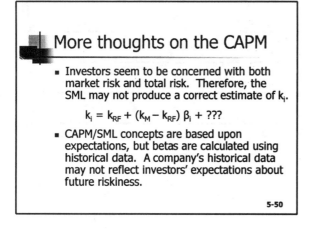

More thoughts on the CAPM

- Investors seem to be concerned with both market risk and total risk. Therefore, the SML may not produce a correct estimate of k_i.

$$k_i = k_{RF} + (k_M - k_{RF})\ \beta_i + ???$$

- CAPM/SML concepts are based upon expectations, but betas are calculated using historical data. A company's historical data may not reflect investors' expectations about future riskiness.

5-50

EXAM-TYPE PROBLEMS

5-1. For markets to be in equilibrium (that is, for there to be no strong pressure for prices to depart from their current levels),

a. The expected rate of return must be equal to the required rate of return; that is, $\hat{k} = k$.

b. The past realized rate of return must be equal to the expected rate of return; that is, $\bar{k} = \hat{k}$.

c. The required rate of return must equal the realized rate of return; that is, $k = \bar{k}$.

d. All three of the above statements must hold for equilibrium to exist; that is, $\hat{k} = k = \bar{k}$.

e. None of the above statements is correct.

5-2. Which of the following statements is most correct?

a. According to CAPM theory, the required rate of return on a given stock can be found by use of the SML equation:

$$k_i = k_{RF} + (k_M - k_{RF})b_i.$$

Expectations for inflation are not reflected anywhere in this equation, even indirectly, and because of that the text notes that the CAPM may not be strictly correct.

b. If the required rate of return is given by the SML equation as set forth in answer a, there is nothing a financial manager can do to change his or her company's cost of capital, because each of the elements in the equation is determined exclusively by the market, not by the type of actions a company's management can take, even in the long run.

c. Assume that the required rate of return on the market is currently $k_M = 15\%$, and that k_M remains fixed at that level. If the yield curve has a steep upward slope, the calculated market risk premium would be larger if the 30-day T-bill rate were used as the risk-free rate than if the 30-year T-bond rate were used as k_{RF}.

d. Statements a and b are true.

e. Statements a and c are true.

5-3. You hold a diversified portfolio consisting of a $5,000 investment in each of 20 different common stocks. The portfolio beta is equal to 1.15. You have decided to sell one of your stocks, a lead mining stock whose b = 1.0, for $5,000 net and to use the proceeds to buy $5,000 of stock in a steel company whose b = 2.0. What will be the portfolio's new beta? (1.20)

5-4.   Electro Inc. has a beta of 1.7, Flowers Galore has a beta of 0.6, the expected rate of return on an average stock is 14 percent, and the risk-free rate of return is 7.8 percent. By how much does the required return on the riskier stock exceed the required return on the less risky stock? (+6.82%)

6-50 Assume that you are nearing graduation and that you have applied for a job with a local bank, First National Bank. As part of the bank's evaluation process, you have been asked to take an examination that covers several financial analysis techniques. The first section of the test addresses time value of money analysis. See how you would do by answering the following questions.

  a. Draw time lines for (1) a $100 lump sum cash flow at the end of Year 2, (2) an ordinary annuity of $100 per year for 3 years, and (3) an uneven cash flow stream of -$50, $100, $75, and $50 at the end of Years 0 through 3.

  b. (1) What is the future value of an initial $100 after 3 years if it is invested in an account paying 10 percent, annual compounding?

  (2) What is the present value of $100 to be received in 3 years if the appropriate interest rate is 10 percent, annual compounding?

  c. We sometimes need to find how long it will take a sum of money (or anything else) to grow to some specified amount. For example, if a company's sales are growing at a rate of 20 percent per year, how long will it take sales to double?

  d. What is the difference between an ordinary annuity and an annuity due? What type of annuity is shown below? How would you change it to the other type of annuity?

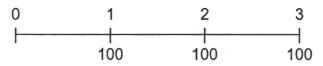

  e. (1) What is the future value of a 3-year ordinary annuity of $100 if the appropriate interest rate is 10 percent, annual compounding?

  (2) What is the present value of the annuity?

  (3) What would the future and present values be if the annuity were an annuity due?

---

f. What is the present value of the following uneven cash flow stream? The appropriate interest rate is 10 percent, compounded annually.

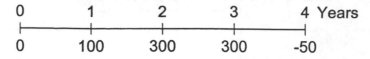

g. What annual interest rate will cause $100 to grow to $125.97 in 3 years?

h. A 20-year-old student wants to begin saving for her retirement. Her plan is to save $3 a day. Every day she places $3 in a drawer. At the end of each year, she invests the accumulated savings ($1,095) in an online stock account that has an expected annual return of 12 percent.
   (1) If she keeps saving in this manner, how much will she have accumulated by age 65?

   (2) If a 40-year-old investor began saving in this manner, how much would he have by age 65?

   (3) How much would the 40-year-old investor have to save each year to accumulate the same amount at age 65 as the 20-year-old investor described above?

i. (1) Will the future value be larger or smaller if we compound an initial amount more often than annually, for example, every 6 months, or *semiannually*, holding the stated interest rate constant? Why?

   (2) Define (a) the stated, or quoted, or nominal, rate, (b) the periodic rate, and (c) the effective annual rate (EAR).

   (3) What is the effective annual rate corresponding to a nominal rate of 10 percent, compounded semiannually? Compounded quarterly? Compounded daily?

   (4) What is the future value of $100 after 3 years under 10 percent semiannual compounding? Quarterly compounding?

j. When will the effective annual rate be equal to the nominal (quoted) rate?

k. (1) What is the value at the end of Year 3 of the following cash flow stream if the quoted interest rate is 10 percent, compounded semiannually?

   (2) What is the PV of the same stream?

   (3) Is the stream an annuity?

(4) An important rule is that you should *never* show a nominal rate on a time line or use it in calculations unless what condition holds? (Hint: Think of annual compounding, when i_{Nom} = EAR = i_{PER}.) What would be wrong with your answer to parts k(1) and k(2) if you used the nominal rate, 10 percent, rather than the periodic rate, $i_{Nom}/2$ = 10%/2 = 5%?

l. (1) Construct an amortization schedule for a $1,000, 10 percent, annual compounding loan with 3 equal installments.

 (2) What is the annual interest expense for the borrower, and the annual interest income for the lender, during Year 2?

m. Suppose a house is on the market for $250,000, and a bank agrees to lend the potential home buyer $220,000 secured by a mortgage on the house. Thus, the buyer must come up with $30,000 to complete the transaction. For purposes of this question, ignore any additional closing costs. Suppose the buyer has only $7,500 cash, and the seller agrees to take a note with the following terms: a face value of $22,500, a 7.5 percent annual interest rate, and payments at the end of the year based on a 20-year amortization schedule, but with the loan maturing at the end of the 10th year.
 (1) What is the balloon portion of the payment due at the end of the 10th year?
 (2) What is the total payment that will be due at the end of the 10th year?

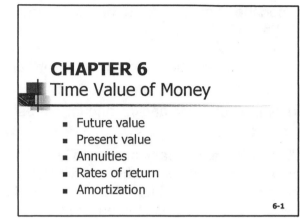

CHAPTER 6
Time Value of Money

- Future value
- Present value
- Annuities
- Rates of return
- Amortization

6-1

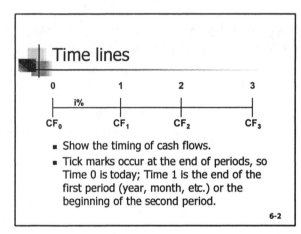

Time lines

0	1	2	3
	i%		
CF_0	CF_1	CF_2	CF_3

- Show the timing of cash flows.
- Tick marks occur at the end of periods, so Time 0 is today; Time 1 is the end of the first period (year, month, etc.) or the beginning of the second period.

6-2

Drawing time lines:
$100 lump sum due in 2 years;
3-year $100 ordinary annuity

$100 lump sum due in 2 years

0	1	2
	i%	
		100

3 year $100 ordinary annuity

0	1	2	3
	i%		
	100	100	100

6-3

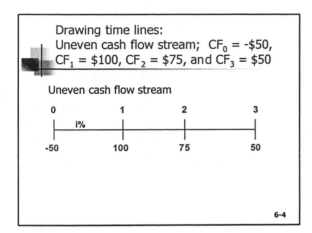

Drawing time lines:
Uneven cash flow stream; $CF_0 = -\$50$,
$CF_1 = \$100$, $CF_2 = \$75$, and $CF_3 = \$50$

Uneven cash flow stream

0	1	2	3
i%			
-50	100	75	50

6-4

What is the future value (FV) of an initial $100 after 3 years, if I/YR = 10%?

- Finding the FV of a cash flow or series of cash flows when compound interest is applied is called compounding.
- FV can be solved by using the arithmetic, financial calculator, and spreadsheet methods.

0	1	2	3
10%			
100			FV = ?

6-5

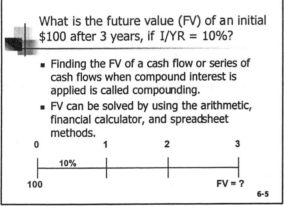

Solving for FV:
The arithmetic method

- After 1 year:
  - $FV_1 = PV(1 + i) = \$100(1.10)$
    $= \$110.00$
- After 2 years:
  - $FV_2 = PV(1 + i)^2 = \$100(1.10)^2$
    $= \$121.00$
- After 3 years:
  - $FV_3 = PV(1 + i)^3 = \$100(1.10)^3$
    $= \$133.10$
- After n years (general case):
  - $FV_n = PV(1 + i)^n$

6-6

Solving for FV: The calculator method

- Solves the general FV equation.
- Requires 4 inputs into calculator, and will solve for the fifth. (Set to P/YR = 1 and END mode.)

6-7

What is the present value (PV) of $100 due in 3 years, if I/YR = 10%?

- Finding the PV of a cash flow or series of cash flows when compound interest is applied is called discounting (the reverse of compounding).
- The PV shows the value of cash flows in terms of today's purchasing power.

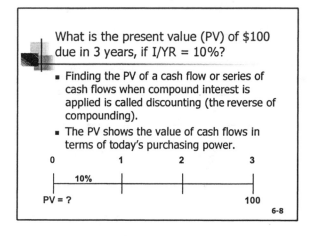

6-8

Solving for PV: The arithmetic method

- Solve the general FV equation for PV:
  - $PV = FV_n / (1 + i)^n$

  - $PV = FV_3 / (1 + i)^3$
    $= \$100 / (1.10)^3$
    $= \$75.13$

6-9

Solving for PV: The calculator method

- Solves the general FV equation for PV.
- Exactly like solving for FV, except we have different input information and are solving for a different variable.

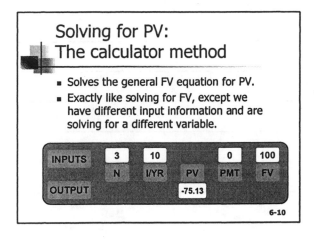

6-10

Solving for N: If sales grow at 20% per year, how long before sales double?

- Solves the general FV equation for N.
- Same as previous problems, but now solving for N.

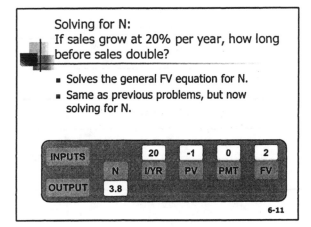

6-11

What is the difference between an ordinary annuity and an annuity due?

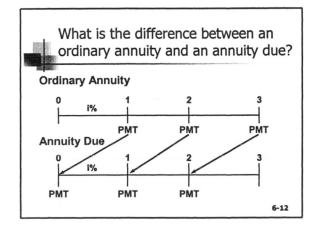

6-12

Solving for FV:
3-year ordinary annuity of $100 at 10%

- $100 payments occur at the end of each period, but there is no PV.

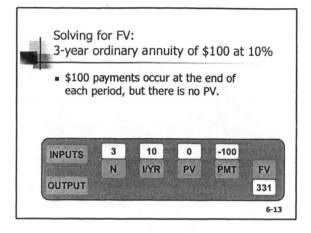

6-13

Solving for PV:
3-year ordinary annuity of $100 at 10%

- $100 payments still occur at the end of each period, but now there is no FV.

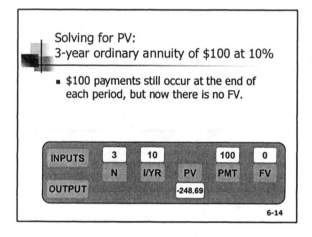

6-14

Solving for FV:
3-year annuity due of $100 at 10%

- Now, $100 payments occur at the beginning of each period.
- Set calculator to "BEGIN" mode.

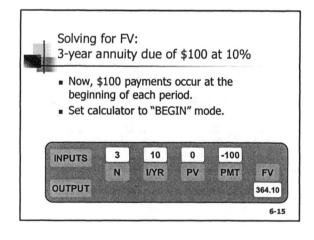

6-15

Solving for PV:
3 year annuity due of $100 at 10%

- Again, $100 payments occur at the beginning of each period.
- Set calculator to "BEGIN" mode.

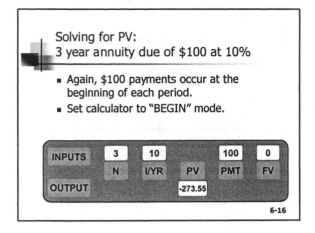

6-16

What is the PV of this uneven cash flow stream?

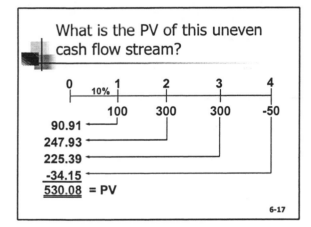

6-17

Solving for PV:
Uneven cash flow stream

- Input cash flows in the calculator's "CFLO" register:
  - $CF_0 = 0$
  - $CF_1 = 100$
  - $CF_2 = 300$
  - $CF_3 = 300$
  - $CF_4 = -50$
- Enter I/YR = 10, press NPV button to get NPV = $530.09. (Here NPV = PV.)

6-18

Solving for I:
What interest rate would cause $100 to grow to $125.97 in 3 years?

- Solves the general FV equation for I.

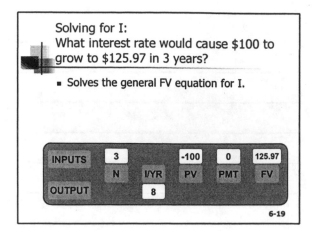

6-19

The Power of Compound Interest

A 20-year-old student wants to start saving for retirement. She plans to save $3 a day. Every day, she puts $3 in her drawer. At the end of the year, she invests the accumulated savings ($1,095) in an online stock account. The stock account has an expected annual return of 12%.

How much money will she have when she is 65 years old?

6-20

Solving for FV:
Savings problem

- If she begins saving today, and sticks to her plan, she will have $1,487,261.89 when she is 65.

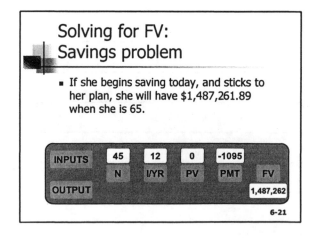

6-21

Solving for FV:
Savings problem, if you wait until you are 40 years old to start

- If a 40-year-old investor begins saving today, and sticks to the plan, he or she will have $146,000.59 at age 65. This is $1.3 million less than if starting at age 20.
- Lesson: It pays to start saving early.

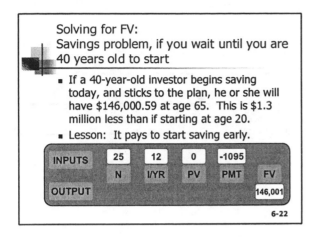

6-22

Solving for PMT:
How much must the 40-year old deposit annually to catch the 20-year old?

- To find the required annual contribution, enter the number of years until retirement and the final goal of $1,487,261.89, and solve for PMT.

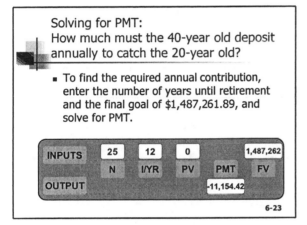

6-23

Will the FV of a lump sum be larger or smaller if compounded more often, holding the stated I% constant?

- LARGER, as the more frequently compounding occurs, interest is earned on interest more often.

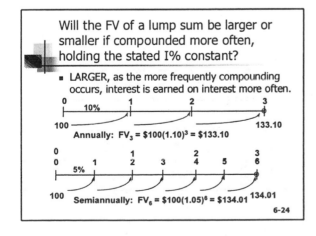

Annually: FV$_3$ = $100(1.10)^3 = $133.10

Semiannually: FV$_6$ = $100(1.05)^6 = $134.01

6-24

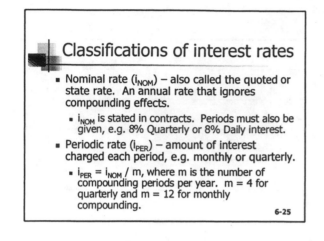

Classifications of interest rates

- Nominal rate (i_{NOM}) – also called the quoted or state rate. An annual rate that ignores compounding effects.
  - i_{NOM} is stated in contracts. Periods must also be given, e.g. 8% Quarterly or 8% Daily interest.
- Periodic rate (i_{PER}) – amount of interest charged each period, e.g. monthly or quarterly.
  - $i_{PER} = i_{NOM} / m$, where m is the number of compounding periods per year. m = 4 for quarterly and m = 12 for monthly compounding.

6-25

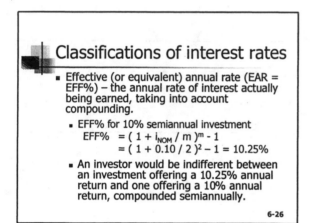

Classifications of interest rates

- Effective (or equivalent) annual rate (EAR = EFF%) – the annual rate of interest actually being earned, taking into account compounding.
  - EFF% for 10% semiannual investment
    $$EFF\% = (1 + i_{NOM} / m)^m - 1$$
    $$= (1 + 0.10 / 2)^2 - 1 = 10.25\%$$
  - An investor would be indifferent between an investment offering a 10.25% annual return and one offering a 10% annual return, compounded semiannually.

6-26

Why is it important to consider effective rates of return?

- An investment with monthly payments is different from one with quarterly payments. Must put each return on an EFF% basis to compare rates of return. Must use EFF% for comparisons. See following values of EFF% rates at various compounding levels.

EAR$_{ANNUAL}$	10.00%
EAR$_{QUARTERLY}$	10.38%
EAR$_{MONTHLY}$	10.47%
EAR$_{DAILY (365)}$	10.52%

6-27

Can the effective rate ever be equal to the nominal rate?

- Yes, but only if annual compounding is used, i.e., if m = 1.
- If m > 1, EFF% will always be greater than the nominal rate.

6-28

When is each rate used?

- i_{NOM} written into contracts, quoted by banks and brokers. Not used in calculations or shown on time lines.
- i_{PER} Used in calculations and shown on time lines. If m = 1, $i_{NOM} = i_{PER} =$ EAR.
- EAR Used to compare returns on investments with different payments per year. Used in calculations when annuity payments don't match compounding periods.

6-29

What is the FV of $100 after 3 years under 10% semiannual compounding? Quarterly compounding?

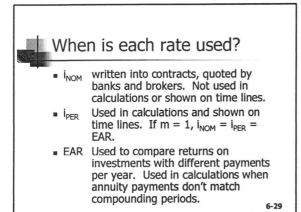

$$FV_n = PV \left(1 + \frac{i_{NOM}}{m} \right)^{m \times n}$$

$$FV_{3S} = \$100 \left(1 + \frac{0.10}{2} \right)^{2 \times 3}$$

$$FV_{3S} = \$100 \, (1.05)^6 = \$134.01$$

$$FV_{3Q} = \$100 \, (1.025)^{12} = \$134.49$$

6-30

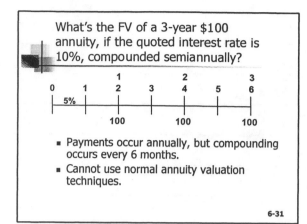

What's the FV of a 3-year $100 annuity, if the quoted interest rate is 10%, compounded semiannually?

- Payments occur annually, but compounding occurs every 6 months.
- Cannot use normal annuity valuation techniques.

6-31

Method 1:
Compound each cash flow

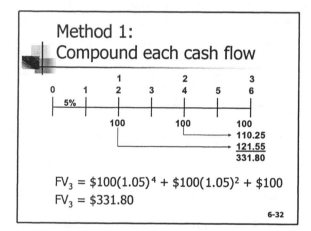

$$FV_3 = \$100(1.05)^4 + \$100(1.05)^2 + \$100$$
$$FV_3 = \$331.80$$

6-32

Method 2:
Financial calculator

- Find the EAR and treat as an annuity.
- $EAR = (1 + 0.10 / 2)^2 - 1 = 10.25\%$.

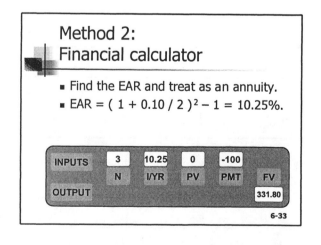

6-33

Find the PV of this 3-year ordinary annuity.

- Could solve by discounting each cash flow, or ...
- Use the EAR and treat as an annuity to solve for PV.

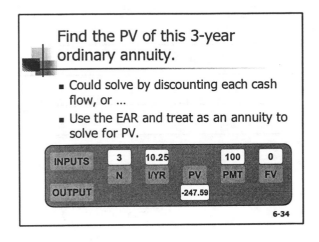

6-34

Loan amortization

- Amortization tables are widely used for home mortgages, auto loans, business loans, retirement plans, etc.
- Financial calculators and spreadsheets are great for setting up amortization tables.

- EXAMPLE: Construct an amortization schedule for a $1,000, 10% annual rate loan with 3 equal payments.

6-35

Step 1:
Find the required annual payment

- All input information is already given, just remember that the FV = 0 because the reason for amortizing the loan and making payments is to retire the loan.

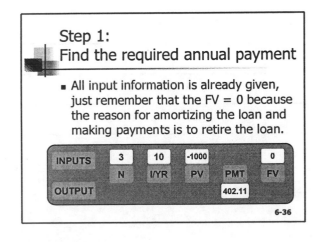

6-36

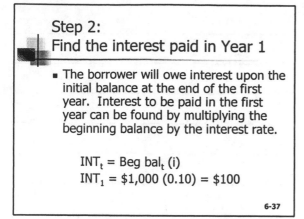

Step 2:

Find the interest paid in Year 1

- The borrower will owe interest upon the initial balance at the end of the first year. Interest to be paid in the first year can be found by multiplying the beginning balance by the interest rate.

$$INT_t = Beg\ bal_t\ (i)$$
$$INT_1 = \$1,000\ (0.10) = \$100$$

6-37

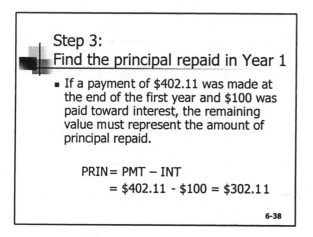

Step 3:

Find the principal repaid in Year 1

- If a payment of \$402.11 was made at the end of the first year and \$100 was paid toward interest, the remaining value must represent the amount of principal repaid.

$$PRIN = PMT - INT$$
$$= \$402.11 - \$100 = \$302.11$$

6-38

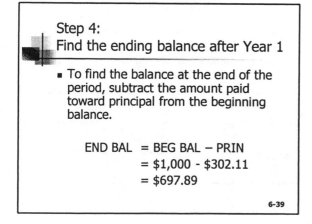

Step 4:

Find the ending balance after Year 1

- To find the balance at the end of the period, subtract the amount paid toward principal from the beginning balance.

$$END\ BAL = BEG\ BAL - PRIN$$
$$= \$1,000 - \$302.11$$
$$= \$697.89$$

6-39

Constructing an amortization table: Repeat steps 1 – 4 until end of loan

Year	BEG BAL	PMT	INT	PRIN	END BAL
1	$1,000	$402	$100	$302	$698
2	698	402	70	332	366
3	366	402	37	366	0
TOTAL		1,206.34	206.34	1,000	-

- Interest paid declines with each payment as the balance declines. What are the tax implications of this?

6-40

Illustrating an amortized payment: Where does the money go?

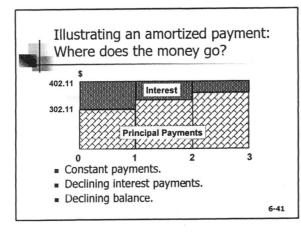

- Constant payments.
- Declining interest payments.
- Declining balance.

6-41

Partial amortization

- Bank agrees to lend a home buyer $220,000 to buy a $250,000 home, requiring a $30,000 down payment.
- The home buyer only has $7,500 in cash, so the seller agrees to take a note with the following terms:
  - Face value = $22,500
  - 7.5% nominal interest rate
  - Payments made at the end of the year, based upon a 20-year amortization schedule.
  - Loan matures at the end of the 10th year.

6-42

Calculating annual loan payments

- Based upon the loan information, the home buyer must make annual payments of $2,207.07 on the loan.

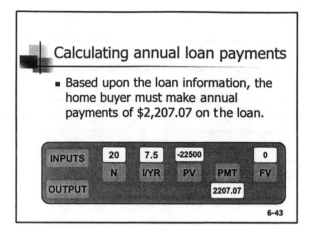

INPUTS	20	7.5	-22500		0
	N	I/YR	PV	PMT	FV
OUTPUT				2207.07	

6-43

_____

_____

_____

_____

_____

_____

_____

Determining the balloon payment

- Using an amortization table (spreadsheet or calculator), it can be found that at the end of the 10th year, the remaining balance on the loan will be $15,149.54.
- Therefore,
  - Balloon payment = $15,149.54
  - Final payment = $17,356.61

6-44

_____

_____

_____

_____

_____

_____

_____

EXAM-TYPE PROBLEMS

6-1.   Which of the following statements is most correct?

   a. The first payment under a 3-year, annual payment, amortized loan for $1,000
       will include a *smaller* percentage (or fraction) of the payment as interest if the
       interest rate is 5 percent than if it is 10 percent.

   b. If you are lending money, then, based on effective interest rates, you should
       prefer to lend at a 10 percent nominal, or quoted, rate but with semiannual
       payments, rather than at a 10.1 percent nominal rate with annual payments.
       However, as a borrower you should prefer the annual payment loan.

   c. The value of a perpetuity (say for $100 per year) will approach infinity as the
       interest rate used to evaluate the perpetuity approaches zero.

   d. Statements a, b, and c are true.

   e. Only statements b and c are true.

6-2.   You want to buy a new BMW sports car on your 27th birthday. You have priced
       these cars and found that they currently sell for $25,000. You believe that the price
       will increase by 10 percent per year until you are ready to buy one. You can
       presently invest to earn 14 percent. If you just turned 20 years old, how much must
       you invest at the end of each of the next 7 years to be able to purchase the BMW in
       7 years? ($4,540.15)

6-3.   On January 1, 2003, a graduate student developed a 5-year financial plan that
       would provide enough money at the end of her graduate work (January 1, 2008) to
       open a business of her own. Her plan was to deposit $8,000 per year for 5 years,
       starting immediately, into an account paying 10 percent compounded annually. Her
       activities proceeded according to plan except that at the end of her third year
       (1/1/06) she withdrew $5,000 to take a Caribbean cruise, at the end of the fourth
       year (1/1/07) she withdrew $5,000 to buy a used Prelude, and at the end of the fifth
       year (1/1/08) she had to withdraw $5,000 for her dissertation to be typed. Her
       account, at the end of the fifth year, was less than the amount she had originally
       planned on by how much? ($16,550)

6-4.   You have just taken out a 30-year, $120,000 mortgage on your new home. This
       mortgage is to be repaid in 360 equal end-of-month installments. If each of the
       monthly installments is $1,500, what is the effective annual interest rate on this
       mortgage? (15.87%)

6-5.   Assume that your father is now 50 years old, that he plans to retire in 10 years, and
       that he expects to live for 25 years after he retires, that is, until he is 85. He wants a
       fixed retirement income that has the same purchasing power at the time he retires

as $40,000 has today. (He realizes that the real value of his retirement income will decline year by year after he retires.) His retirement income will begin the day he retires, 10 years from today, and he will then get 24 additional annual payments. Inflation is expected to be 5 percent per year from today forward; he currently has $100,000 saved up; and he expects to earn a return on his savings of 8 percent per year, annual compounding. To the nearest dollar, how much must he save during each of the next 10 years (with deposits being made at the end of each year) to meet his retirement goal? ($36,950)

6-6. An investment pays you 10 percent interest, compounded quarterly.

a. What is the periodic rate of interest? (2.5%)

b. What is the nominal rate of interest? (10%)

c. What is the effective annual rate of interest? (10.38%)

7-23 Robert Black and Carol Alvarez are vice-presidents of Western Money Management and codirectors of the company's pension fund management division. A major new client, the California League of Cities, has requested that Western present an investment seminar to the mayors of the represented cities, and Black and Alvarez, who will make the actual presentation, have asked you to help them by answering the following questions.

a. What are the key features of a bond?

b. What are call provisions and sinking fund provisions? Do these provisions make bonds more or less risky?

c. How is the value of any asset whose value is based on expected future cash flows determined?

d. How is the value of a bond determined? What is the value of a 10-year, $1,000 par value bond with a 10 percent annual coupon if its required rate of return is 10 percent?

e. (1) What would be the value of the bond described in part d if, just after it had been issued, the expected inflation rate rose by 3 percentage points, causing investors to require a 13 percent return? Would we now have a discount or a premium bond?

(2) What would happen to the bond's value if inflation fell, and k_d declined to 7 percent? Would we now have a premium or a discount bond?

(3) What would happen to the value of the 10-year bond over time if the required rate of return remained at 13 percent, or if it remained at 7 percent? (Hint: With a financial calculator, enter PMT, I, FV, and N, and then change (override) N to see what happens to the PV as the bond approaches maturity.)

f. (1) What is the yield to maturity on a 10-year, 9 percent, annual coupon, $1,000 par value bond that sells for $887.00? That sells for $1,134.20? What does the fact that a bond sells at a discount or at a premium tell you about the relationship between k_d and the bond's coupon rate?

(2) What are the total return, the current yield, and the capital gains yield for the discount bond? (Assume the bond is held to maturity and the company does not default on the bond.)

g. What is *interest rate (or price) risk*? Which bond has more interest rate risk, an annual payment 1-year bond or a 10-year bond? Why?

h. What is *reinvestment rate risk*? Which has more reinvestment rate risk, a 1-year bond or a 10-year bond?

i. How does the equation for valuing a bond change if semiannual payments are made? Find the value of a 10-year, semiannual payment, 10 percent coupon bond if nominal k_d = 13%.

j. Suppose you could buy, for $1,000, either a 10 percent, 10-year, annual payment bond or a 10 percent, 10-year, semiannual payment bond. They are equally risky. Which would you prefer? If $1,000 is the proper price for the semiannual bond, what is the equilibrium price for the annual payment bond?

k. Suppose a 10-year, 10 percent, semiannual coupon bond with a par value of $1,000 is currently selling for $1,135.90, producing a nominal yield to maturity of 8 percent. However, the bond can be called after 4 years for a price of $1,050.

(1) What is the bond's *nominal yield to call (YTC)*?

(2) If you bought this bond, do you think you would be more likely to earn the YTM or the YTC? Why?

l. Does the yield to maturity represent the promised or expected return on the bond?

m. These bonds were rated AA- by S&P. Would you consider these bonds investment grade or junk bonds?

n. What factors determine a company's bond rating?

o. If this firm were to default on the bonds, would the company be immediately liquidated? Would the bondholders be assured of receiving all of their promised payments?

CHAPTER 7
Bonds and Their Valuation

- Key features of bonds
- Bond valuation
- Measuring yield
- Assessing risk

7-1

What is a bond?

- A long-term debt instrument in which a borrower agrees to make payments of principal and interest, on specific dates, to the holders of the bond.

7-2

Bond markets

- Primarily traded in the over-the-counter (OTC) market.
- Most bonds are owned by and traded among large financial institutions.
- Full information on bond trades in the OTC market is not published, but a representative group of bonds is listed and traded on the bond division of the NYSE.

7-3

Key Features of a Bond

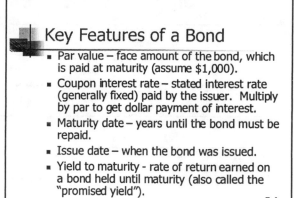

- Par value – face amount of the bond, which is paid at maturity (assume $1,000).
- Coupon interest rate – stated interest rate (generally fixed) paid by the issuer. Multiply by par to get dollar payment of interest.
- Maturity date – years until the bond must be repaid.
- Issue date – when the bond was issued.
- Yield to maturity - rate of return earned on a bond held until maturity (also called the "promised yield").

7-4

Effect of a call provision

- Allows issuer to refund the bond issue if rates decline (helps the issuer, but hurts the investor).
- Borrowers are willing to pay more, and lenders require more, for callable bonds.
- Most bonds have a deferred call and a declining call premium.

7-5

What is a sinking fund?

- Provision to pay off a loan over its life rather than all at maturity.
- Similar to amortization on a term loan.
- Reduces risk to investor, shortens average maturity.
- But not good for investors if rates decline after issuance.

7-6

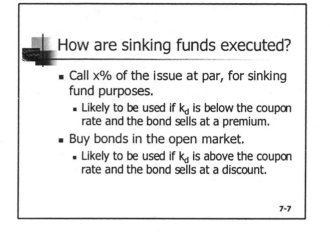

How are sinking funds executed?

- Call x% of the issue at par, for sinking fund purposes.
  - Likely to be used if k_d is below the coupon rate and the bond sells at a premium.
- Buy bonds in the open market.
  - Likely to be used if k_d is above the coupon rate and the bond sells at a discount.

7-7

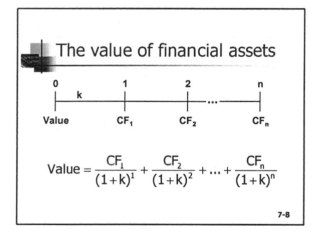

The value of financial assets

$$Value = \frac{CF_1}{(1+k)^1} + \frac{CF_2}{(1+k)^2} + \dots + \frac{CF_n}{(1+k)^n}$$

7-8

Other types (features) of bonds

- Convertible bond – may be exchanged for common stock of the firm, at the holder's option.
- Warrant – long-term option to buy a stated number of shares of common stock at a specified price.
- Putable bond – allows holder to sell the bond back to the company prior to maturity.
- Income bond – pays interest only when interest is earned by the firm.
- Indexed bond – interest rate paid is based upon the rate of inflation.

7-9

What is the opportunity cost of debt capital?

- The discount rate (k_i) is the opportunity cost of capital, and is the rate that could be earned on alternative investments of equal risk.

$$k_i = k^* + IP + MRP + DRP + LP$$

7-10

What is the value of a 10-year, 10% annual coupon bond, if $k_d = 10\%$?

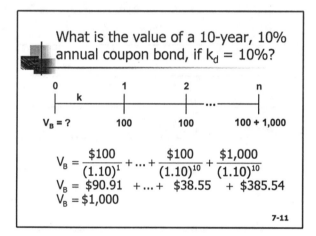

$$V_B = \frac{\$100}{(1.10)^1} + ... + \frac{\$100}{(1.10)^{10}} + \frac{\$1,000}{(1.10)^{10}}$$
$$V_B = \$90.91 \quad + ... + \quad \$38.55 \quad + \$385.54$$
$$V_B = \$1,000$$

7-11

Using a financial calculator to value a bond

- This bond has a $1,000 lump sum due at t = 10, and annual $100 coupon payments beginning at t = 1 and continuing through t = 10, the price of the bond can be found by solving for the PV of these cash flows.

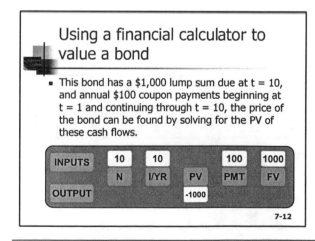

7-12

An example: Increasing inflation and k_d

- Suppose inflation rises by 3%, causing k_d = 13%. When k_d rises above the coupon rate, the bond's value falls below par, and sells at a discount.

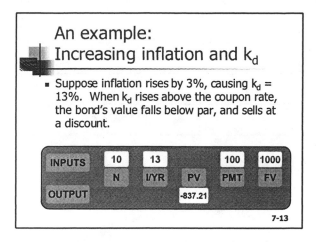

7-13

An example: Decreasing inflation and k_d

- Suppose inflation falls by 3%, causing k_d = 7%. When k_d falls below the coupon rate, the bond's value rises above par, and sells at a premium.

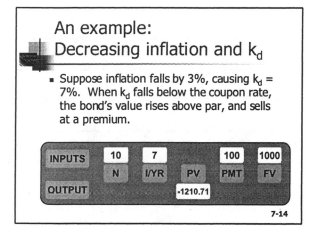

7-14

The price path of a bond

- What would happen to the value of this bond if its required rate of return remained at 10%, or at 13%, or at 7% until maturity?

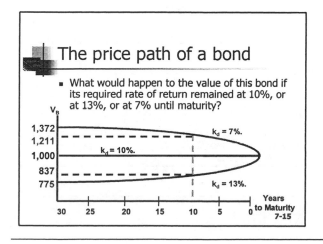

7-15

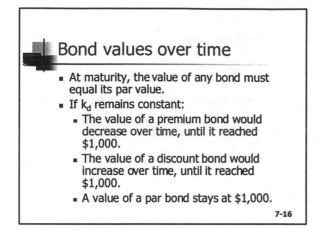

Bond values over time

- At maturity, the value of any bond must equal its par value.
- If k_d remains constant:
  - The value of a premium bond would decrease over time, until it reached $1,000.
  - The value of a discount bond would increase over time, until it reached $1,000.
  - A value of a par bond stays at $1,000.

7-16

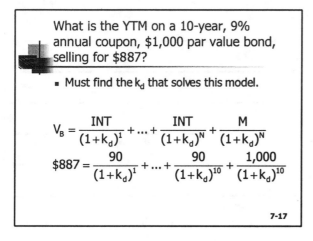

What is the YTM on a 10-year, 9% annual coupon, $1,000 par value bond, selling for $887?

- Must find the k_d that solves this model.

$$V_B = \frac{INT}{(1+k_d)^1} + ... + \frac{INT}{(1+k_d)^N} + \frac{M}{(1+k_d)^N}$$

$$\$887 = \frac{90}{(1+k_d)^1} + ... + \frac{90}{(1+k_d)^{10}} + \frac{1,000}{(1+k_d)^{10}}$$

7-17

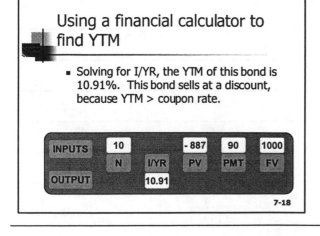

Using a financial calculator to find YTM

- Solving for I/YR, the YTM of this bond is 10.91%. This bond sells at a discount, because YTM > coupon rate.

INPUTS	10		- 887	90	1000
	N	I/YR	PV	PMT	FV
OUTPUT		10.91			

7-18

Find YTM, if the bond price was $1,134.20.

- Solving for I/YR, the YTM of this bond is 7.08%. This bond sells at a premium, because YTM < coupon rate.

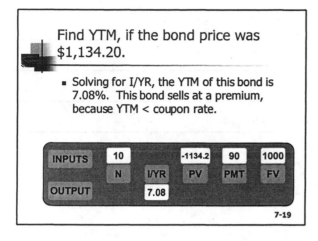

7-19

Definitions

$$\text{Current yield (CY)} = \frac{\text{Annual coupon payment}}{\text{Current price}}$$

$$\text{Capital gains yield (CGY)} = \frac{\text{Change in price}}{\text{Beginning price}}$$

$$\text{Expected total return} = \text{YTM} = \begin{pmatrix} \text{Expected} \\ \text{CY} \end{pmatrix} + \begin{pmatrix} \text{Expected} \\ \text{CGY} \end{pmatrix}$$

7-20

An example: Current and capital gains yield

- Find the current yield and the capital gains yield for a 10-year, 9% annual coupon bond that sells for $887, and has a face value of $1,000.

Current yield = $90 / $887

= 0.1015 = 10.15%

7-21

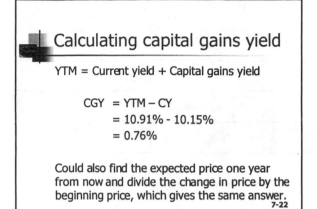

Calculating capital gains yield

YTM = Current yield + Capital gains yield

$$CGY = YTM - CY$$
$$= 10.91\% - 10.15\%$$
$$= 0.76\%$$

Could also find the expected price one year from now and divide the change in price by the beginning price, which gives the same answer.

7-22

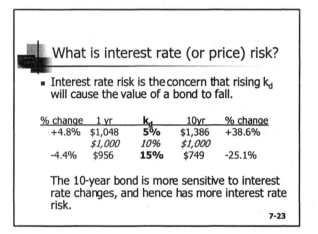

What is interest rate (or price) risk?

- Interest rate risk is the concern that rising k_d will cause the value of a bond to fall.

% change	1 yr	k_d	10yr	% change
+4.8%	$1,048	5%	$1,386	+38.6%
	$1,000	10%	$1,000	
-4.4%	$956	15%	$749	-25.1%

The 10-year bond is more sensitive to interest rate changes, and hence has more interest rate risk.

7-23

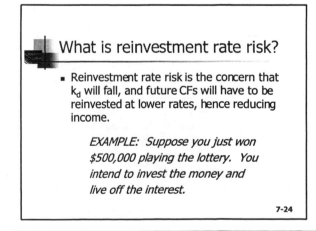

What is reinvestment rate risk?

- Reinvestment rate risk is the concern that k_d will fall, and future CFs will have to be reinvested at lower rates, hence reducing income.

    EXAMPLE: Suppose you just won $500,000 playing the lottery. You intend to invest the money and live off the interest.

7-24

Reinvestment rate risk example

- You may invest in either a 10-year bond or a series of ten 1-year bonds. Both 10-year and 1-year bonds currently yield 10%.
- If you choose the 1-year bond strategy:
  - After Year 1, you receive $50,000 in income and have $500,000 to reinvest. But, if 1-year rates fall to 3%, your annual income would fall to $15,000.
- If you choose the 10-year bond strategy:
  - You can lock in a 10% interest rate, and $50,000 annual income.

7-25

Conclusions about interest rate and reinvestment rate risk

	Short-term AND/OR High coupon bonds	Long-term AND/OR Low coupon bonds
Interest rate risk	Low	High
Reinvestment rate risk	High	Low

- CONCLUSION: Nothing is riskless!

7-26

Semiannual bonds

1. Multiply years by 2 : number of periods = 2n.
2. Divide nominal rate by 2 : periodic rate (I/YR) = k_d / 2.
3. Divide annual coupon by 2 : PMT = ann cpn / 2.

7-27

What is the value of a 10-year, 10% semiannual coupon bond, if k_d = 13%?

1. Multiply years by 2 : N = 2 * 10 = 20.
2. Divide nominal rate by 2 : I/YR = 13 / 2 = 6.5.
3. Divide annual coupon by 2 : PMT = 100 / 2 = 50.

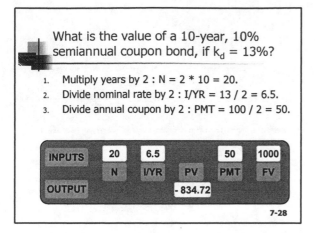

7-28

Would you prefer to buy a 10-year, 10% annual coupon bond or a 10-year, 10% semiannual coupon bond, all else equal?

The semiannual bond's effective rate is:

$$EFF\% = \left(1 + \frac{i_{Nom}}{m}\right)^m - 1 = \left(1 + \frac{0.10}{2}\right)^2 - 1 = 10.25\%$$

10.25% > 10% (the annual bond's effective rate), so you would prefer the semiannual bond.

7-29

If the proper price for this semiannual bond is $1,000, what would be the proper price for the annual coupon bond?

- The semiannual coupon bond has an effective rate of 10.25%, and the annual coupon bond should earn the same EAR. At these prices, the annual and semiannual coupon bonds are in equilibrium, as they earn the same effective return.

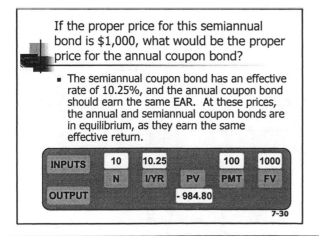

7-30

A 10-year, 10% semiannual coupon bond selling for $1,135.90 can be called in 4 years for $1,050, what is its yield to call (YTC)?

- The bond's yield to maturity can be determined to be 8%. Solving for the YTC is identical to solving for YTM, except the time to call is used for N and the call premium is FV.

INPUTS	8		- 1135.90	50	1050
	N	I/YR	PV	PMT	FV
OUTPUT		3.568			

7-31

Yield to call

- 3.568% represents the periodic semiannual yield to call.
- $YTC_{NOM} = k_{NOM} = 3.568\% \times 2 = 7.137\%$ is the rate that a broker would quote.
- The effective yield to call can be calculated
  - $YTC_{EFF} = (1.03568)^2 - 1 = 7.26\%$

7-32

If you bought these callable bonds, would you be more likely to earn the YTM or YTC?

- The coupon rate = 10% compared to YTC = 7.137%. The firm could raise money by selling new bonds which pay 7.137%.
- Could replace bonds paying $100 per year with bonds paying only $71.37 per year.
- Investors should expect a call, and to earn the YTC of 7.137%, rather than the YTM of 8%.

7-33

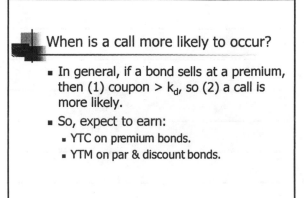

When is a call more likely to occur?

- In general, if a bond sells at a premium, then (1) coupon > k_d, so (2) a call is more likely.
- So, expect to earn:
  - YTC on premium bonds.
  - YTM on par & discount bonds.

7-34

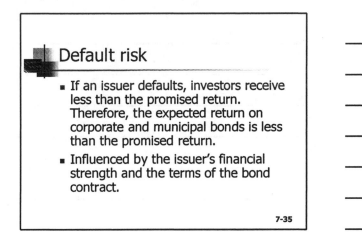

Default risk

- If an issuer defaults, investors receive less than the promised return. Therefore, the expected return on corporate and municipal bonds is less than the promised return.
- Influenced by the issuer's financial strength and the terms of the bond contract.

7-35

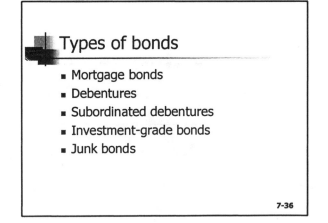

Types of bonds

- Mortgage bonds
- Debentures
- Subordinated debentures
- Investment-grade bonds
- Junk bonds

7-36

Evaluating default risk: Bond ratings

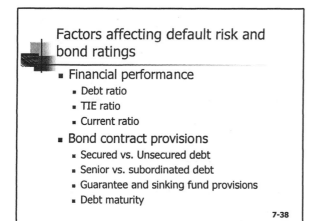

	Investment Grade	Junk Bonds
Moody's	Aaa Aa A Baa	Ba B Caa C
S & P	AAA AA A BBB	BB B CCC D

- Bond ratings are designed to reflect the probability of a bond issue going into default.

7-37

Factors affecting default risk and bond ratings

- Financial performance
  - Debt ratio
  - TIE ratio
  - Current ratio
- Bond contract provisions
  - Secured vs. Unsecured debt
  - Senior vs. subordinated debt
  - Guarantee and sinking fund provisions
  - Debt maturity

7-38

Other factors affecting default risk

- Earnings stability
- Regulatory environment
- Potential antitrust or product liabilities
- Pension liabilities
- Potential labor problems
- Accounting policies

7-39

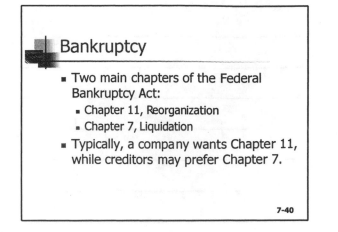

Bankruptcy

- Two main chapters of the Federal Bankruptcy Act:
  - Chapter 11, Reorganization
  - Chapter 7, Liquidation
- Typically, a company wants Chapter 11, while creditors may prefer Chapter 7.

7-40

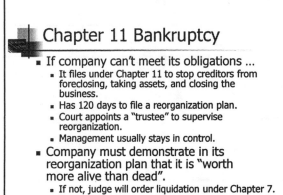

Chapter 11 Bankruptcy

- If company can't meet its obligations ...
  - It files under Chapter 11 to stop creditors from foreclosing, taking assets, and closing the business.
  - Has 120 days to file a reorganization plan.
  - Court appoints a "trustee" to supervise reorganization.
  - Management usually stays in control.
- Company must demonstrate in its reorganization plan that it is "worth more alive than dead".
  - If not, judge will order liquidation under Chapter 7.

7-41

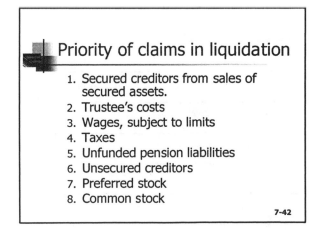

Priority of claims in liquidation

1. Secured creditors from sales of secured assets.
2. Trustee's costs
3. Wages, subject to limits
4. Taxes
5. Unfunded pension liabilities
6. Unsecured creditors
7. Preferred stock
8. Common stock

7-42

Reorganization

- In a liquidation, unsecured creditors generally get zero. This makes them more willing to participate in reorganization even though their claims are greatly scaled back.
- Various groups of creditors vote on the reorganization plan. If both the majority of the creditors and the judge approve, company "emerges" from bankruptcy with lower debts, reduced interest charges, and a chance for success.

7-43

EXAM-TYPE PROBLEMS

7-1. Gator Services Unlimited (GSU) needs to raise $25 million in new debt capital. GSU's currently outstanding bonds have a $1,000 par value, an 8 percent coupon rate, pay interest semiannually, and have 30 years remaining to maturity. The bonds are callable after 5 years at a price of $1,080, and currently sell at a price of $676.77. Right now, the yield curve is flat and is expected to remain flat for a while. The risk on GSU's new bonds is the same as for its old bonds. On the basis of these data, what is the best estimate of GSU's nominal interest rate on new bonds? (12%)

7-2. Florida Financial Corporation (FFC) purchases packages of guaranteed student loans from banks for its portfolio. FFC is considering a package with the following characteristics. The securities, which are similar to bonds, have a $1,000 par value, pay 8 percent interest semiannually for 5 years, and then pay a stepped-up interest rate of 10 percent semiannually for the next 7 years. The maturity value is $1,000, paid at the end of 12 years. FFC's alternatives to this investment are 9 percent coupon bonds, selling at par of $1,000, which pay interest quarterly. Assuming that the investments are of similar risk, how much should FFC be willing to pay for the student loan package? ($985.97)

7-3. Trickle Corporation's 12 percent coupon rate, semiannual payment, $1,000 par value bonds that mature in 25 years, are callable at a price of $1,080 five years from now. The bonds currently sell for $1,230.51 in the market, and the yield curve is flat. Assuming that the yield curve is expected to remain flat, what is Trickle's most likely *before-tax cost* of debt if it issues new bonds today? (7.70%)

7-4. Recycler Battery Corporation (RBC) issued zero coupon bonds 5 years ago at a price of $214.50 per bond. RBC's zeros had a 20-year original maturity, and a $1,000 par value. The bonds were callable 10 years after the issue date at a price 7 percent over their accrued value on the call date. If the bonds sell for $239.39 in the market today, what annual rate of return should an investor who buys the bonds today expect to earn on them? (Hint: Material covered in Web Appendix 7A.) (10%)

7-5. Suppose a new company decides to raise its initial $200 million of capital as $100 million of common equity and $100 million of long-term debt. By an iron-clad provision in its charter, the company can never borrow any more money. Which of the following statements is most correct?

   a. If the debt were raised by issuing $50 million of debentures and $50 million of first mortgage bonds, we could be absolutely certain that the firm's total interest expense would be lower than if the debt were raised by issuing $100 million of debentures.

---

b. If the debt were raised by issuing $50 million of debentures and $50 million of first mortgage bonds, we could be absolutely certain that the firm's total interest expense would be lower than if the debt were raised by issuing $100 million of first mortgage bonds.

c. The higher the percentage of total debt represented by debentures, the greater the risk of, and hence the interest rate on, the debentures.

d. The higher the percentage of total debt represented by mortgage bonds, the riskier both types of bonds will be, and, consequently, the higher the firms' total dollar interest charges will be.

e. In this situation, we cannot tell for sure how, or whether, the firm's total interest expense on the $100 million of debt would be affected by the mix of debentures versus first mortgage bonds. Interest rates on the two types of bonds would vary as their percentages were changed, but the result might well be such that the firm's total interest charges would not be affected materially by the mix between the two.

7-6. Which of the following statements is most correct?

a. Because bonds can generally be called only at a premium, meaning that the bondholder will enjoy a capital gain, including a call provision (other than a sinking fund call) in the indenture increases the value of the bond and lowers the bond's required rate of return.

b. You are considering two bonds. Both are rated AA, both mature in 20 years, both have a 10 percent coupon, and both are offered to you at their $1,000 par value. However, Bond X has a sinking fund while Bond Y does not. This is probably not an equilibrium situation, as Bond X, which has the sinking fund, would generally be expected to have a higher yield than Bond Y.

c. A sinking fund provides for the orderly retirement of a debt (or preferred stock) issue. Sinking funds generally force the firm to call a percentage of the issue each year. However, the call price for sinking fund purposes is generally higher than the call price for refunding purposes.

d. Zero coupon bonds are bought primarily by pension funds and other tax-exempt investors because they avoid the tax that non-tax exempt investors must pay on the accrued value each year.

e. All of the above statements are false.

7-7. Research Technologies' noncallable bonds have 10 years remaining to maturity. The bonds have a face value of $1,000, a yield to maturity of 12 percent, pay interest semiannually, and have a 10 percent coupon rate. What is their current yield? (11.30%)

8-27 Robert Balik and Carol Kiefer are senior vice-presidents of the Mutual of Chicago Insurance Company. They are co-directors of the company's pension fund management division, with Balik having responsibility for fixed income securities (primarily bonds) and Kiefer being responsible for equity investments. A major new client, the California League of Cities, has requested that Mutual of Chicago present an investment seminar to the mayors of the represented cities, and Balik and Kiefer, who will make the actual presentation, have asked you to help them.

To illustrate the common stock valuation process, Balik and Kiefer have asked you to analyze the Bon Temps Company, an employment agency that supplies word processor operators and computer programmers to businesses with temporarily heavy workloads. You are to answer the following questions.

a. Describe briefly the legal rights and privileges of common stockholders.

b. (1) Write out a formula that can be used to value any stock, regardless of its dividend pattern.

(2) What is a constant growth stock? How are constant growth stocks valued?

(3) What happens if a company has a constant g that exceeds its k_s? Will many stocks have expected $g > k_s$ in the short run (that is, for the next few years)? In the long run (that is, forever)?

c. Assume that Bon Temps has a beta coefficient of 1.2, that the risk-free rate (the yield on T-bonds) is 7 percent, and that the required rate of return on the market is 12 percent. What is the required rate of return on the firm's stock?

d. Assume that Bon Temps is a constant growth company whose last dividend (D_0, which was paid yesterday) was $2.00 and whose dividend is expected to grow indefinitely at a 6 percent rate.

(1) What is the firm's expected dividend stream over the next 3 years?

(2) What is the firm's current stock price?

(3) What is the stock's expected value 1 year from now?

(4) What are the expected dividend yield, the capital gains yield, and the total return during the first year?

---

e. Now assume that the stock is currently selling at $30.29. What is the expected rate of return on the stock?

f. What would the stock price be if its dividends were expected to have zero growth?

g. Now assume that Bon Temps is expected to experience supernormal growth of 30 percent for the next 3 years, then to return to its long-run constant growth rate of 6 percent. What is the stock's value under these conditions? What is its expected dividend yield and capital gains yield in Year 1? Year 4?

h. Suppose Bon Temps is expected to experience zero growth during the first 3 years and then to resume its steady-state growth of 6 percent in the fourth year. What is the stock's value now? What is its expected dividend yield and its capital gains yield in Year 1? Year 4?

i. Finally, assume that Bon Temps' earnings and dividends are expected to decline by a constant 6 percent per year, that is, $g = -6\%$. Why would anyone be willing to buy such a stock, and at what price should it sell? What would be the dividend yield and capital gains yield in each year?

j. Bon Temps embarks on an aggressive expansion that requires additional capital. Management decides to finance the expansion by borrowing $40 million and by halting dividend payments to increase retained earnings. The projected free cash flows for the next three years are -$5 million, $10 million, and $20 million. After the third year, free cash flow is projected to grow at a constant 6 percent. The overall cost of capital is 10 percent. What is Bon Temps' total value? If it has 10 million shares of stock and $40 million total debt, what is the price per share?

k. What does market equilibrium mean?

l. If equilibrium does not exist, how will it be established?

m. What is the Efficient Markets Hypothesis, what are its three forms, and what are its implications?

n. Phyfe Company recently issued preferred stock. It pays an annual dividend of $5, and the issue price was $50 per share. What is the expected return to an investor on this preferred stock?

CHAPTER 8
Stocks and Their Valuation

- Features of common stock
- Determining common stock values
- Efficient markets
- Preferred stock

8-1

Facts about common stock

- Represents ownership
- Ownership implies control
- Stockholders elect directors
- Directors elect management
- Management's goal: Maximize the stock price

8-2

Social/Ethical Question

- Should management be equally concerned about employees, customers, suppliers, and "the public," or just the stockholders?
- In an enterprise economy, management should work for stockholders subject to constraints (environmental, fair hiring, etc.) and competition.

8-3

Types of stock market transactions

- Secondary market
- Primary market
- Initial public offering market ("going public")

8-4

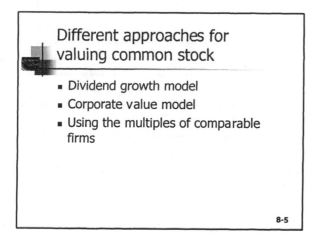

Different approaches for valuing common stock

- Dividend growth model
- Corporate value model
- Using the multiples of comparable firms

8-5

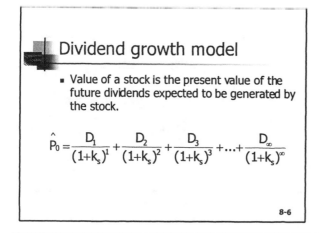

Dividend growth model

- Value of a stock is the present value of the future dividends expected to be generated by the stock.

$$\hat{P}_0 = \frac{D_1}{(1+k_s)^1} + \frac{D_2}{(1+k_s)^2} + \frac{D_3}{(1+k_s)^3} + \ldots + \frac{D_\infty}{(1+k_s)^\infty}$$

8-6

Constant growth stock

- A stock whose dividends are expected to grow forever at a constant rate, g.

$$D_1 = D_0 (1+g)^1$$
$$D_2 = D_0 (1+g)^2$$
$$D_t = D_0 (1+g)^t$$

- If g is constant, the dividend growth formula converges to:

$$\hat{P}_0 = \frac{D_0(1+g)}{k_s - g} = \frac{D_1}{k_s - g}$$

8-7

Future dividends and their present values

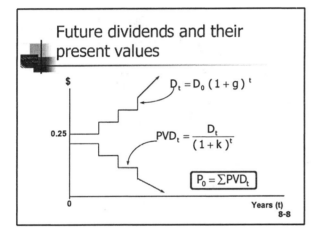

$$D_t = D_0 (1+g)^t$$

$$PVD_t = \frac{D_t}{(1+k)^t}$$

$$\boxed{P_0 = \sum PVD_t}$$

Years (t)
8-8

What happens if $g > k_s$?

- If $g > k_s$, the constant growth formula leads to a negative stock price, which does not make sense.
- The constant growth model can only be used if:
  - $k_s > g$
  - g is expected to be constant forever

8-9

If k_{RF} = 7%, k_M = 12%, and β = 1.2, what is the required rate of return on the firm's stock?

- Use the SML to calculate the required rate of return (k_s):

$$k_s = k_{RF} + (k_M - k_{RF})\beta$$
$$= 7\% + (12\% - 7\%)1.2$$
$$= 13\%$$

8-10

If D_0 = $2 and g is a constant 6%, find the expected dividend stream for the next 3 years, and their PVs.

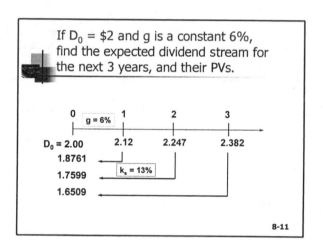

8-11

What is the stock's market value?

- Using the constant growth model:

$$P_0 = \frac{D_1}{k_s - g} = \frac{\$2.12}{0.13 - 0.06}$$
$$= \frac{\$2.12}{0.07}$$
$$= \$30.29$$

8-12

What is the expected market price of the stock, one year from now?

- D_1 will have been paid out already. So, P_1 is the present value (as of year 1) of D_2, D_3, D_4, etc.

$$\hat{P}_1 = \frac{D_2}{k_s - g} = \frac{\$2.247}{0.13 - 0.06}$$
$$= \$32.10$$

- Could also find expected P_1 as:

$$\hat{P}_1 = P_0 \, (1.06) = \$32.10$$

8-13

What is the expected dividend yield, capital gains yield, and total return during the first year?

- Dividend yield
  $$= D_1 / P_0 = \$2.12 / \$30.29 = 7.0\%$$
- Capital gains yield
  $$= (P_1 - P_0) / P_0$$
  $$= (\$32.10 - \$30.29) / \$30.29 = 6.0\%$$
- Total return (k_s)
  $$= \text{Dividend Yield} + \text{Capital Gains Yield}$$
  $$= 7.0\% + 6.0\% = 13.0\%$$

8-14

What would the expected price today be, if g = 0?

- The dividend stream would be a perpetuity.

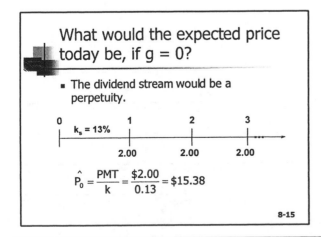

$$\hat{P}_0 = \frac{PMT}{k} = \frac{\$2.00}{0.13} = \$15.38$$

8-15

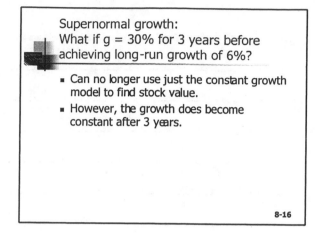

Supernormal growth:
What if g = 30% for 3 years before achieving long-run growth of 6%?

- Can no longer use just the constant growth model to find stock value.
- However, the growth does become constant after 3 years.

8-16

Valuing common stock with nonconstant growth

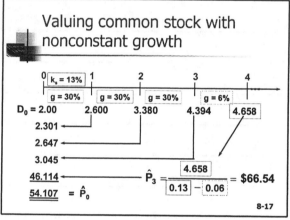

8-17

Find expected dividend and capital gains yields during the first and fourth years.

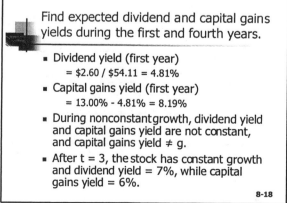

- Dividend yield (first year)
  = \$2.60 / \$54.11 = 4.81%
- Capital gains yield (first year)
  = 13.00% - 4.81% = 8.19%
- During nonconstant growth, dividend yield and capital gains yield are not constant, and capital gains yield ≠ g.
- After t = 3, the stock has constant growth and dividend yield = 7%, while capital gains yield = 6%.

8-18

Nonconstant growth:
What if g = 0% for 3 years before long-run growth of 6%?

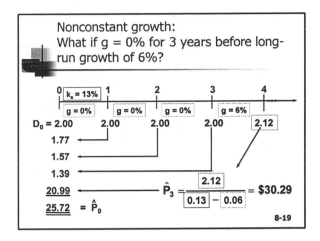

$$\hat{P}_3 = \frac{2.12}{0.13 - 0.06} = \$30.29$$

8-19

Find expected dividend and capital gains yields during the first and fourth years.

- Dividend yield (first year)
  = $2.00 / $25.72 = 7.78%
- Capital gains yield (first year)
  = 13.00% - 7.78% = 5.22%
- After t = 3, the stock has constant growth and dividend yield = 7%, while capital gains yield = 6%.

8-20

If the stock was expected to have negative growth (g = -6%), would anyone buy the stock, and what is its value?

- The firm still has earnings and pays dividends, even though they may be declining, they still have value.

$$\hat{P}_0 = \frac{D_1}{k_s - g} = \frac{D_0(1+g)}{k_s - g}$$

$$= \frac{\$2.00\,(0.94)}{0.13 - (-0.06)} = \frac{\$1.88}{0.19} = \$9.89$$

8-21

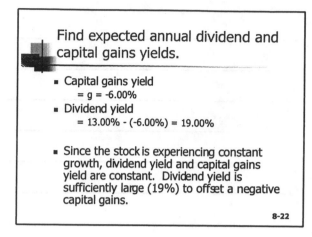

Find expected annual dividend and capital gains yields.

- Capital gains yield
  = g = -6.00%
- Dividend yield
  = 13.00% - (-6.00%) = 19.00%

- Since the stock is experiencing constant growth, dividend yield and capital gains yield are constant. Dividend yield is sufficiently large (19%) to offset a negative capital gains.

8-22

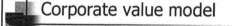

Corporate value model

- Also called the free cash flow method. Suggests the value of the entire firm equals the present value of the firm's free cash flows.
- Remember, free cash flow is the firm's after-tax operating income less the net capital investment
  - FCF = NOPAT – Net capital investment

8-23

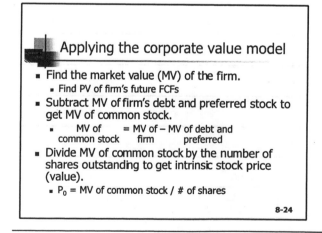

Applying the corporate value model

- Find the market value (MV) of the firm.
  - Find PV of firm's future FCFs
- Subtract MV of firm's debt and preferred stock to get MV of common stock.
  - MV of   = MV of – MV of debt and
    common stock   firm   preferred
- Divide MV of common stock by the number of shares outstanding to get intrinsic stock price (value).
  - P_0 = MV of common stock / # of shares

8-24

Issues regarding the corporate value model

- Often preferred to the dividend growth model, especially when considering number of firms that don't pay dividends or when dividends are hard to forecast.
- Similar to dividend growth model, assumes at some point free cash flow will grow at a constant rate.
- Terminal value (TV_n) represents value of firm at the point that growth becomes constant.

8-25

Given the long-run g_{FCF} = 6%, and WACC of 10%, use the corporate value model to find the firm's intrinsic value.

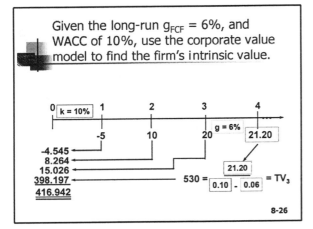

8-26

If the firm has $40 million in debt and has 10 million shares of stock, what is the firm's intrinsic value per share?

- MV of equity = MV of firm − MV of debt
  = $416.94m - $40m
  = $376.94 million
- Value per share = MV of equity / # of shares
  = $376.94m / 10m
  = $37.69

8-27

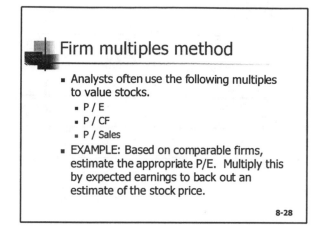

Firm multiples method

- Analysts often use the following multiples to value stocks.
  - P / E
  - P / CF
  - P / Sales
- EXAMPLE: Based on comparable firms, estimate the appropriate P/E. Multiply this by expected earnings to back out an estimate of the stock price.

8-28

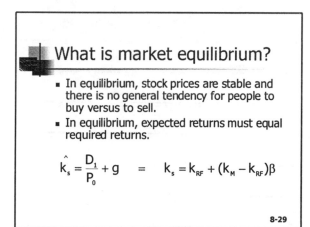

What is market equilibrium?

- In equilibrium, stock prices are stable and there is no general tendency for people to buy versus to sell.
- In equilibrium, expected returns must equal required returns.

$$\hat{k}_s = \frac{D_1}{P_0} + g \quad = \quad k_s = k_{RF} + (k_M - k_{RF})\beta$$

8-29

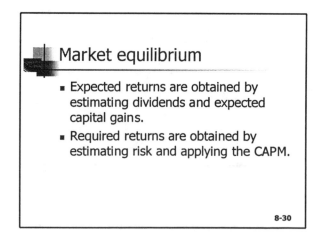

Market equilibrium

- Expected returns are obtained by estimating dividends and expected capital gains.
- Required returns are obtained by estimating risk and applying the CAPM.

8-30

How is market equilibrium established?

- If expected return exceeds required return ...
  - The current price (P_0) is "too low" and offers a bargain.
  - Buy orders will be greater than sell orders.
  - P_0 will be bid up until expected return equals required return

8-31

Factors that affect stock price

- Required return (k_s) could change
  - Changing inflation could cause k_{RF} to change
  - Market risk premium or exposure to market risk (β) could change
- Growth rate (g) could change
  - Due to economic (market) conditions
  - Due to firm conditions

8-32

What is the Efficient Market Hypothesis (EMH)?

- Securities are normally in equilibrium and are "fairly priced."
- Investors cannot "beat the market" except through good luck or better information.
- Levels of market efficiency
  - Weak-form efficiency
  - Semistrong-form efficiency
  - Strong-form efficiency

8-33

Weak-form efficiency

- Can't profit by looking at past trends. A recent decline is no reason to think stocks will go up (or down) in the future.
- Evidence supports weak-form EMH, but "technical analysis" is still used.

8-34

Semistrong-form efficiency

- All publicly available information is reflected in stock prices, so it doesn't pay to over analyze annual reports looking for undervalued stocks.
- Largely true, but superior analysts can still profit by finding and using new information

8-35

Strong-form efficiency

- All information, even inside information, is embedded in stock prices.
- Not true--insiders can gain by trading on the basis of insider information, but that's illegal.

8-36

Is the stock market efficient?

- Empirical studies have been conducted to test the three forms of efficiency. Most of which suggest the stock market was:
  - Highly efficient in the weak form.
  - Reasonably efficient in the semistrong form.
  - Not efficient in the strong form. Insiders could and did make abnormal (and sometimes illegal) profits.
- Behavioral finance – incorporates elements of cognitive psychology to better understand how individuals and markets respond to different situations.

8-37

Preferred stock

- Hybrid security
- Like bonds, preferred stockholders receive a fixed dividend that must be paid before dividends are paid to common stockholders.
- However, companies can omit preferred dividend payments without fear of pushing the firm into bankruptcy.

8-38

If preferred stock with an annual dividend of $5 sells for $50, what is the preferred stock's expected return?

$V_p = D / k_p$
$\$50 = \$5 / k_p$

$k_p = \$5 / \$50$
$= 0.10 = 10\%$

8-39

EXAM-TYPE PROBLEMS

8-1. Carlson Products, a constant growth company, has a current market (and equilibrium) stock price of $20.00. Carlson's next dividend, D_1, is forecasted to be $2.00, and Carlson is growing at an annual rate of 6 percent. Carlson has a beta coefficient of 1.2, and the required rate of return on the market is 15 percent. As Carlson's financial manager, you have access to insider information concerning a switch in product lines that would not change the growth rate, but would cut Carlson's beta coefficient in half. If you buy the stock at the current market price, what is your expected percentage capital gain? (43%)

8-2. The Hart Mountain Company has recently discovered a new type of kitty litter that is extremely absorbent. It is expected that the firm will experience (beginning now) an unusually high growth rate of 20 percent during the 3-year period it has exclusive rights to the property where the raw material used to make this kitty litter is found. However, beginning with the fourth year the firm's competition will have access to the material, and from that time on, the firm will achieve a normal growth rate of 8 percent annually. During the rapid growth period, the firm's dividend payout ratio will be a relatively low 20 percent to conserve funds for reinvestment. However, the decrease in growth in the fourth year will be accompanied by an increase in the dividend payout to 50 percent. Last year's earnings were $E_0 = \$2.00$ per share, and the firm's required return is 10 percent. What should be the current price of the common stock? ($71.54)

8-3. Which of the following statements is most correct?

a. One of the advantages of common stock financing is that there is no dilution of owner's equity, as there is with debt.

b. If the market price of a stock falls below its book value, the firm can be liquidated, with the book value proceeds then distributed to the shareholders. Thus, a stock's book value per share sets a floor below which the stock's market price is unlikely to fall.

c. The preemptive right gives a firm's preferred stockholders preference to assets over common stockholders in the event the firm is liquidated.

d. All of the above statements are true.

e. All of the above statements are false.

8-4. Bosio Enterprises has preferred stock outstanding that pays a dividend of $8.75 at the end of each year. If the preferred stock's required return is 12.5 percent, for how much does each share of preferred stock sell? ($70)

8-5. Today is December 31, 2002. The following information applies to Harberford Enterprises:

- After-tax, operating income [EBIT(1 − T)] for the Year 2003 is expected to be $800 million.
- The company's depreciation expense for the Year 2003 is expected to be $160 million.
- The company's capital expenditures for the Year 2003 are expected to be $320 million.
- No change is expected in the company's net operating working capital.
- The company's free cash flow is expected to grow at a constant rate of 4 percent per year.
- The company's cost of equity is 12 percent.
- The company's WACC is 9 percent.
- The market value of the company's debt is $4.8 billion.
- The company has 320 million shares of stock outstanding.

Using the free cash flow approach, what should the company's stock price be today? ($25)

9-22 Coleman Technologies is considering a major expansion program that has been proposed by the company's information technology group. Before proceeding with the expansion, the company needs to develop an estimate of its cost of capital. Assume that you are an assistant to Jerry Lehman, the financial vice-president. Your first task is to estimate Coleman's cost of capital. Lehman has provided you with the following data, which he believes may be relevant to your task:

1. The firm's tax rate is 40 percent.

2. The current price of Coleman's 12 percent coupon, semiannual payment, noncallable bonds with 15 years remaining to maturity is $1,153.72. Coleman does not use short-term interest-bearing debt on a permanent basis. New bonds would be privately placed with no flotation cost.

3. The current price of the firm's 10 percent, $100 par value, quarterly dividend, perpetual preferred stock is $111.10.

4. Coleman's common stock is currently selling at $50 per share. Its last dividend (D_0) was $4.19, and dividends are expected to grow at a constant rate of 5 percent in the foreseeable future. Coleman's beta is 1.2, the yield on T-bonds is 7 percent, and the market risk premium is estimated to be 6 percent. For the bond-yield-plus-risk-premium approach, the firm uses a 4 percentage point risk premium.

5. Coleman's target capital structure is 30 percent long-term debt, 10 percent preferred stock, and 60 percent common equity.

To structure the task somewhat, Lehman has asked you to answer the following questions.

a. (1) What sources of capital should be included when you estimate Coleman's weighted average cost of capital (WACC)?

   (2) Should the component costs be figured on a before-tax or an after-tax basis?

   (3) Should the costs be historical (embedded) costs or new (marginal) costs?

b. What is the market interest rate on Coleman's debt and its component cost of debt?

c. (1) What is the firm's cost of preferred stock?

---

(2) Coleman's preferred stock is riskier to investors than its debt, yet the preferred's yield to investors is lower than the yield to maturity on the debt. Does this suggest that you have made a mistake? (Hint: Think about taxes.)

d. (1) Why is there a cost associated with retained earnings?

   (2) What is Coleman's estimated cost of common equity using the CAPM approach?

e. What is the estimated cost of common equity using the discounted cash flow (DCF) approach?

f. What is the bond-yield-plus-risk-premium estimate for Coleman's cost of common equity?

g. What is your final estimate for k_s?

h. Explain in words why new common stock has a higher percentage cost than retained earnings.

i. (1) What are two approaches that can be used to account for flotation costs?

   (2) Coleman estimates that if it issues new common stock, the flotation cost will be 15 percent. Coleman incorporates the flotation costs into the DCF approach. What is the estimated cost of newly issued common stock, taking into account the flotation cost?

j. What is Coleman's overall, or weighted average, cost of capital (WACC)? Ignore flotation costs.

k. What factors influence Coleman's composite WACC?

l. Should the company use the composite WACC as the hurdle rate for each of its projects?

m. What are three types of project risk? How is each type of risk used?

n. Coleman is interested in establishing a new division, which will focus primarily on developing new Internet-based projects. In trying to determine the cost of capital for this new division, you discover that stand-alone firms involved in similar projects have on average the following characteristics:

   • Their capital structure is 40 percent debt and 60 percent common equity.

   • Their cost of debt is typically 12 percent.

- The beta is 1.7.

Given this information, what would your estimate be for the division's cost of capital? Note that Coleman uses the CAPM to calculate the division's cost of capital.

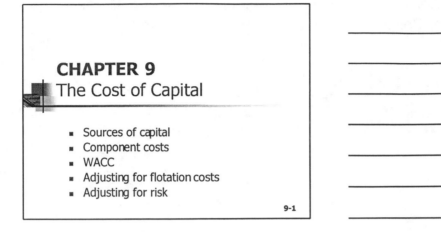

CHAPTER 9
The Cost of Capital

- Sources of capital
- Component costs
- WACC
- Adjusting for flotation costs
- Adjusting for risk

9-1

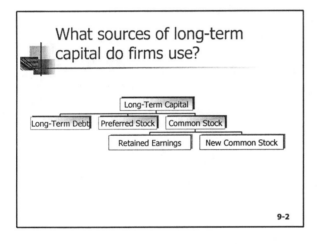

What sources of long-term capital do firms use?

Long-Term Capital

Long-Term Debt   Preferred Stock   Common Stock

Retained Earnings   New Common Stock

9-2

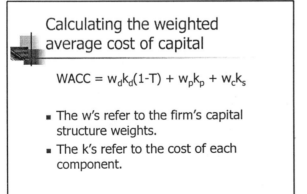

Calculating the weighted average cost of capital

$$WACC = w_d k_d (1-T) + w_p k_p + w_c k_s$$

- The w's refer to the firm's capital structure weights.
- The k's refer to the cost of each component.

9-3

Should our analysis focus on before-tax or after-tax capital costs?

- Stockholders focus on A-T CFs. Therefore, we should focus on A-T capital costs, i.e. use A-T costs of capital in WACC. Only k_d needs adjustment, because interest is tax deductible.

9-4

Should our analysis focus on historical (embedded) costs or new (marginal) costs?

- The cost of capital is used primarily to make decisions that involve raising new capital. So, focus on today's marginal costs (for WACC).

9-5

How are the weights determined?

$$WACC = w_d k_d (1-T) + w_p k_p + w_c k_s$$

- Use accounting numbers or market value (book vs. market weights)?
- Use actual numbers or target capital structure?

9-6

Component cost of debt

$$WACC = w_d k_d (1-T) + w_p k_p + w_c k_s$$

- k_d is the marginal cost of debt capital.
- The yield to maturity on outstanding L-T debt is often used as a measure of k_d.
- Why tax-adjust, i.e. why $k_d(1-T)$?

9-7

A 15-year, 12% semiannual coupon bond sells for $1,153.72. What is the cost of debt (k_d)?

- Remember, the bond pays a semiannual coupon, so $k_d = 5.0\% \times 2 = 10\%$.

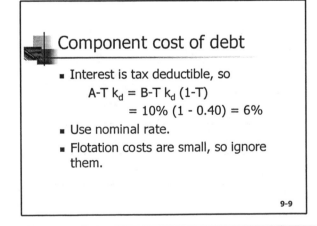

9-8

Component cost of debt

- Interest is tax deductible, so
  A-T k_d = B-T k_d (1-T)
  = 10% (1 - 0.40) = 6%
- Use nominal rate.
- Flotation costs are small, so ignore them.

9-9

Component cost of preferred stock

$$WACC = w_d k_d (1-T) + w_p k_p + w_c k_s$$

- k_p is the marginal cost of preferred stock.
- The rate of return investors require on the firm's preferred stock.

9-10

What is the cost of preferred stock?

- The cost of preferred stock can be solved by using this formula:

$$k_p = D_p / P_p$$
$$= \$10 / \$111.10$$
$$= 9\%$$

9-11

Component cost of preferred stock

- Preferred dividends are not tax-deductible, so no tax adjustments necessary. Just use k_p.
- Nominal k_p is used.
- Our calculation ignores possible flotation costs.

9-12

Is preferred stock more or less risky to investors than debt?

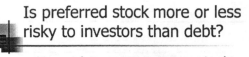

- More risky; company not required to pay preferred dividend.
- However, firms try to pay preferred dividend. Otherwise, (1) cannot pay common dividend, (2) difficult to raise additional funds, (3) preferred stockholders may gain control of firm.

9-13

Why is the yield on preferred stock lower than debt?

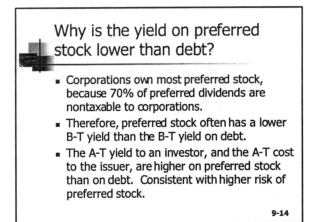

- Corporations own most preferred stock, because 70% of preferred dividends are nontaxable to corporations.
- Therefore, preferred stock often has a lower B-T yield than the B-T yield on debt.
- The A-T yield to an investor, and the A-T cost to the issuer, are higher on preferred stock than on debt. Consistent with higher risk of preferred stock.

9-14

Illustrating the differences between A-T costs of debt and preferred stock

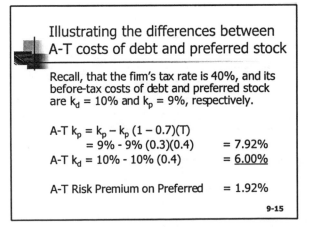

Recall, that the firm's tax rate is 40%, and its before-tax costs of debt and preferred stock are k_d = 10% and k_p = 9%, respectively.

A-T k_p = k_p − k_p (1 − 0.7)(T)
       = 9% - 9% (0.3)(0.4)   = 7.92%
A-T k_d = 10% - 10% (0.4)   = <u>6.00%</u>

A-T Risk Premium on Preferred   = 1.92%

9-15

Component cost of equity

$$WACC = w_d k_d (1-T) + w_p k_p + w_c k_s$$

- k_s is the marginal cost of common equity using retained earnings.
- The rate of return investors require on the firm's common equity using new equity is k_e.

9-16

Why is there a cost for retained earnings?

- Earnings can be reinvested or paid out as dividends.
- Investors could buy other securities, earn a return.
- If earnings are retained, there is an opportunity cost (the return that stockholders could earn on alternative investments of equal risk).
  - Investors could buy similar stocks and earn k_s.
  - Firm could repurchase its own stock and earn k_s.
  - Therefore, k_s is the cost of retained earnings.

9-17

Three ways to determine the cost of common equity, k_s

- CAPM: $k_s = k_{RF} + (k_M - k_{RF})\ \beta$

- DCF: $k_s = D_1 / P_0 + g$

- Own-Bond-Yield-Plus-Risk Premium:
  $$k_s = k_d + RP$$

9-18

If the k_{RF} = 7%, RP_M = 6%, and the firm's beta is 1.2, what's the cost of common equity based upon the CAPM?

$$k_s = k_{RF} + (k_M - k_{RF})\ \beta$$
$$= 7.0\% + (6.0\%)1.2 = 14.2\%$$

9-19

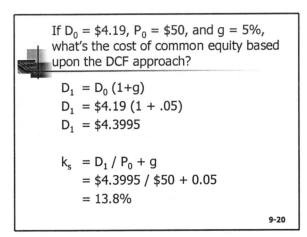

If D_0 = $4.19, P_0 = $50, and g = 5%, what's the cost of common equity based upon the DCF approach?

D_1 = D_0 (1+g)
D_1 = $4.19 (1 + .05)
D_1 = $4.3995

k_s = D_1 / P_0 + g
  = $4.3995 / $50 + 0.05
  = 13.8%

9-20

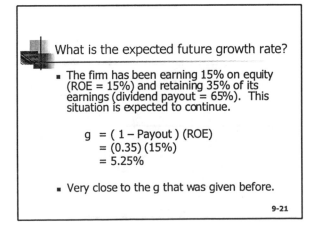

What is the expected future growth rate?

- The firm has been earning 15% on equity (ROE = 15%) and retaining 35% of its earnings (dividend payout = 65%). This situation is expected to continue.

  g = (1 – Payout) (ROE)
    = (0.35) (15%)
    = 5.25%

- Very close to the g that was given before.

9-21

Can DCF methodology be applied if growth is not constant?

- Yes, nonconstant growth stocks are expected to attain constant growth at some point, generally in 5 to 10 years.
- May be complicated to compute.

9-22

If k_d = 10% and RP = 4%, what is k_s using the own-bond-yield-plus-risk-premium method?

- This RP is not the same as the CAPM RP_M.
- This method produces a ballpark estimate of k_s, and can serve as a useful check.

$$k_s = k_d + RP$$
$$k_s = 10.0\% + 4.0\% = 14.0\%$$

9-23

What is a reasonable final estimate of k_s?

Method	Estimate
CAPM	14.2%
DCF	13.8%
k_d + RP	14.0%
Average	14.0%

9-24

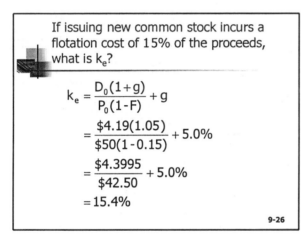

Why is the cost of retained earnings cheaper than the cost of issuing new common stock?

- When a company issues new common stock they also have to pay flotation costs to the underwriter.
- Issuing new common stock may send a negative signal to the capital markets, which may depress the stock price.

9-25

If issuing new common stock incurs a flotation cost of 15% of the proceeds, what is k_e?

$$k_e = \frac{D_0(1+g)}{P_0(1-F)} + g$$

$$= \frac{\$4.19(1.05)}{\$50(1-0.15)} + 5.0\%$$

$$= \frac{\$4.3995}{\$42.50} + 5.0\%$$

$$= 15.4\%$$

9-26

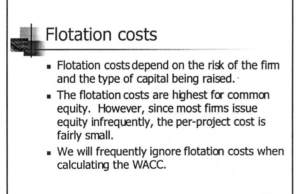

Flotation costs

- Flotation costs depend on the risk of the firm and the type of capital being raised. ·
- The flotation costs are highest for common equity. However, since most firms issue equity infrequently, the per-project cost is fairly small.
- We will frequently ignore flotation costs when calculating the WACC.

9-27

Ignoring flotation costs, what is the firm's WACC?

$$\begin{aligned} \text{WACC} &= w_d k_d (1\text{-}T) + w_p k_p + w_c k_s \\ &= 0.3(10\%)(0.6) + 0.1(9\%) + 0.6(14\%) \\ &= 1.8\% + 0.9\% + 8.4\% \\ &= 11.1\% \end{aligned}$$

9-28

What factors influence a company's composite WACC?

- Market conditions.
- The firm's capital structure and dividend policy.
- The firm's investment policy. Firms with riskier projects generally have a higher WACC.

9-29

Should the company use the composite WACC as the hurdle rate for each of its projects?

- NO! The composite WACC reflects the risk of an average project undertaken by the firm. Therefore, the WACC only represents the "hurdle rate" for a typical project with average risk.
- Different projects have different risks. The project's WACC should be adjusted to reflect the project's risk.

9-30

Risk and the Cost of Capital

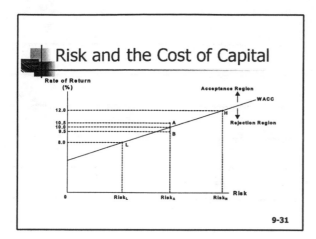

9-31

What are the three types of project risk?

- Stand-alone risk
- Corporate risk
- Market risk

9-32

How is each type of risk used?

- Market risk is theoretically best in most situations.
- However, creditors, customers, suppliers, and employees are more affected by corporate risk.
- Therefore, corporate risk is also relevant.

9-33

Problem areas in cost of capital

- Depreciation-generated funds
- Privately owned firms
- Measurement problems
- Adjusting costs of capital for different risk
- Capital structure weights

9-34

How are risk-adjusted costs of capital determined for specific projects or divisions?

- Subjective adjustments to the firm's composite WACC.
- Attempt to estimate what the cost of capital would be if the project/division were a stand-alone firm. This requires estimating the project's beta.

9-35

Finding a divisional cost of capital: Using similar stand-alone firms to estimate a project's cost of capital

- Comparison firms have the following characteristics:
  - Target capital structure consists of 40% debt and 60% equity.
  - $k_d = 12\%$
  - $k_{RF} = 7\%$
  - $RP_M = 6\%$
  - $\beta_{DIV} = 1.7$
  - Tax rate = 40%

9-36

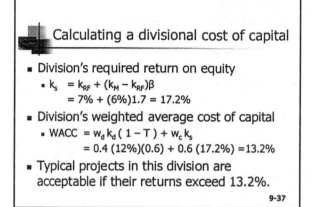

Calculating a divisional cost of capital

- Division's required return on equity
  - $k_s = k_{RF} + (k_M - k_{RF})\beta$
    $= 7\% + (6\%)1.7 = 17.2\%$
- Division's weighted average cost of capital
  - $WACC = w_d k_d (1 - T) + w_c k_s$
    $= 0.4 (12\%)(0.6) + 0.6 (17.2\%) = 13.2\%$
- Typical projects in this division are acceptable if their returns exceed 13.2%.

9-37

EXAM-TYPE PROBLEMS

9-1. Barak Company's 8 percent coupon rate, quarterly payment, $1,000 par value bond, which matures in 20 years, currently sells at a price of $686.86. The company's tax rate is 40 percent. Based on the nominal interest rate, not the EAR, what is the firm's component cost of debt for purposes of calculating the WACC? (7.32%)

9-2. Allison Engines Corporation has established a target capital structure of 40 percent debt and 60 percent common equity. The current market price of the firm's stock is P_0 = $28; its last dividend was D_0 = $2.20, and its expected dividend growth rate is 6 percent. Allison can issue new common stock at a flotation cost of 15 percent. What is Allison's marginal cost of outside equity capital, k_e? (15.8%)

9-3. Gator Services Unlimited's (GSU) financial analyst must determine the firm's WACC for use in capital budgeting. She has gathered the following relevant data:

(1) Target capital structure: Debt 55 percent, Common equity 45 percent.

(2) Interest rate on new debt = 10%.

(3) GSU's current stock price = $42.50; its last dividend was $3.00.

(4) The firm's constant growth rate is 10 percent; its tax rate is 35 percent.

What is GSU's WACC? (11.57%)

9-4. The Hiers Company has a target capital structure of 42 percent debt and 58 percent equity. The yield to maturity on the company's bonds is 11 percent, and the company's tax rate is 40 percent. Hiers' treasurer has calculated the company's WACC as 10.53 percent. What is the company's cost of equity capital, according to the treasurer's calculation? (13.38%)

BLUEPRINTS: CHAPTER 10
THE BASICS OF CAPITAL BUDGETING

10-25 Assume that you recently went to work for Allied Components Company, a supplier of auto repair parts used in the after-market with products from DaimlerChrysler, Ford, and other auto makers. Your boss, the chief financial officer (CFO), has just handed you the estimated cash flows for two proposed projects. Project L involves adding a new item to the firm's ignition system line; it would take some time to build up the market for this product, so the cash inflows would increase over time. Project S involves an add-on to an existing line, and its cash flows would decrease over time. Both projects have 3-year lives, because Allied is planning to introduce entirely new models after 3 years.

Here are the projects' net cash flows (in thousands of dollars):

	Expected Net Cash Flow	
Year	Project L	Project S
0	($100)	($100)
1	10	70
2	60	50
3	80	20

Depreciation, salvage values, net operating working capital requirements, and tax effects are all included in these cash flows.

The CFO also made subjective risk assessments of each project, and he concluded that both projects have risk characteristics that are similar to the firm's average project. Allied's weighted average cost of capital is 10 percent. You must now determine whether one or both of the projects should be accepted.

a. What is capital budgeting? Are there any similarities between a firm's capital budgeting decisions and an individual's investment decisions?

b. What is the difference between independent and mutually exclusive projects? Between projects with normal and nonnormal cash flows?

c. (1) What is the payback period? Find the paybacks for Projects L and S.

   (2) What is the rationale for the payback method? According to the payback criterion, which project or projects should be accepted if the firm's maximum acceptable payback is 2 years, and if Projects L and S are independent? If they are mutually exclusive?

   (3) What is the difference between the regular and discounted payback periods?

---

(4) What is the main disadvantage of discounted payback? Is the payback method of any real usefulness in capital budgeting decisions?

d. (1) Define the term *net present value (NPV)*. What is each project's NPV?

(2) What is the rationale behind the NPV method? According to NPV, which project or projects should be accepted if they are independent? Mutually exclusive?

(3) Would the NPVs change if the cost of capital changed?

e. (1) Define the term *internal rate of return (IRR)*. What is each project's IRR?

(2) How is the IRR on a project related to the YTM on a bond?

(3) What is the logic behind the IRR method? According to IRR, which projects should be accepted if they are independent? Mutually exclusive?

(4) Would the projects' IRRs change if the cost of capital changed?

f. (1) Draw NPV profiles for Projects L and S. At what discount rate do the profiles cross?

(2) Look at your NPV profile graph without referring to the actual NPVs and IRRs. Which project or projects should be accepted if they are independent? Mutually exclusive? Explain. Are your answers correct at any cost of capital less than 23.6 percent?

g. (1) What is the underlying cause of ranking conflicts between NPV and IRR?

(2) What is the "reinvestment rate assumption," and how does it affect the NPV versus IRR conflict?

(3) Which method is the best? Why?

h. (1) Define the term *modified IRR (MIRR)*. Find the MIRRs for Projects L and S.

(2) What are the MIRR's advantages and disadvantages vis-à-vis the regular IRR? What are the MIRR's advantages and disadvantages vis-à-vis the NPV?

i. As a separate project (Project P), the firm is considering sponsoring a pavilion at the upcoming World's Fair. The pavilion would cost $800,000, and it is expected to result in $5 million of incremental cash inflows during its 1 year of operation. However, it would then take another year, and $5 million of costs, to demolish the site and return it to its original condition. Thus, Project P's expected net cash flows look like this (in millions of dollars):

Year	Net Cash Flows
0	($0.8)
1	5.0
2	(5.0)

The project is estimated to be of average risk, so its cost of capital is 10 percent.

(1) What is Project P's NPV? What is its IRR? Its MIRR?

(2) Draw Project P's NPV profile. Does Project P have normal or nonnormal cash flows? Should this project be accepted?

CHAPTER 10
The Basics of Capital Budgeting

Should we build this plant?

10-1

What is capital budgeting?

- Analysis of potential additions to fixed assets.
- Long-term decisions; involve large expenditures.
- Very important to firm's future.

10-2

Steps to capital budgeting

1. Estimate CFs (inflows & outflows).
2. Assess riskiness of CFs.
3. Determine the appropriate cost of capital.
4. Find NPV and/or IRR.
5. Accept if NPV > 0 and/or IRR > WACC.

10-3

What is the difference between independent and mutually exclusive projects?

- Independent projects – if the cash flows of one are unaffected by the acceptance of the other.
- Mutually exclusive projects – if the cash flows of one can be adversely impacted by the acceptance of the other.

10-4

What is the difference between normal and nonnormal cash flow streams?

- Normal cash flow stream – Cost (negative CF) followed by a series of positive cash inflows. One change of signs.
- Nonnormal cash flow stream – Two or more changes of signs. Most common: Cost (negative CF), then string of positive CFs, then cost to close project. Nuclear power plant, strip mine, etc.

10-5

What is the payback period?

- The number of years required to recover a project's cost, or "How long does it take to get our money back?"
- Calculated by adding project's cash inflows to its cost until the cumulative cash flow for the project turns positive.

10-6

Calculating payback

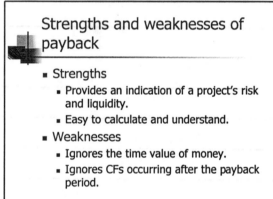

Project L

	0		1		2	2.4	3
CF_t	-100		10		60	100	80
Cumulative	-100		-90		-30	0	50

$Payback_L$ = 2 + 30 / 80 = 2.375 years

Project S

	0		1	1.6	2		3
CF_t	-100		70	100	50		20
Cumulative	-100		-30	0	20		40

$Payback_S$ = 1 + 30 / 50 = 1.6 years

10-7

Strengths and weaknesses of payback

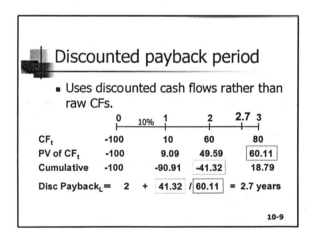

- Strengths
  - Provides an indication of a project's risk and liquidity.
  - Easy to calculate and understand.
- Weaknesses
  - Ignores the time value of money.
  - Ignores CFs occurring after the payback period.

10-8

Discounted payback period

- Uses discounted cash flows rather than raw CFs.

	0	10%	1	2	2.7	3
CF_t	-100		10	60		80
PV of CF_t	-100		9.09	49.59		60.11
Cumulative	-100		-90.91	-41.32		18.79

$Disc\ Payback_L$ = 2 + 41.32 / 60.11 = 2.7 years

10-9

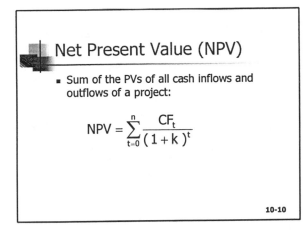

Net Present Value (NPV)

- Sum of the PVs of all cash inflows and outflows of a project:

$$NPV = \sum_{t=0}^{n} \frac{CF_t}{(1+k)^t}$$

10-10

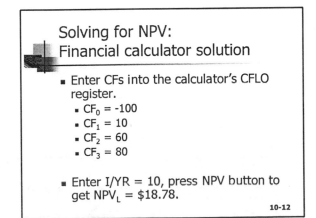

What is Project L's NPV?

Year	CF_t	PV of CF_t
0	-100	-$100
1	10	9.09
2	60	49.59
3	80	60.11
	NPV_L =	$18.79

NPV_S = $19.98

10-11

Solving for NPV: Financial calculator solution

- Enter CFs into the calculator's CFLO register.
  - CF_0 = -100
  - CF_1 = 10
  - CF_2 = 60
  - CF_3 = 80

- Enter I/YR = 10, press NPV button to get NPV_L = $18.78.

10-12

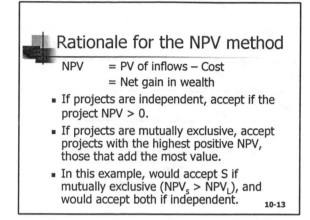

Rationale for the NPV method

NPV   = PV of inflows – Cost
         = Net gain in wealth

- If projects are independent, accept if the project NPV > 0.
- If projects are mutually exclusive, accept projects with the highest positive NPV, those that add the most value.
- In this example, would accept S if mutually exclusive (NPV$_s$ > NPV$_L$), and would accept both if independent.

10-13

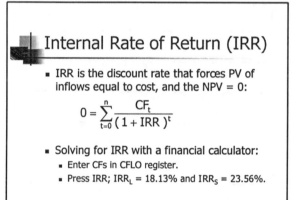

Internal Rate of Return (IRR)

- IRR is the discount rate that forces PV of inflows equal to cost, and the NPV = 0:

$$0 = \sum_{t=0}^{n} \frac{CF_t}{(1 + IRR)^t}$$

- Solving for IRR with a financial calculator:
  - Enter CFs in CFLO register.
  - Press IRR; IRR$_L$ = 18.13% and IRR$_S$ = 23.56%.

10-14

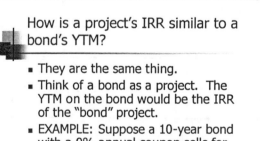

How is a project's IRR similar to a bond's YTM?

- They are the same thing.
- Think of a bond as a project. The YTM on the bond would be the IRR of the "bond" project.
- EXAMPLE: Suppose a 10-year bond with a 9% annual coupon sells for $1,134.20.
  - Solve for IRR = YTM = 7.08%, the annual return for this project/bond.

10-15

Rationale for the IRR method

- If IRR > WACC, the project's rate of return is greater than its costs. There is some return left over to boost stockholders' returns.

10-16

IRR Acceptance Criteria

- If IRR > k, accept project.
- If IRR < k, reject project.

- If projects are independent, accept both projects, as both IRR > k = 10%.
- If projects are mutually exclusive, accept S, because $IRR_s > IRR_L$.

10-17

NPV Profiles

- A graphical representation of project NPVs at various different costs of capital.

k	NPV_L	NPV_S
0	$50	$40
5	33	29
10	19	20
15	7	12
20	(4)	5

10-18

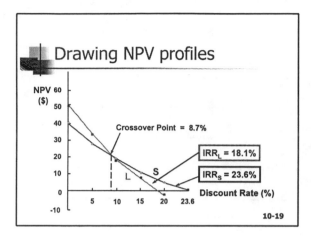

Drawing NPV profiles

Comparing the NPV and IRR methods

- If projects are independent, the two methods always lead to the same accept/reject decisions.
- If projects are mutually exclusive …
  - If k > crossover point, the two methods lead to the same decision and there is no conflict.
  - If k < crossover point, the two methods lead to different accept/reject decisions.

10-20

Finding the crossover point

1. Find cash flow differences between the projects for each year.
2. Enter these differences in CFLO register, then press IRR. Crossover rate = 8.68%, rounded to 8.7%.
3. Can subtract S from L or vice versa, but better to have first CF negative.
4. If profiles don't cross, one project dominates the other.

10-21

Reasons why NPV profiles cross

- Size (scale) differences – the smaller project frees up funds at t = 0 for investment. The higher the opportunity cost, the more valuable these funds, so high k favors small projects.
- Timing differences – the project with faster payback provides more CF in early years for reinvestment. If k is high, early CF especially good, $NPV_S > NPV_L$.

10-22

Reinvestment rate assumptions

- NPV method assumes CFs are reinvested at k, the opportunity cost of capital.
- IRR method assumes CFs are reinvested at IRR.
- Assuming CFs are reinvested at the opportunity cost of capital is more realistic, so NPV method is the best. NPV method should be used to choose between mutually exclusive projects.
- Perhaps a hybrid of the IRR that assumes cost of capital reinvestment is needed.

10-23

Since managers prefer the IRR to the NPV method, is there a better IRR measure?

- Yes, MIRR is the discount rate that causes the PV of a project's terminal value (TV) to equal the PV of costs. TV is found by compounding inflows at WACC.
- MIRR assumes cash flows are reinvested at the WACC.

10-24

Calculating MIRR

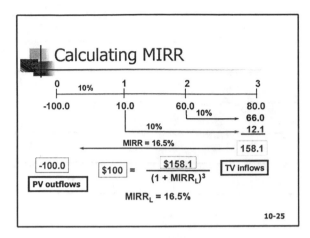

Why use MIRR versus IRR?

- MIRR correctly assumes reinvestment at opportunity cost = WACC. MIRR also avoids the problem of multiple IRRs.
- Managers like rate of return comparisons, and MIRR is better for this than IRR.

10-26

Project P has cash flows (in 000s): CF_0 = -$800, CF_1 = $5,000, and CF_2 = -$5,000. Find Project P's NPV and IRR.

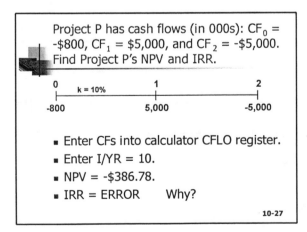

- Enter CFs into calculator CFLO register.
- Enter I/YR = 10.
- NPV = -$386.78.
- IRR = ERROR   Why?

10-27

Multiple IRRs

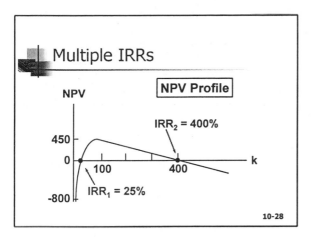

NPV Profile

IRR$_2$ = 400%

IRR$_1$ = 25%

10-28

Why are there multiple IRRs?

- At very low discount rates, the PV of CF$_2$ is large & negative, so NPV < 0.
- At very high discount rates, the PV of both CF$_1$ and CF$_2$ are low, so CF$_0$ dominates and again NPV < 0.
- In between, the discount rate hits CF$_2$ harder than CF$_1$, so NPV > 0.
- Result: 2 IRRs.

10-29

Solving the multiple IRR problem

- Using a calculator
  - Enter CFs as before.
  - Store a "guess" for the IRR (try 10%)
    - 10 ▪ STO
      - ▪ IRR = 25% (the lower IRR)
  - Now guess a larger IRR (try 200%)
    - 200 ▪ STO
      - ▪ IRR = 400% (the higher IRR)
  - When there are nonnormal CFs and more than one IRR, use the MIRR.

10-30

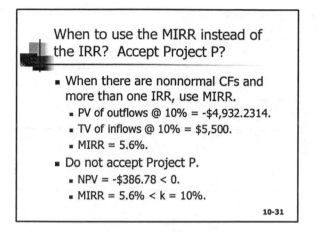

When to use the MIRR instead of the IRR? Accept Project P?

- When there are nonnormal CFs and more than one IRR, use MIRR.
  - PV of outflows @ 10% = -$4,932.2314.
  - TV of inflows @ 10% = $5,500.
  - MIRR = 5.6%.
- Do not accept Project P.
  - NPV = -$386.78 < 0.
  - MIRR = 5.6% < k = 10%.

10-31

_____

_____

_____

_____

_____

_____

_____

EXAM-TYPE PROBLEMS

10-1. A company is analyzing two mutually exclusive projects, S and L, whose cash flows are shown below:

Years	0	1	2	3	4
	12%				
S	-1,100	900	350	50	10
L	-1,100	0	300	500	850

The company's cost of capital is 12 percent, and it can get an unlimited amount of capital at that cost. What is the *regular IRR* (not MIRR) of the *better* project? (Hint: Note that the better project may or may not be the one with the higher IRR.) (13.09%)

10-2. As the director of capital budgeting for Lasser Company, you are evaluating two mutually exclusive projects with the following net cash flows:

Year	Project X	Project Z
0	-$100	-$100
1	50	10
2	40	30
3	30	40
4	10	60

Do the two NPV profiles cross in the relevant part of the NPV profile graph (the upper right quadrant) and, if they do cross, at what rate do the profiles cross? (7.17%)

10-3. Below are the returns of Nulook Cosmetics and the "market" over a 3-year period:

Year	Nulook	Market
1	9%	6%
2	15	10
3	36	24

Nulook finances internally using only retained earnings, and it uses the Capital Asset Pricing Model with a historical beta to determine its cost of equity. Currently, the risk-free rate is 7 percent, and the estimated market risk premium is 6 percent. Nulook is evaluating a project that has a cost today of $2,028 and will provide estimated after-tax cash inflows of $1,000 at the end of each of the next 3 years. What is this project's MIRR? (20.01%)

11-18 After seeing Snapple's success with noncola soft drinks and learning of Coke's and Pepsi's interest, Allied Food Products has decided to consider an expansion of its own in the fruit juice business. The product being considered is fresh lemon juice. Assume that you were recently hired as assistant to the director of capital budgeting, and you must evaluate the new project.

The lemon juice would be produced in an unused building adjacent to Allied's Fort Myers plant; Allied owns the building, which is fully depreciated. The required equipment would cost $200,000, plus an additional $40,000 for shipping and installation. In addition, inventories would rise by $25,000, while accounts payable would go up by $5,000. All of these costs would be incurred at t = 0. By a special ruling, the machinery could be depreciated under the MACRS system as 3-year property. The applicable depreciation rates are 33%, 45%, 15%, and 7%.

The project is expected to operate for 4 years, at which time it will be terminated. The cash inflows are assumed to begin 1 year after the project is undertaken, or at t = 1, and to continue out to t = 4. At the end of the project's life (t = 4), the equipment is expected to have a salvage value of $25,000.

Unit sales are expected to total 100,000 cans per year, and the expected sales price is $2.00 per can. Cash operating costs for the project (total operating costs less depreciation) are expected to total 60 percent of dollar sales. Allied's tax rate is 40 percent, and its weighted average cost of capital is 10 percent. Tentatively, the lemon juice project is assumed to be of equal risk to Allied's other assets.

You have been asked to evaluate the project and to make a recommendation as to whether it should be accepted or rejected. To guide you in your analysis, your boss gave you the following set of questions.

a. Draw a time line that shows when the net cash inflows and outflows will occur, and explain how the time line can be used to help structure the analysis.

b. Allied has a standard form that is used in the capital budgeting process; see Table IC11-1. Part of the table has been completed, but you must replace the blanks with the missing numbers.

Table IC11-1. Allied's Lemon Juice Project
(Total Cost in Thousands)

End of Year:	0	1	2	3	4
I. Investment Outlay					
Equipment cost					
Installation					
Increase in inventory					
Increase in accounts payable	‾‾‾				
Total net investment	══				
II. Operating Cash Flows					
Unit sales (thousands)			100		
Price/unit		$ 2.00	$ 2.00	‾‾‾	
Total revenues		‾‾‾	‾‾‾	‾‾‾	$200.0
Operating costs, excluding depreciation			$120.0		
Depreciation				36.0	16.8
Total costs		$199.2	$228.0	‾‾‾	‾‾‾
Oper. income bef. taxes				$ 44.0	
Taxes on oper. income		0.3	‾‾‾		25.3
Oper. income after taxes				$ 26.4	
Depreciation		79.2		36.0	
Operating cash flow	$ 0.0	$ 79.7	══	══	$ 54.7
III. Terminal Year Cash Flows					
Return of net operating working capital					
Salvage value					
Tax on salvage value					
Total termination cash flows					‾‾‾ ══
IV. Net Cash Flows					
Net cash flow	($260.0)	‾‾‾	‾‾‾	‾‾‾	$ 89.7
V. Results					
NPV =					
IRR =					
MIRR =					
Payback =					

Complete the table in the following steps:

(1) Fill in the blanks under Year 0 for the initial investment outlay.

(2) Complete the table for unit sales, sales price, total revenues, and operating costs excluding depreciation.

(3) Complete the depreciation data.

(4) Now complete the table down to operating income after taxes, and then down to net cash flows.

(5) Now fill in the blanks under Year 4 for the terminal cash flows, and complete the net cash flow line. Discuss net operating working capital. What would have happened if the machinery were sold for less than its book value?

c. (1) Allied uses debt in its capital structure, so some of the money used to finance the project will be debt. Given this fact, should the projected cash flows be revised to show projected interest charges? Explain.

(2) Suppose you learned that Allied had spent $50,000 to renovate the building last year, expensing these costs. Should this cost be reflected in the analysis? Explain.

(3) Now suppose you learned that Allied could lease its building to another party and earn $25,000 per year. Should that fact be reflected in the analysis? If so, how?

(4) Now assume that the lemon juice project would take away profitable sales from Allied's fresh orange juice business. Should that fact be reflected in your analysis? If so, how?

d. Disregard all the assumptions made in part c, and assume there was no alternative use for the building over the next 4 years. Now calculate the project's NPV, IRR, MIRR, and regular payback. Do these indicators suggest that the project should be accepted?

e. If this project had been a replacement rather than an expansion project, how would the analysis have changed? Think about the changes that would have to occur in the cash flow table.

f. Assume that inflation is expected to average 5 percent over the next 4 years; that this expectation is reflected in the WACC; and that inflation will increase variable costs and revenues by the same percentage, 5 percent. Does it appear that inflation has been dealt with properly in the analysis? If not, what should be done, and how would the required adjustment affect the decision? You can modify the numbers in the table to quantify your results.

Although inflation was considered in the initial analysis, the riskiness of the project was not considered. The expected cash flows, considering inflation (in thousands of dollars), are given in Table IC11-2. Allied's overall cost of capital (WACC) is 10 percent.

Table IC11-2. Allied's Lemon Juice Project Considering Inflation
(in Thousands)

			Year		
	0	1	2	3	4
Investment in:					
Fixed assets	($240)				
Net operating					
working capital	(20)				
Unit sales (thousands)		100	100	100	100
Sale price (dollars)		$2.100	$2.205	$2.315	$2.431
Total revenues		$210.0	$220.5	$231.5	$243.1
Cash operating costs (60%)		126.0	132.3	138.9	145.9
Depreciation		79.2	108.0	36.0	16.8
Operating income before taxes		$ 4.8	($ 19.8)	$ 56.6	$ 80.4
Taxes on operating income (40%)		1.9	(7.9)	22.6	32.1
Operating income after taxes		$ 2.9	($ 11.9)	$ 34.0	$ 48.3
Plus depreciation		79.2	108.0	36.0	16.8
Operating cash flow		$ 82.1	$ 96.1	$ 70.0	$ 65.1
Salvage value					25.0
Tax on SV (40%)					(10.0)
Recovery of NOWC					20.0
Net cash flow	($260)	$ 82.1	$ 96.1	$ 70.0	$100.1
Cumulative cash flows					
for payback:	(260.0)	(177.9)	(81.8)	(11.8)	88.3
Compounded inflows					
for MIRR:		109.2	116.3	77.0	100.1
Terminal value of inflows:					402.6

NPV at 10% cost of capital = $15.0
IRR   = 12.6%
MIRR   = 11.6%

You have been asked to answer the following questions.

g. (1) What are the three levels, or types, of project risk that are normally considered?

    (2) Which type is most relevant?

    (3) Which type is easiest to measure?

    (4) Are the three types of risk generally highly correlated?

h. (1) What is sensitivity analysis?

   (2) Discuss how one would perform a sensitivity analysis on the unit sales, salvage value, and cost of capital for the project. Assume that each of these variables deviates from its base-case, or expected, value by plus and minus 10, 20, and 30 percent. Explain how you would calculate the NPV, IRR, MIRR, and payback for each case.

   (3) What is the primary weakness of sensitivity analysis? What are its primary advantages?

i. Assume that you are confident about the estimates of all the variables that affect the cash flows except unit sales. If product acceptance is poor, sales would be only 75,000 units a year, while a strong consumer response would produce sales of 125,000 units. In either case, cash costs would still amount to 60 percent of revenues. You believe that there is a 25 percent chance of poor acceptance, a 25 percent chance of excellent acceptance, and a 50 percent chance of average acceptance (the base case).

   (1) What is the worst-case NPV? The best-case NPV?

   (2) Use the worst-, most likely (or base), and best-case NPVs, with their probabilities of occurrence, to find the project's expected NPV, standard deviation, and coefficient of variation.

j. (1) Assume that Allied's average project has a coefficient of variation (CV) in the range of 1.25 to 1.75. Would the lemon juice project be classified as high risk, average risk, or low risk? What type of risk is being measured here?

   (2) Based on common sense, how highly correlated do you think the project would be with the firm's other assets? (Give a correlation coefficient or range of coefficients, based on your judgment.)

   (3) How would this correlation coefficient and the previously calculated σ combine to affect the project's contribution to corporate, or within-firm, risk? Explain.

k. (1) Based on your judgment, what do you think the project's correlation coefficient would be with respect to the general economy and thus with returns on "the market"?

   (2) How would correlation with the economy affect the project's market risk?

l. (1) Allied typically adds or subtracts 3 percentage points to the overall cost of capital to adjust for risk. Should the lemon juice project be accepted?

   (2) What subjective risk factors should be considered before the final decision is made?

m. In recent months, Allied's group has begun to focus on real option analysis.

    (1) What is real option analysis?

    (2) What are some examples of projects with embedded real options?

CHAPTER 11
Cash Flow Estimation and Risk Analysis

- Relevant cash flows
- Incorporating inflation
- Types of risk
- Risk Analysis

11-1

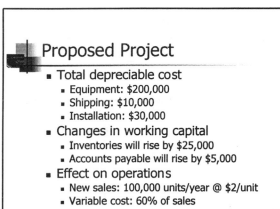

Proposed Project

- Total depreciable cost
  - Equipment: $200,000
  - Shipping: $10,000
  - Installation: $30,000
- Changes in working capital
  - Inventories will rise by $25,000
  - Accounts payable will rise by $5,000
- Effect on operations
  - New sales: 100,000 units/year @ $2/unit
  - Variable cost: 60% of sales

11-2

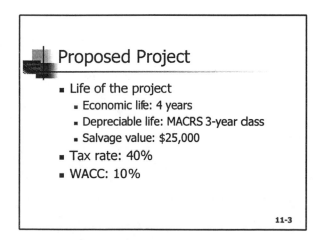

Proposed Project

- Life of the project
  - Economic life: 4 years
  - Depreciable life: MACRS 3-year class
  - Salvage value: $25,000
- Tax rate: 40%
- WACC: 10%

11-3

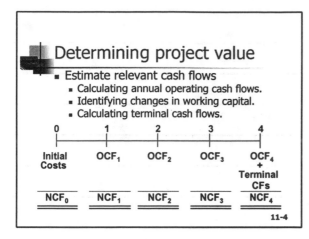

Determining project value

- Estimate relevant cash flows
  - Calculating annual operating cash flows.
  - Identifying changes in working capital.
  - Calculating terminal cash flows.

0	1	2	3	4
Initial Costs	OCF_1	OCF_2	OCF_3	OCF_4 + Terminal CFs
NCF_0	NCF_1	NCF_2	NCF_3	NCF_4

11-4

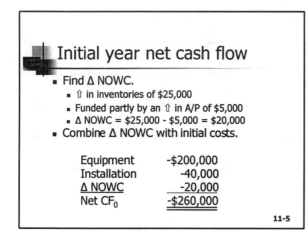

Initial year net cash flow

- Find Δ NOWC.
  - ⇧ in inventories of $25,000
  - Funded partly by an ⇧ in A/P of $5,000
  - Δ NOWC = $25,000 - $5,000 = $20,000
- Combine Δ NOWC with initial costs.

Equipment	-$200,000
Installation	-40,000
Δ NOWC	-20,000
Net CF_0	-$260,000

11-5

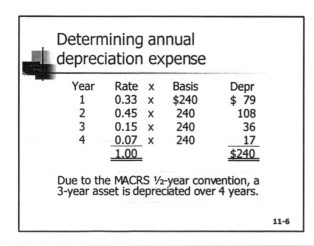

Determining annual depreciation expense

Year	Rate	x	Basis	Depr
1	0.33	x	$240	$ 79
2	0.45	x	240	108
3	0.15	x	240	36
4	0.07	x	240	17
	1.00			$240

Due to the MACRS ½-year convention, a 3-year asset is depreciated over 4 years.

11-6

Annual operating cash flows

	1	2	3	4
Revenues	200	200	200	200
- Op. Costs (60%)	-120	-120	-120	-120
- Deprn Expense	-79	-108	-36	-17
Oper. Income (BT)	1	-28	44	63
- Tax (40%)	-	-11	18	25
Oper. Income (AT)	1	-17	26	38
+ Deprn Expense	79	108	36	17
Operating CF	80	91	62	55

11-7

Terminal net cash flow

Recovery of NOWC	$20,000
Salvage value	25,000
Tax on SV (40%)	-10,000
Terminal CF	$35,000

Q. How is NOWC recovered?
Q. Is there always a tax on SV?
Q. Is the tax on SV ever a positive cash flow?

11-8

Should financing effects be included in cash flows?

- No, dividends and interest expense should not be included in the analysis.
- Financing effects have already been taken into account by discounting cash flows at the WACC of 10%.
- Deducting interest expense and dividends would be "double counting" financing costs.

11-9

Should a $50,000 improvement cost from the previous year be included in the analysis?

- No, the building improvement cost is a sunk cost and should not be considered.
- This analysis should only include incremental investment.

11-10

If the facility could be leased out for $25,000 per year, would this affect the analysis?

- Yes, by accepting the project, the firm foregoes a possible annual cash flow of $25,000, which is an opportunity cost to be charged to the project.
- The relevant cash flow is the annual after-tax opportunity cost.
  - A-T opportunity cost = $25,000 (1 – T)
    - = $25,000(0.6)
    - = $15,000

11-11

If the new product line were to decrease the sales of the firm's other lines, would this affect the analysis?

- Yes. The effect on other projects' CFs is an "externality."
- Net CF loss per year on other lines would be a cost to this project.
- Externalities can be positive (in the case of complements) or negative (substitutes).

11-12

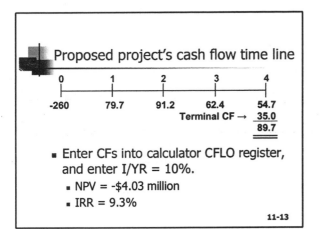

Proposed project's cash flow time line

0	1	2	3	4
-260	79.7	91.2	62.4	54.7
			Terminal CF →	35.0
				89.7

- Enter CFs into calculator CFLO register, and enter I/YR = 10%.
  - NPV = -$4.03 million
  - IRR = 9.3%

11-13

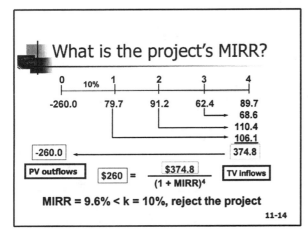

What is the project's MIRR?

0	10%	1	2	3	4
-260.0		79.7	91.2	62.4	89.7
					68.6
					110.4
					106.1
-260.0					374.8

$$\boxed{\text{PV outflows}} \quad \boxed{\$260} = \frac{\boxed{\$374.8}}{(1 + \text{MIRR})^4} \quad \boxed{\text{TV inflows}}$$

MIRR = 9.6% < k = 10%, reject the project

11-14

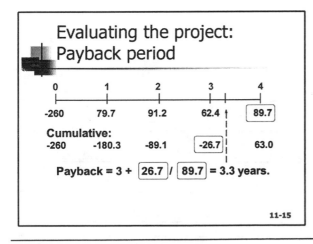

Evaluating the project: Payback period

0	1	2	3	4
-260	79.7	91.2	62.4	89.7

Cumulative:

-260	-180.3	-89.1	-26.7	63.0

Payback = 3 + 26.7 / 89.7 = 3.3 years.

11-15

If this were a replacement rather than a new project, would the analysis change?

- Yes, the old equipment would be sold, and new equipment purchased.
- The incremental CFs would be the changes from the old to the new situation.
- The relevant depreciation expense would be the change with the new equipment.
- If the old machine was sold, the firm would not receive the SV at the end of the machine's life. This is the opportunity cost for the replacement project.

11-16

What if there is expected annual inflation of 5%, is NPV biased?

- Yes, inflation causes the discount rate to be upwardly revised.
- Therefore, inflation creates a downward bias on PV.
- Inflation should be built into CF forecasts.

11-17

Annual operating cash flows, if expected annual inflation = 5%

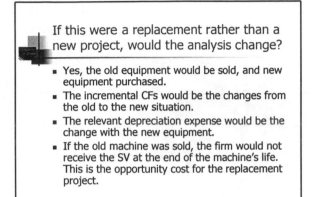

	1	2	3	4
Revenues	210	220	232	243
Op. Costs (60%)	-126	-132	-139	-146
- Deprn Expense	-79	-108	-36	-17
- Oper. Income (BT)	5	-20	57	80
- Tax (40%)	2	-8	23	32
Oper. Income (AT)	3	-12	34	48
+ Deprn Expense	79	108	36	17
Operating CF	82	96	70	65

11-18

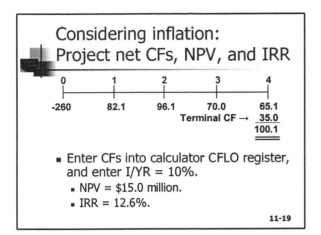

Considering inflation:
Project net CFs, NPV, and IRR

```
    0       1       2       3       4
    |-------|-------|-------|-------|
  -260    82.1    96.1    70.0    65.1
                          Terminal CF →   35.0
                                         100.1
```

- Enter CFs into calculator CFLO register, and enter I/YR = 10%.
  - NPV = $15.0 million.
  - IRR = 12.6%.

11-19

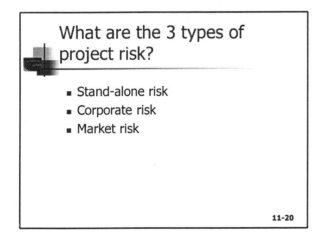

What are the 3 types of project risk?

- Stand-alone risk
- Corporate risk
- Market risk

11-20

What is stand-alone risk?

- The project's total risk, if it were operated independently.
- Usually measured by standard deviation (or coefficient of variation).
- However, it ignores the firm's diversification among projects and investor's diversification among firms.

11-21

What is corporate risk?

- The project's risk when considering the firm's other projects, i.e., diversification within the firm.
- Corporate risk is a function of the project's NPV and standard deviation and its correlation with the returns on other projects in the firm.

11-22

What is market risk?

- The project's risk to a well-diversified investor.
- Theoretically, it is measured by the project's beta and it considers both corporate and stockholder diversification.

11-23

Which type of risk is most relevant?

- Market risk is the most relevant risk for capital projects, because management's primary goal is shareholder wealth maximization.
- However, since total risk affects creditors, customers, suppliers, and employees, it should not be completely ignored.

11-24

Which risk is the easiest to measure?

- Stand-alone risk is the easiest to measure. Firms often focus on stand-alone risk when making capital budgeting decisions.
- Focusing on stand-alone risk is not theoretically correct, but it does not necessarily lead to poor decisions.

11-25

Are the three types of risk generally highly correlated?

- Yes, since most projects the firm undertakes are in its core business, stand-alone risk is likely to be highly correlated with its corporate risk.
- In addition, corporate risk is likely to be highly correlated with its market risk.

11-26

What is sensitivity analysis?

- Sensitivity analysis measures the effect of changes in a variable on the project's NPV.
- To perform a sensitivity analysis, all variables are fixed at their expected values, except for the variable in question which is allowed to fluctuate.
- Resulting changes in NPV are noted.

11-27

What are the advantages and disadvantages of sensitivity analysis?

- Advantage
  - Identifies variables that may have the greatest potential impact on profitability and allows management to focus on these variables.
- Disadvantages
  - Does not reflect the effects of diversification.
  - Does not incorporate any information about the possible magnitudes of the forecast errors.

11-28

Perform a scenario analysis of the project, based on changes in the sales forecast

- Suppose we are confident of all the variable estimates, except unit sales. The actual unit sales are expected to follow the following probability distribution:

Case	Probability	Unit Sales
Worst	0.25	75,000
Base	0.50	100,000
Best	0.25	125,000

11-29

Scenario analysis

- All other factors shall remain constant and the NPV under each scenario can be determined.

Case	Probability	NPV
Worst	0.25	($27.8)
Base	0.50	$15.0
Best	0.25	$57.8

11-30

Determining expected NPV, σ_{NPV}, and CV_{NPV} from the scenario analysis

- E(NPV) = 0.25(-$27.8)+0.5($15.0)+0.25($57.8)
  = $15.0

- σ_{NPV} = [0.25(-$27.8-$15.0)^2 + 0.5($15.0-$15.0)^2 + 0.25($57.8-$15.0)^2]$^{1/2}$
  = $30.3.

- CV_{NPV} = $30.3 /$15.0 = 2.0.

11-31

If the firm's average projects have CV_{NPV} ranging from 1.25 to 1.75, would this project be of high, average, or low risk?

- With a CV_{NPV} of 2.0, this project would be classified as a high-risk project.
- Perhaps, some sort of risk correction is required for proper analysis.

11-32

Is this project likely to be correlated with the firm's business? How would it contribute to the firm's overall risk?

- We would expect a positive correlation with the firm's aggregate cash flows.
- As long as correlation is not perfectly positive (i.e., $\rho \neq 1$), we would expect it to contribute to the lowering of the firm's total risk.

11-33

If the project had a high correlation with the economy, how would corporate and market risk be affected?

- The project's corporate risk would not be directly affected. However, when combined with the project's high stand-alone risk, correlation with the economy would suggest that market risk (beta) is high.

11-34

If the firm uses a +/- 3% risk adjustment for the cost of capital, should the project be accepted?

- Reevaluating this project at a 13% cost of capital (due to high stand-alone risk), the NPV of the project is -$2.2 .
- If, however, it were a low-risk project, we would use a 7% cost of capital and the project NPV is $34.1.

11-35

What subjective risk factors should be considered before a decision is made?

- Numerical analysis sometimes fails to capture all sources of risk for a project.
- If the project has the potential for a lawsuit, it is more risky than previously thought.
- If assets can be redeployed or sold easily, the project may be less risky.

11-36

What is Monte Carlo simulation?

- A risk analysis technique in which probable future events are simulated on a computer, generating estimated rates of return and risk indexes.
- Simulation software packages are often add-ons to spreadsheet programs.

11-37

What is real option analysis?

- Real options exist when managers can influence the size and riskiness of a project's cash flows by taking different actions during the project's life.
- Real option analysis incorporates typical NPV budgeting analysis with an analysis for opportunities resulting from managers' decisions.

11-38

What are some examples of real options?

- Investment timing options
- Abandonment/shutdown options
- Growth/expansion options
- Flexibility options

11-39

EXAM-TYPE PROBLEMS

11-1. General Communications encounters significant uncertainty in its sales volume and price with its primary product. The firm uses scenario analysis to determine an expected NPV, which it then uses in its capital budget. The base-case, best-case, and worst-case scenarios and probabilities are provided in the following table. What are this product's expected NPV, standard deviation, and coefficient of variation? ($23,411,250; $19,682,424.70; 0.8407)

Scenario	Probability of Outcome	Unit Sales Volume	Sales Price	NPV (in 000's)
Worst case	0.20	9,000	$5,750	-$9,000
Base case	0.45	15,600	$7,000	+$20,500
Best case	0.35	21,500	$8,150	+$45,675

11-2. The Merry Milling Company is evaluating the proposed acquisition of a new milling machine. The machine's base price is $540,000, and it would cost another $62,500 to modify it for special use by your firm. The machine falls into the MACRS 3-year class, and it would be sold after 3 years for $325,000. (See Table 11A-2 for MACRS recovery allowance percentages.) The machine would require an increase in net operating working capital (inventory) of $27,500. The milling machine would have no effect on revenues, but it is expected to save the firm $220,000 per year in before-tax operating costs, mainly labor. The firm's marginal tax rate is 35 percent. If the project's cost of capital is 12 percent, should the machine be purchased? (Yes, NPV = $54,202)

11-3. The Metropolitan Oil Company is deciding whether to drill for oil on a tract of land that the company owns. The company estimates that the project would cost $13.6 million today. Metropolitan estimates that once drilled, the oil will generate positive net cash flows of $6.8 million a year at the end of each of the next 4 years. While the company is fairly confident about its cash flow forecast, it recognizes that if it waits 2 years, it would have more information about the local geology as well as the price of oil. Metropolitan estimates that if it waits 2 years, the project would cost $15.3 million. Moreover, if it waits 2 years, there is a 90 percent chance that the net cash flows would be $7.14 million a year for 4 years, and there is a 10 percent chance that the cash flows will be $3.74 million a year for 4 years. Assume that all cash flows are discounted at 10 percent.

   a. If the company chooses to drill today, what is the project's net present value? ($7.9551 million)

   b. Would it make sense to wait 2 years before deciding whether to drill? (No, NPV = $5.4542 million)

12-16 Assume that you have just been hired as business manager of Campus Deli (CD), which is located adjacent to the campus. Sales were $1,100,000 last year; variable costs were 60 percent of sales; and fixed costs were $40,000. Therefore, EBIT totaled $400,000. Because the university's enrollment is capped, EBIT is expected to be constant over time. Since no expansion capital is required, CD pays out all earnings as dividends. Assets are $2 million, and 80,000 shares are outstanding. The management group owns about 50 percent of the stock, which is traded in the over-the-counter market.

CD currently has no debt—it is an all-equity firm—and its 80,000 shares outstanding sell at a price of $25 per share, which is also the book value. The firm's federal-plus-state tax rate is 40 percent. On the basis of statements made in your finance text, you believe that CD's shareholders would be better off if some debt financing were used. When you suggested this to your new boss, she encouraged you to pursue the idea, but to provide support for the suggestion.

In today's market, the risk-free rate, k_{RF}, is 6 percent and the market risk premium, $k_M - k_{RF}$, is 6 percent. CD's unlevered beta, b_U, is 1.0. Since CD currently has no debt, its cost of equity (and WACC) is 12 percent.

If the firm were recapitalized, debt would be issued, and the borrowed funds would be used to repurchase stock. Stockholders, in turn, would use funds provided by the repurchase to buy equities in other fast-food companies similar to CD. You plan to complete your report by asking and then answering the following questions.

a. (1) What is business risk? What factors influence a firm's business risk?

(2) What is operating leverage, and how does it affect a firm's business risk?

b. (1) What is meant by the terms "financial leverage" and "financial risk"?

(2) How does financial risk differ from business risk?

c. Now, to develop an example that can be presented to CD's management as an illustration, consider two hypothetical firms, Firm U, with zero debt financing, and Firm L, with $10,000 of 12 percent debt. Both firms have $20,000 in total assets and a 40 percent federal-plus-state tax rate, and they have the following EBIT probability distribution for next year:

	Probability	EBIT
	0.25	$2,000
	0.50	3,000
	0.25	4,000

(1) Complete the partial income statements and the firms' ratios in Table IC12-1.

Table IC12-1. Income Statements and Ratios

	Firm U			Firm L		
Assets	$20,000	$20,000	$20,000	$20,000	$20,000	$20,000
Equity	$20,000	$20,000	$20,000	$10,000	$10,000	$10,000
Probability	0.25	0.50	0.25	0.25	0.50	0.25
Sales	$ 6,000	$ 9,000	$12,000	$ 6,000	$ 9,000	$12,000
Oper. costs	4,000	6,000	8,000	4,000	6,000	8,000
EBIT	$ 2,000	$ 3,000	$ 4,000	$ 2,000	$ 3,000	$ 4,000
Interest (12%)	0	0	0	1,200		1,200
EBT	$ 2,000	$ 3,000	$ 4,000	$ 800	$	$ 2,800
Taxes (40%)	800	1,200	1,600	320		1,120
Net income	$ 1,200	$ 1,800	$ 2,400	$ 480	$	$ 1,680
BEP						
(BEP = EBIT/Assets)	10.0%	15.0%	20.0%	10.0%	%	20.0%
ROE	6.0%	9.0%	12.0%	4.8%	%	16.8%
TIE	∞	∞	∞	1.7×	×	3.3×
E(BEP)		15.0%			%	
E(ROE)		9.0%			10.8%	
E(TIE)		∞			2.5×	
σ(BEP)		3.5%			%	
σ(ROE)		2.1%			4.2%	
σ(TIE)		0			0.6×	

(2) Be prepared to discuss each entry in the table and to explain how this example illustrates the impact of financial leverage on expected rate of return and risk.

d. After speaking with a local investment banker, you obtain the following estimates of the cost of debt at different debt levels (in thousands of dollars):

Amount Borrowed	Debt/Assets Ratio	Debt/Equity Ratio	Bond Rating	k_d
$ 0	0	0	--	--
250	0.125	0.1429	AA	8.0%
500	0.250	0.3333	A	9.0
750	0.375	0.6000	BBB	11.5
1,000	0.500	1.0000	BB	14.0

Now consider the optimal capital structure for CD.

(1) To begin, define the terms "optimal capital structure" and "target capital structure."

(2) Why does CD's bond rating and cost of debt depend on the amount of money borrowed?

(3) Assume that shares could be repurchased at the current market price of $25 per share. Calculate CD's expected EPS and TIE at debt levels of $0, $250,000, $500,000, $750,000, and $1,000,000. How many shares would remain after recapitalization under each scenario?

(4) Using the Hamada equation, what is the cost of equity if CD recapitalizes with $250,000 of debt? $500,000? $750,000? $1,000,000?

(5) Considering only the levels of debt discussed, what is the capital structure that minimizes CD's WACC?

(6) What would be the new stock price if CD recapitalizes with $250,000 of debt? $500,000? $750,000? $1,000,000? Recall that the payout ratio is 100 percent, so g = 0.

(7) Is EPS maximized at the debt level that maximizes share price? Why or why not?

(8) Considering only the levels of debt discussed, what is CD's optimal capital structure?

(9) What is the WACC at the optimal capital structure?

e. Suppose you discovered that CD had more business risk than you originally estimated. Describe how this would affect the analysis. What if the firm had less business risk than originally estimated?

f. What are some factors a manager should consider when establishing his or her firm's target capital structure?

g. Put labels on Figure IC12-1, and then discuss the graph as you might use it to explain to your boss why CD might want to use some debt.

Figure IC12-1
Relationship between Capital Structure and Stock Price

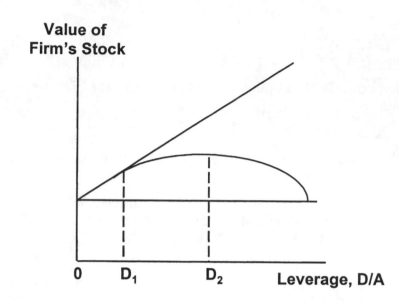

h.   How does the existence of asymmetric information and signaling affect capital structure?

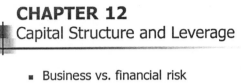

CHAPTER 12
Capital Structure and Leverage

- Business vs. financial risk
- Optimal capital structure
- Operating leverage
- Capital structure theory

12-1

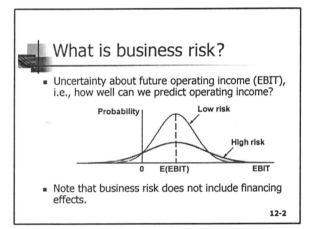

What is business risk?

- Uncertainty about future operating income (EBIT), i.e., how well can we predict operating income?

- Note that business risk does not include financing effects.

12-2

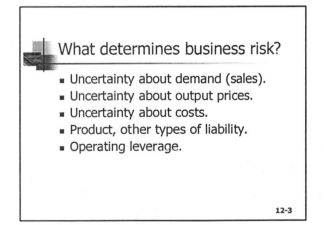

What determines business risk?

- Uncertainty about demand (sales).
- Uncertainty about output prices.
- Uncertainty about costs.
- Product, other types of liability.
- Operating leverage.

12-3

What is operating leverage, and how does it affect a firm's business risk?

- Operating leverage is the use of fixed costs rather than variable costs.
- If most costs are fixed, hence do not decline when demand falls, then the firm has high operating leverage.

12-4

Effect of operating leverage

- More operating leverage leads to more business risk, for then a small sales decline causes a big profit decline.

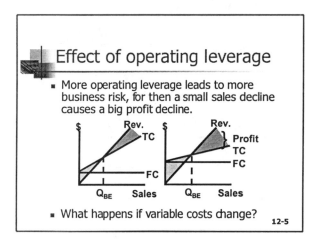

- What happens if variable costs change?

12-5

Using operating leverage

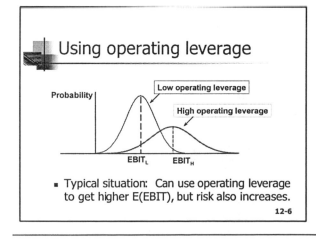

- Typical situation: Can use operating leverage to get higher E(EBIT), but risk also increases.

12-6

What is financial leverage? Financial risk?

- Financial leverage is the use of debt and preferred stock.
- Financial risk is the additional risk concentrated on common stockholders as a result of financial leverage.

12-7

Business risk vs. Financial risk

- Business risk depends on business factors such as competition, product liability, and operating leverage.
- Financial risk depends only on the types of securities issued.
  - More debt, more financial risk.
  - Concentrates business risk on stockholders.

12-8

An example:
Illustrating effects of financial leverage

- Two firms with the same operating leverage, business risk, and probability distribution of EBIT.
- Only differ with respect to their use of debt (capital structure).

Firm U	Firm L
No debt	$10,000 of 12% debt
$20,000 in assets	$20,000 in assets
40% tax rate	40% tax rate

12-9

Firm U: Unleveraged

	Economy		
	Bad	Avg.	Good
Prob.	0.25	0.50	0.25
EBIT	$2,000	$3,000	$4,000
Interest	0	0	0
EBT	$2,000	$3,000	$4,000
Taxes (40%)	800	1,200	1,600
NI	$1,200	$1,800	$2,400

12-10

Firm L: Leveraged

	Economy		
	Bad	Avg.	Good
Prob.*	0.25	0.50	0.25
EBIT*	$2,000	$3,000	$4,000
Interest	1,200	1,200	1,200
EBT	$ 800	$1,800	$2,800
Taxes (40%)	320	720	1,120
NI	$ 480	$1,080	$1,680

*Same as for Firm U.

12-11

Ratio comparison between leveraged and unleveraged firms

FIRM U	Bad	Avg	Good
BEP	10.0%	15.0%	20.0%
ROE	6.0%	9.0%	12.0%
TIE	∞	∞	∞

FIRM L	Bad	Avg	Good
BEP	10.0%	15.0%	20.0%
ROE	4.8%	10.8%	16.8%
TIE	1.67x	2.50x	3.30x

12-12

Risk and return for leveraged and unleveraged firms

Expected Values:

	Firm U	Firm L
E(BEP)	15.0%	15.0%
E(ROE)	9.0%	10.8%
E(TIE)	∞	2.5x

Risk Measures:

	Firm U	Firm L
σ_{ROE}	2.12%	4.24%
CV_{ROE}	0.24	0.39

12-13

The effect of leverage on profitability and debt coverage

- For leverage to raise expected ROE, must have BEP > k_d.
- Why? If k_d > BEP, then the interest expense will be higher than the operating income produced by debt-financed assets, so leverage will depress income.
- As debt increases, TIE decreases because EBIT is unaffected by debt, and interest expense increases (Int Exp = k_dD).

12-14

Conclusions

- Basic earning power (BEP) is unaffected by financial leverage.
- L has higher expected ROE because BEP > k_d.
- L has much wider ROE (and EPS) swings because of fixed interest charges. Its higher expected return is accompanied by higher risk.

12-15

Optimal Capital Structure

- That capital structure (mix of debt, preferred, and common equity) at which P_0 is maximized. Trades off higher E(ROE) and EPS against higher risk. The tax-related benefits of leverage are exactly offset by the debt's risk-related costs.
- The target capital structure is the mix of debt, preferred stock, and common equity with which the firm intends to raise capital.

12-16

Describe the sequence of events in a recapitalization.

- Campus Deli announces the recapitalization.
- New debt is issued.
- Proceeds are used to repurchase stock.
  - The number of shares repurchased is equal to the amount of debt issued divided by price per share.

12-17

Cost of debt at different levels of debt, after the proposed recapitalization

Amount borrowed	D/A ratio	D/E ratio	Bond rating	k_d
$ 0	0	0	--	--
250	0.125	0.1429	AA	8.0%
500	0.250	0.3333	A	9.0%
750	0.375	0.6000	BBB	11.5%
1,000	0.500	1.0000	BB	14.0%

12-18

Why do the bond rating and cost of debt depend upon the amount borrowed?

- As the firm borrows more money, the firm increases its financial risk causing the firm's bond rating to decrease, and its cost of debt to increase.

12-19

Analyze the proposed recapitalization at various levels of debt. Determine the EPS and TIE at each level of debt.

$D = \$0$

$$EPS = \frac{(EBIT - k_d D)(1 - T)}{Shares\ outstanding}$$

$$= \frac{(\$400,000)(0.6)}{80,000}$$

$$= \$3.00$$

12-20

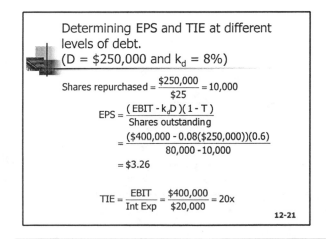

Determining EPS and TIE at different levels of debt.

($D = \$250,000$ and $k_d = 8\%$)

$$Shares\ repurchased = \frac{\$250,000}{\$25} = 10,000$$

$$EPS = \frac{(EBIT - k_d D)(1 - T)}{Shares\ outstanding}$$

$$= \frac{(\$400,000 - 0.08(\$250,000))(0.6)}{80,000 - 10,000}$$

$$= \$3.26$$

$$TIE = \frac{EBIT}{Int\ Exp} = \frac{\$400,000}{\$20,000} = 20x$$

12-21

Determining EPS and TIE at different levels of debt.
(D = $500,000 and k_d = 9%)

$$\text{Shares repurchased} = \frac{\$500,000}{\$25} = 20,000$$

$$\text{EPS} = \frac{(\text{EBIT} - k_d D)(1 - T)}{\text{Shares outstanding}}$$

$$= \frac{(\$400,000 - 0.09(\$500,000))(0.6)}{80,000 - 20,000}$$

$$= \$3.55$$

$$\text{TIE} = \frac{\text{EBIT}}{\text{Int Exp}} = \frac{\$400,000}{\$45,000} = 8.9x$$

12-22

Determining EPS and TIE at different levels of debt.
(D = $750,000 and k_d = 11.5%)

$$\text{Shares repurchased} = \frac{\$750,000}{\$25} = 30,000$$

$$\text{EPS} = \frac{(\text{EBIT} - k_d D)(1 - T)}{\text{Shares outstanding}}$$

$$= \frac{(\$400,000 - 0.115(\$750,000))(0.6)}{80,000 - 30,000}$$

$$= \$3.77$$

$$\text{TIE} = \frac{\text{EBIT}}{\text{Int Exp}} = \frac{\$400,000}{\$86,250} = 4.6x$$

12-23

Determining EPS and TIE at different levels of debt.
(D = $1,000,000 and k_d = 14%)

$$\text{Shares repurchased} = \frac{\$1,000,000}{\$25} = 40,000$$

$$\text{EPS} = \frac{(\text{EBIT} - k_d D)(1 - T)}{\text{Shares outstanding}}$$

$$= \frac{(\$400,000 - 0.14(\$1,000,000))(0.6)}{80,000 - 40,000}$$

$$= \$3.90$$

$$\text{TIE} = \frac{\text{EBIT}}{\text{Int Exp}} = \frac{\$400,000}{\$140,000} = 2.9x$$

12-24

Stock Price, with zero growth

$$P_0 = \frac{D_1}{k_s - g} = \frac{EPS}{k_s} = \frac{DPS}{k_s}$$

- If all earnings are paid out as dividends, $E(g) = 0$.
- EPS = DPS
- To find the expected stock price (P_0), we must find the appropriate k_s at each of the debt levels discussed.

12-25

What effect does increasing debt have on the cost of equity for the firm?

- If the level of debt increases, the riskiness of the firm increases.
- We have already observed the increase in the cost of debt.
- However, the riskiness of the firm's equity also increases, resulting in a higher k_s.

12-26

The Hamada Equation

- Because the increased use of debt causes both the costs of debt and equity to increase, we need to estimate the new cost of equity.
- The Hamada equation attempts to quantify the increased cost of equity due to financial leverage.
- Uses the unlevered beta of a firm, which represents the business risk of a firm as if it had no debt.

12-27

The Hamada Equation

$$\beta_L = \beta_U[\, 1 + (1 - T)\,(D/E)\,]$$

- Suppose, the risk-free rate is 6%, as is the market risk premium. The unlevered beta of the firm is 1.0. We were previously told that total assets were $2,000,000.

12-28

Calculating levered betas and costs of equity

If D = $250,

$$\beta_L = 1.0\,[\, 1 + (0.6)(\$250/\$1,750)\,]$$
$$\beta_L = 1.0857$$

$$k_s = k_{RF} + (k_M - k_{RF})\,\beta_L$$
$$k_s = 6.0\% + (6.0\%)\,1.0857$$
$$k_s = 12.51\%$$

12-29

Table for calculating levered betas and costs of equity

Amount borrowed	D/A ratio	D/E ratio	Levered Beta	k_s
$ 0	0.00%	0.00%	1.00	12.00%
250	12.50	14.29	1.09	12.51
500	25.00	33.33	1.20	13.20
750	37.50	60.00	1.36	14.16
1,000	50.00	100.00	1.60	15.60

12-30

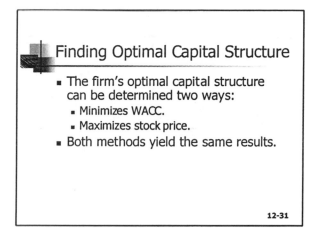

Finding Optimal Capital Structure

- The firm's optimal capital structure can be determined two ways:
  - Minimizes WACC.
  - Maximizes stock price.
- Both methods yield the same results.

12-31

Table for calculating WACC and determining the minimum WACC

Amount borrowed	D/A ratio	E/A ratio	k_s	$k_d (1-T)$	WACC
$ 0	0.00%	100.00%	12.00%	0.00%	12.00%
250	12.50	87.50	12.51	4.80	11.55
500	25.00	75.00	13.20	5.40	11.25
750	37.50	62.50	14.16	6.90	11.44
1,000	50.00	50.00	15.60	8.40	12.00

* Amount borrowed expressed in terms of thousands of dollars

12-32

Table for determining the stock price maximizing capital structure

Amount Borrowed	DPS	k_s	P_0
$ 0	$3.00	12.00%	$25.00
250,000	3.26	12.51	26.03
500,000	3.55	13.20	26.89
750,000	3.77	14.16	26.59
1,000,000	3.90	15.60	25.00

12-33

What debt ratio maximizes EPS?

- Maximum EPS = $3.90 at D = $1,000,000, and D/A = 50%. (Remember DPS = EPS because payout = 100%.)
- Risk is too high at D/A = 50%.

12-34

What is Campus Deli's optimal capital structure?

- P_0 is maximized ($26.89) at D/A = $500,000/$2,000,000 = 25%, so optimal D/A = 25%.
- EPS is maximized at 50%, but primary interest is stock price, not E(EPS).
- The example shows that we can push up E(EPS) by using more debt, but the risk resulting from increased leverage more than offsets the benefit of higher E(EPS).

12-35

What if there were more/less business risk than originally estimated, how would the analysis be affected?

- If there were higher business risk, then the probability of financial distress would be greater at any debt level, and the optimal capital structure would be one that had less debt. On the other hand, lower business risk would lead to an optimal capital structure with more debt.

12-36

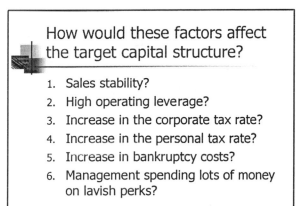

Other factors to consider when establishing the firm's target capital structure

1. Industry average debt ratio
2. TIE ratios under different scenarios
3. Lender/rating agency attitudes
4. Reserve borrowing capacity
5. Effects of financing on control
6. Asset structure
7. Expected tax rate

12-37

How would these factors affect the target capital structure?

1. Sales stability?
2. High operating leverage?
3. Increase in the corporate tax rate?
4. Increase in the personal tax rate?
5. Increase in bankruptcy costs?
6. Management spending lots of money on lavish perks?

12-38

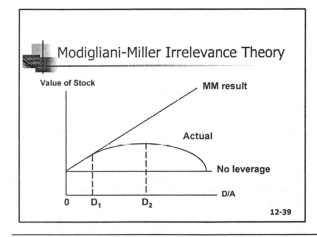

Modigliani-Miller Irrelevance Theory

Value of Stock

MM result

Actual

No leverage

D/A

0   D₁   D₂

12-39

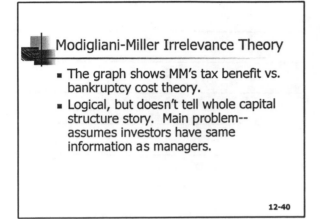

Modigliani-Miller Irrelevance Theory

- The graph shows MM's tax benefit vs. bankruptcy cost theory.
- Logical, but doesn't tell whole capital structure story. Main problem-- assumes investors have same information as managers.

12-40

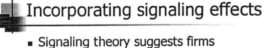

Incorporating signaling effects

- Signaling theory suggests firms should use less debt than MM suggest.
- This unused debt capacity helps avoid stock sales, which depress stock price because of signaling effects.

12-41

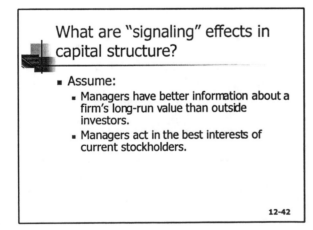

What are "signaling" effects in capital structure?

- Assume:
  - Managers have better information about a firm's long-run value than outside investors.
  - Managers act in the best interests of current stockholders.

12-42

What can managers be expected to do?

- Issue stock if they think stock is overvalued.
- Issue debt if they think stock is undervalued.
- As a result, investors view a common stock offering as a negative signal-- managers think stock is overvalued.

12-43

Conclusions on Capital Structure

- Need to make calculations as we did, but should also recognize inputs are "guesstimates."
- As a result of imprecise numbers, capital structure decisions have a large judgmental content.
- We end up with capital structures varying widely among firms, even similar ones in same industry.

12-44

EXAM-TYPE PROBLEMS

12-1. If you know that your firm is facing relatively poor prospects but needs new capital, and you know that investors do not have this information, signaling theory would predict that you would

  a. Issue debt to maintain the returns of equity holders.

  b. Issue equity to share the burden of decreased equity returns between old and new shareholders.

  c. Be indifferent between issuing debt and equity.

  d. Postpone going into the capital markets until your firm's prospects improve.

  e. Convey your inside information to investors using the media to eliminate the information asymmetry.

12-2. Howell Enterprises is forecasting EPS of $4.00 per share for next year. The firm has 10,000 shares outstanding; it pays 12 percent interest on its debt; and it faces a 40 percent marginal tax rate. Its estimated fixed costs are $80,000, while its variable costs are estimated at 40 percent of revenues. The firm's target capital structure is 40 percent equity and 60 percent debt, and it has total assets of $400,000. On what level of sales is Howell basing its EPS forecast? ($292,445)

12-3. A company estimates that its fixed operating costs are $900,000, and its variable costs are $3.25 per unit sold. Each unit produced sells for $4.75. What is the company's breakeven point? In other words, how many units must it sell before its operating income becomes positive? (600,000)

12-4. Harris Enterprises is trying to estimate its optimal capital structure. The firm's current capital structure consists of 30 percent debt and 70 percent equity; however, management believes the firm should use more debt. The risk-free rate, k_{RF}, is 6 percent, the market risk premium, $k_M - k_{RF}$, is 5 percent, and the firm's tax rate is 40 percent. Currently, Harris' cost of equity is 12 percent, which is determined on the basis of the CAPM. What would be Harris' estimated cost of equity if it were to change from its present capital structure to a capital structure consisting of 45 percent debt and 55 percent equity? (13.12%)

13-12 Southeastern Steel Company (SSC) was formed 5 years ago to exploit a new continuous-casting process. SSC's founders, Donald Brown and Margo Valencia, had been employed in the research department of a major integrated-steel company, but when that company decided against using the new process (which Brown and Valencia had developed), they decided to strike out on their own. One advantage of the new process was that it required relatively little capital in comparison with the typical steel company, so Brown and Valencia have been able to avoid issuing new stock, and thus they own all of the shares. However, SSC has now reached the stage in which outside equity capital is necessary if the firm is to achieve its growth targets yet still maintain its target capital structure of 60 percent equity and 40 percent debt. Therefore, Brown and Valencia have decided to take the company public. Until now, Brown and Valencia have paid themselves reasonable salaries but routinely reinvested all after-tax earnings in the firm, so dividend policy has not been an issue. However, before talking with potential outside investors, they must decide on a dividend policy.

Assume that you were recently hired by Arthur Adamson & Company (AA), a national consulting firm, which has been asked to help SSC prepare for its public offering. Martha Millon, the senior AA consultant in your group, has asked you to make a presentation to Brown and Valencia in which you review the theory of dividend policy and discuss the following questions.

a. (1) What is meant by the term "dividend policy"?

(2) The terms "irrelevance," "bird-in-the-hand," and "tax preference" have been used to describe three major theories regarding the way dividend policy affects a firm's value. Explain what these terms mean, and briefly describe each theory.

(3) What do the three theories indicate regarding the actions management should take with respect to dividend policy?

(4) What results have empirical studies of the dividend theories produced? How does all this affect what we can tell managers about dividend policy?

b. Discuss (1) the information content, or signaling, hypothesis, (2) the clientele effect, and (3) their effects on dividend policy.

c. (1) Assume that SSC has an $800,000 capital budget planned for the coming year. You have determined that its present capital structure (60 percent equity and 40 percent debt) is optimal, and its net income is forecasted at $600,000. Use the residual dividend model approach to determine SSC's total dollar dividend and payout ratio. In the process, explain what the residual dividend model is. Then, explain what would happen if net income were forecasted at $400,000, or at $800,000.

    (2) In general terms, how would a change in investment opportunities affect the payout ratio under the residual payment policy?

    (3) What are the advantages and disadvantages of the residual policy? (Hint: Don't neglect signaling and clientele effects.)

d. What is a dividend reinvestment plan (DRIP), and how does it work?

e. Describe the series of steps that most firms take in setting dividend policy in practice.

f. What are stock repurchases? Discuss the advantages and disadvantages of a firm's repurchasing its own shares.

g. What are stock dividends and stock splits? What are the advantages and disadvantages of stock dividends and stock splits?

CHAPTER 13
Distributions to shareholders:
Dividends and share repurchases

- Theories of investor preferences
- Signaling effects
- Residual model
- Dividend reinvestment plans
- Stock dividends and stock splits
- Stock repurchases

13-1

What is dividend policy?

- The decision to pay out earnings versus retaining and reinvesting them.
- Dividend policy includes
  - High or low dividend payout?
  - Stable or irregular dividends?
  - How frequent to pay dividends?
  - Announce the policy?

13-2

Do investors prefer high or low dividend payouts?

- Three theories of dividend policy:
  - Dividend irrelevance: Investors don't care about payout.
  - Bird-in-the-hand: Investors prefer a high payout.
  - Tax preference: Investors prefer a low payout.

13-3

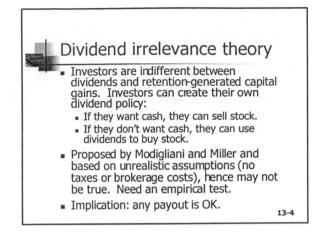

Dividend irrelevance theory

- Investors are indifferent between dividends and retention-generated capital gains. Investors can create their own dividend policy:
  - If they want cash, they can sell stock.
  - If they don't want cash, they can use dividends to buy stock.
- Proposed by Modigliani and Miller and based on unrealistic assumptions (no taxes or brokerage costs), hence may not be true. Need an empirical test.
- Implication: any payout is OK.

13-4

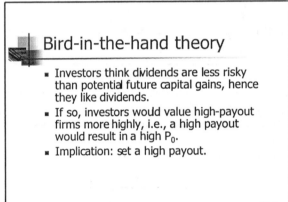

Bird-in-the-hand theory

- Investors think dividends are less risky than potential future capital gains, hence they like dividends.
- If so, investors would value high-payout firms more highly, i.e., a high payout would result in a high P_0.
- Implication: set a high payout.

13-5

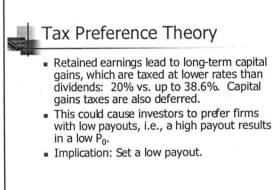

Tax Preference Theory

- Retained earnings lead to long-term capital gains, which are taxed at lower rates than dividends: 20% vs. up to 38.6%. Capital gains taxes are also deferred.
- This could cause investors to prefer firms with low payouts, i.e., a high payout results in a low P_0.
- Implication: Set a low payout.

13-6

Possible stock price effects

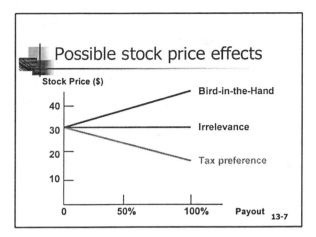

Possible cost of equity effects

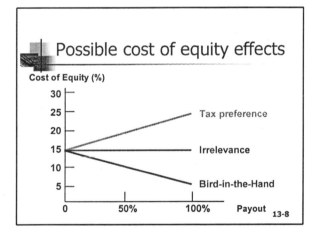

Which theory is most correct?

- Empirical testing has not been able to determine which theory, if any, is correct.
- Thus, managers use judgment when setting policy.
- Analysis is used, but it must be applied with judgment.

13-9

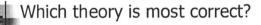

What's the "information content," or "signaling," hypothesis?

- Managers hate to cut dividends, so they won't raise dividends unless they think raise is sustainable. So, investors view dividend increases as signals of management's view of the future.

- Therefore, a stock price increase at time of a dividend increase could reflect higher expectations for future EPS, not a desire for dividends.

13-10

What's the "clientele effect"?

- Different groups of investors, or clienteles, prefer different dividend policies.

- Firm's past dividend policy determines its current clientele of investors.

- Clientele effects impede changing dividend policy. Taxes & brokerage costs hurt investors who have to switch companies.

13-11

What is the "residual dividend model"?

- Find the retained earnings needed for the capital budget.

- Pay out any leftover earnings (the residual) as dividends.

- This policy minimizes flotation and equity signaling costs, hence minimizes the WACC.

13-12

Residual dividend model

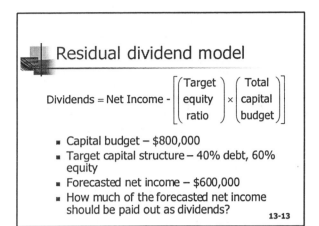

$$\text{Dividends} = \text{Net Income} - \left[\left(\begin{array}{c} \text{Target} \\ \text{equity} \\ \text{ratio} \end{array} \right) \times \left(\begin{array}{c} \text{Total} \\ \text{capital} \\ \text{budget} \end{array} \right) \right]$$

- Capital budget – $800,000
- Target capital structure – 40% debt, 60% equity
- Forecasted net income – $600,000
- How much of the forecasted net income should be paid out as dividends?

13-13

Residual dividend model: Calculating dividends paid

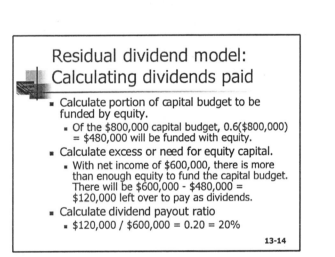

- Calculate portion of capital budget to be funded by equity.
  - Of the $800,000 capital budget, 0.6($800,000) = $480,000 will be funded with equity.
- Calculate excess or need for equity capital.
  - With net income of $600,000, there is more than enough equity to fund the capital budget. There will be $600,000 - $480,000 = $120,000 left over to pay as dividends.
- Calculate dividend payout ratio
  - $120,000 / $600,000 = 0.20 = 20%

13-14

Residual dividend model: What if net income drops to $400,000? Rises to $800,000?

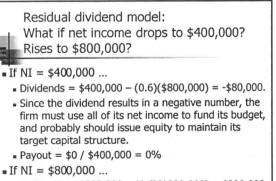

- If NI = $400,000 …
  - Dividends = $400,000 – (0.6)($800,000) = -$80,000.
  - Since the dividend results in a negative number, the firm must use all of its net income to fund its budget, and probably should issue equity to maintain its target capital structure.
  - Payout = $0 / $400,000 = 0%
- If NI = $800,000 …
  - Dividends = $800,000 – (0.6)($800,000) = $320,000.
  - Payout = $320,000 / $800,000 = 40%

13-15

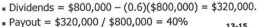

How would a change in investment opportunities affect dividend under the residual policy?

- Fewer good investments would lead to smaller capital budget, hence to a higher dividend payout.
- More good investments would lead to a lower dividend payout.

13-16

Comments on Residual Dividend Policy

- Advantage – Minimizes new stock issues and flotation costs.
- Disadvantages – Results in variable dividends, sends conflicting signals, increases risk, and doesn't appeal to any specific clientele.
- Conclusion – Consider residual policy when setting target payout, but don't follow it rigidly.

13-17

What's a "dividend reinvestment plan (DRIP)"?

- Shareholders can automatically reinvest their dividends in shares of the company's common stock. Get more stock than cash.
- There are two types of plans:
  - Open market
  - New stock

13-18

Open Market Purchase Plan

- Dollars to be reinvested are turned over to trustee, who buys shares on the open market.
- Brokerage costs are reduced by volume purchases.
- Convenient, easy way to invest, thus useful for investors.

13-19

New Stock Plan

- Firm issues new stock to DRIP enrollees (usually at a discount from the market price), keeps money and uses it to buy assets.
- Firms that need new equity capital use new stock plans.
- Firms with no need for new equity capital use open market purchase plans.
- Most NYSE listed companies have a DRIP. Useful for investors.

13-20

Setting Dividend Policy

- Forecast capital needs over a planning horizon, often 5 years.
- Set a target capital structure.
- Estimate annual equity needs.
- Set target payout based on the residual model.
- Generally, some dividend growth rate emerges. Maintain target growth rate if possible, varying capital structure somewhat if necessary.

13-21

Stock Repurchases

- Buying own stock back from stockholders
- Reasons for repurchases:
  - As an alternative to distributing cash as dividends.
  - To dispose of one-time cash from an asset sale.
  - To make a large capital structure change.

13-22

Advantages of Repurchases

- Stockholders can tender or not.
- Helps avoid setting a high dividend that cannot be maintained.
- Repurchased stock can be used in takeovers or resold to raise cash as needed.
- Income received is capital gains rather than higher-taxed dividends.
- Stockholders may take as a positive signal-- management thinks stock is undervalued.

13-23

Disadvantages of Repurchases

- May be viewed as a negative signal (firm has poor investment opportunities).
- IRS could impose penalties if repurchases were primarily to avoid taxes on dividends.
- Selling stockholders may not be well informed, hence be treated unfairly.
- Firm may have to bid up price to complete purchase, thus paying too much for its own stock.

13-24

Stock dividends vs. Stock splits

- Stock dividend: Firm issues new shares in lieu of paying a cash dividend. If 10%, get 10 shares for each 100 shares owned.
- Stock split: Firm increases the number of shares outstanding, say 2:1. Sends shareholders more shares.

13-25

Stock dividends vs. Stock splits

- Both stock dividends and stock splits increase the number of shares outstanding, so "the pie is divided into smaller pieces."
- Unless the stock dividend or split conveys information, or is accompanied by another event like higher dividends, the stock price falls so as to keep each investor's wealth unchanged.
- But splits/stock dividends may get us to an "optimal price range."

13-26

When and why should a firm consider splitting its stock?

- There's a widespread belief that the optimal price range for stocks is $20 to $80. Stock splits can be used to keep the price in this optimal range.
- Stock splits generally occur when management is confident, so are interpreted as positive signals.
- On average, stocks tend to outperform the market in the year following a split.

13-27

EXAM-TYPE PROBLEMS

13-1. If you were to argue that the firm's cost of equity, k_s, increases as the dividend payout decreases, you would be making an argument _____ with MM's dividend irrelevance theory, and _____ with Gordon and Lintner's "bird-in-the-hand" theory.

    a. consistent; consistent

    b. inconsistent; consistent

    c. consistent; inconsistent

    d. inconsistent; inconsistent

    e. The argument above does not make sense, neither theory involves the cost of equity capital.

13-2. Which of the following statements is most correct?

    a. The *tax preference* and *bird-in-the-hand* theories lead to identical conclusions as to the optimal dividend policy.

    b. If a company raises its dividend by an unexpectedly large amount, the announcement of this new and higher dividend is generally accompanied by an increase in the stock price. This is consistent with the bird-in-the-hand theory, and Modigliani and Miller used these findings to support their position on dividend theory.

    c. If it could be demonstrated that a *clientele effect* exists, this would suggest that firms could alter their dividend payment policies from year to year to take advantage of investment opportunities without having to worry about the effects of changing dividends on capital costs.

    d. Each of the above statements is false.

13-3. Driver Corporation is considering a number of positive NPV projects for a total capital budget of $60 million. Its optimal capital structure is 60 percent equity and 40 percent debt. Its earnings before interest and taxes (EBIT) were $98 million for the year. The firm has $200 million in assets, pays an average of 10 percent on all its debt, and faces a marginal tax rate of 34 percent. If the firm maintains a residual dividend policy and will finance its capital budget so as to keep its optimal capital structure intact, what will be the amount of the dividends it pays out? ($23.4 million)

14-21 Dan Barnes, financial manager of Ski Equipment Inc. (SKI), is excited, but apprehensive. The company's founder recently sold his 51 percent controlling block of stock to Kent Koren, who is a big fan of EVA (Economic Value Added). EVA is found by taking the after-tax operating profit and then subtracting the dollar cost of all the capital the firm uses:

$$EVA = EBIT(1 - T) - \text{Capital costs}$$
$$= EBIT(1 - T) - WACC \text{ (Capital employed).}$$

If EVA is positive, then the firm is creating value. On the other hand, if EVA is negative, the firm is not covering its cost of capital, and stockholders' value is being eroded. Koren rewards managers handsomely if they create value, but those whose operations produce negative EVAs are soon looking for work. Koren frequently points out that if a company can generate its current level of sales with less assets, it would need less capital. That would, other things held constant, lower capital costs and increase its EVA.

Shortly after he took control of SKI, Kent Koren met with SKI's senior executives to tell them of his plans for the company. First, he presented some EVA data that convinced everyone that SKI had not been creating value in recent years. He then stated, in no uncertain terms, that this situation must change. He noted that SKI's designs of skis, boots, and clothing are acclaimed throughout the industry, but something is seriously amiss elsewhere in the company. Costs are too high, prices are too low, or the company employs too much capital, and he wants SKI's managers to correct the problem or else.

Barnes has long felt that SKI's working capital situation should be studied—the company may have the optimal amounts of cash, securities, receivables, and inventories, but it may also have too much or too little of these items. In the past, the production manager resisted Barnes' efforts to question his holdings of raw materials inventories, the marketing manager resisted questions about finished goods, the sales staff resisted questions about credit policy (which affects accounts receivable), and the treasurer did not want to talk about her cash and securities balances. Koren's speech made it clear that such resistance would no longer be tolerated.

Barnes also knows that decisions about working capital cannot be made in a vacuum. For example, if inventories could be lowered without adversely affecting operations, then less capital would be required, the dollar cost of capital would decline, and EVA would increase. However, lower raw materials inventories might lead to production slowdowns and higher costs, while lower finished goods inventories might lead to the loss of profitable sales. So, before inventories are changed, it will be necessary to study operating as well as financial effects. The situation is the same with regard to cash and receivables.

a. Barnes plans to use the ratios in Table IC14-1 as the starting point for discussions with SKI's operating executives. He wants everyone to think about the pros and cons of changing each type of current asset and how changes would interact to affect profits and EVA. Based on the Table IC14-1 data, does SKI seem to be following a relaxed, moderate, or restricted working capital policy?

Table IC14-1. Selected Ratios: SKI and Industry Average

	SKI	Industry
Current	1.75×	2.25×
Debt/assets	58.76%	50.00%
Turnover of cash and securities	16.67×	22.22×
Days sales outstanding (365-day basis)	45.63	32.00
Inventory turnover	4.82×	7.00×
Fixed assets turnover	11.35×	12.00×
Total assets turnover	2.08×	3.00×
Profit margin on sales	2.07%	3.50%
Return on equity (ROE)	10.45%	21.00%

b. How can one distinguish between a relaxed but rational working capital policy and a situation in which a firm simply has a lot of current assets because it is inefficient? Does SKI's working capital policy seem appropriate?

c. Assume that SKI's payables deferral period is 30 days. Now, calculate the firm's cash conversion cycle.

d. What might SKI do to reduce its cash and securities without harming operations?

In an attempt to better understand SKI's cash position, Barnes developed a cash budget. Data for the first two months of the year are shown in Table IC14-2. (Note that Barnes' preliminary cash budget does not account for interest income or interest expense.) He has the figures for the other months, but they are not shown in Table IC14-2.

Table IC14-2. SKI's Cash Budget for January and February

	NOV	DEC	JAN	FEB	MAR	APR
I. COLLECTIONS AND PURCHASES WORKSHEET						
(1) Sales (gross)	$71,218	$68,212	$65,213.00	$52,475.00	$42,909	$30,524
Collections:						
(2) During month of sale (0.2)(0.98)(month's sales)			12,781.75	10,285.10		
(3) During first month after sale 0.7(previous month's sales)			47,748.40	45,649.10		
(4) During second month after sale 0.1(sales 2 months ago)			7,121.80	6,821.20		
(5) Total collections (Lines 2 + 3 + 4)			$67,651.95	$62,755.40		
Purchases:						
(6) 0.85(forecasted sales 2 months from now)		$44,603.75	$36,472.65	$25,945.40		
(7) Payments (1-month lag)			44,603.75	36,472.65		
II. CASH GAIN OR LOSS FOR MONTH						
(8) Collections (from Section I)			$67,651.95	$62,755.40		
(9) Payments for purchases (from Section I)			44,603.75	36,472.65		
(10) Wages and salaries			6,690.56	5,470.90		
(11) Rent			2,500.00	2,500.00		
(12) Taxes						
(13) Total payments			$53,794.31	$44,443.55		
(14) Net cash gain (loss) during month (Line 8 - Line 13)			$13,857.64	$18,311.85		
III. CASH SURPLUS OR LOAN REQUIREMENT						
(15) Cash at beginning of month if no borrowing is done			$ 3,000.00	$16,857.64		
(16) Cumulative cash (cash at start, + gain or - loss = Line 14 + Line 15)			16,857.64	35,169.49		
(17) Target cash balance			1,500.00	1,500.00		
(18) Cumulative surplus cash or loans outstanding to maintain $1,500 target cash balance (Line 16 - Line 17)			$15,357.64	$33,669.49		

e. Should depreciation expense be explicitly included in the cash budget? Why or why not?

f. In his preliminary cash budget, Barnes has assumed that all sales are collected and, thus, that SKI has no bad debts. Is this realistic? If not, how would bad debts be dealt with in a cash budgeting sense? (Hint: Bad debts will affect collections but not purchases.)

g. Barnes' cash budget for the entire year, although not given here, is based heavily on his forecast for monthly sales. Sales are expected to be extremely low between May and September but then increase dramatically in the fall and winter. November is typically the firm's best month, when SKI ships equipment to retailers for the holiday season. Interestingly, Barnes' forecasted cash budget indicates that the company's cash holdings will exceed the targeted cash balance every month except for October and November, when shipments will be high but collections will not be coming in until later. Based on the ratios in

Table IC14-1, does it appear that SKI's target cash balance is appropriate? In addition to possibly lowering the target cash balance, what actions might SKI take to better improve its cash management policies, and how might that affect its EVA?

h. What reasons might SKI have for maintaining a relatively high amount of cash?

i. What are the three categories of inventory costs? If the company reduces its inventory, what effect would this have on the various costs of holding inventory?

j. Is there any reason to think that SKI may be holding too much inventory? If so, how would that affect EVA and ROE?

k. If the company reduces its inventory without adversely affecting sales, what effect should this have on the company's cash position (1) in the short run and (2) in the long run? Explain in terms of the cash budget and the balance sheet.

l. Barnes knows that SKI sells on the same credit terms as other firms in its industry. Use the ratios presented in Table IC14-1 to explain whether SKI's customers pay more or less promptly than those of its competitors. If there are differences, does that suggest that SKI should tighten or loosen its credit policy? What four variables make up a firm's credit policy, and in what direction should each be changed by SKI?

m. Does SKI face any risks if it tightens its credit policy?

n. If the company reduces its DSO without seriously affecting sales, what effect would this have on its cash position (1) in the short run and (2) in the long run? Answer in terms of the cash budget and the balance sheet. What effect should this have on EVA in the long run?

In addition to improving the management of its current assets, SKI is also reviewing the ways in which it finances its current assets. With this concern in mind, Dan is also trying to answer the following questions.

o. SKI tries to match the maturity of its assets and liabilities. Describe how SKI could adopt either a more aggressive or more conservative financing policy.

p. What are the advantages and disadvantages of using short-term credit as a source of financing?

q. Is it likely that SKI could make significantly greater use of accrued liabilities?

r. Assume that SKI buys on terms of 1/10, net 30, but that it can get away with paying on the 40th day if it chooses not to take discounts. Also, assume that it purchases $506,985 of equipment per year, net of discounts. How much free trade credit can the company get, how much costly trade credit can it get, and what is the percentage cost of the costly credit? Should SKI take discounts?

s. Would it be feasible for SKI to finance with commercial paper?

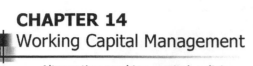

CHAPTER 14
Working Capital Management

- Alternative working capital policies
- Cash management
- Inventory management
- Accounts receivable management
- Working capital financing policies
- Trade credit

14-1

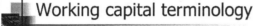

Working capital terminology

- Gross working capital – total current assets.
- Net working capital – current assets minus non-interest bearing current liabilities.
- Working capital policy – deciding the level of each type of current asset to hold, and how to finance current assets.
- Working capital management – controlling cash, inventories, and A/R, plus short-term liability management.

14-2

Selected ratios for SKI Inc.

	SKI	Ind. Avg.
Current	1.75x	2.25x
Debt/Assets	58.76%	50.00%
Turnover of cash & securities	16.67x	22.22x
DSO (days)	45.63	32.00
Inv. turnover	4.82x	7.00x
F. A. turnover	11.35x	12.00x
T. A. turnover	2.08x	3.00x
Profit margin	2.07%	3.50%
ROE	10.45%	21.00%

14-3

How does SKI's working capital policy compare with its industry?

- SKI appears to have large amounts of working capital given its level of sales.
- Working capital policy is reflected in current ratio, turnover of cash and securities, inventory turnover, and DSO.
- These ratios indicate SKI has large amounts of working capital relative to its level of sales. SKI is either very conservative or inefficient.

14-4

Is SKI inefficient or just conservative?

- A conservative (relaxed) policy may be appropriate if it leads to greater profitability.
- However, SKI is not as profitable as the average firm in the industry. This suggests the company has excessive working capital.

14-5

Cash conversion cycle

- The cash conversion model focuses on the length of time between when a company makes payments to its creditors and when a company receives payments from its customers.

$$CCC = \begin{matrix} \text{Inventory} \\ \text{conversion} \\ \text{period} \end{matrix} + \begin{matrix} \text{Receivables} \\ \text{collection} \\ \text{period} \end{matrix} - \begin{matrix} \text{Payables} \\ \text{deferral} \\ \text{period} \end{matrix}$$

14-6

Cash conversion cycle

$$CCC = \begin{array}{c}\text{Inventory} \\ \text{conversion} \\ \text{period}\end{array} + \begin{array}{c}\text{Receivables} \\ \text{collection} \\ \text{period}\end{array} - \begin{array}{c}\text{Payables} \\ \text{deferral} \\ \text{period}\end{array}$$

$$CCC = \frac{\text{Days per year}}{\text{Inv. turnover}} + \begin{array}{c}\text{Days sales} \\ \text{outstanding}\end{array} - \begin{array}{c}\text{Payables} \\ \text{deferral} \\ \text{period}\end{array}$$

$$CCC = \frac{365}{4.82} + 46 - 30$$

$$CCC = 76 + 46 - 30$$

$$CCC = 92 \text{ days.}$$

14-7

Cash doesn't earn a profit, so why hold it?

1. Transactions – must have some cash to operate.
2. Precaution – "safety stock". Reduced by line of credit and marketable securities.
3. Compensating balances – for loans and/or services provided.
4. Speculation – to take advantage of bargains and to take discounts. Reduced by credit lines and marketable securities.

14-8

What is the goal of cash management?

- To meet above objectives, especially to have cash for transactions, yet not have any excess cash.
- To minimize transactions balances in particular, and also needs for cash to meet other objectives.

14-9

Ways to minimize cash holdings

- Use a lockbox.
- Insist on wire transfers from customers.
- Synchronize inflows and outflows.
- Use a remote disbursement account.
- Increase forecast accuracy to reduce need for "safety stock" of cash.
- Hold marketable securities (also reduces need for "safety stock").
- Negotiate a line of credit (also reduces need for "safety stock").

14-10

Cash budget:
The primary cash management tool

- Purpose: Forecasts cash inflows, outflows, and ending cash balances. Used to plan loans needed or funds available to invest.
- Timing: Daily, weekly, or monthly, depending upon purpose of forecast. Monthly for annual planning, daily for actual cash management.

14-11

SKI's cash budget:
For January and February

	Net Cash Inflows	
	Jan	Feb
Collections	$67,651.95	$62,755.40
Purchases	44,603.75	36,472.65
Wages	6,690.56	5,470.90
Rent	2,500.00	2,500.00
Total payments	$53,794.31	$44,443.55
Net CF	$13,857.64	$18,311.85

14-12

SKI's cash budget

	Net Cash Inflows	
	Jan	Feb
Cash at start if no borrowing	$ 3,000.00	$16,857.64
Net CF	13,857.64	18,311.85
Cumulative cash	16,857.64	35,169.49
Less: target cash	1,500.00	1,500.00
Surplus	$15,357.64	$33,669.49

14-13

Should depreciation be explicitly included in the cash budget?

- No. Depreciation is a noncash charge. Only cash payments and receipts appear on cash budget.
- However, depreciation does affect taxes, which appear in the cash budget.

14-14

What are some other potential cash inflows besides collections?

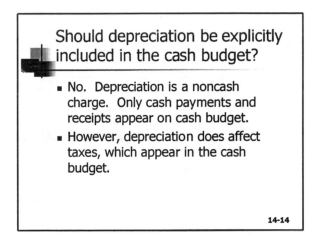

- Proceeds from the sale of fixed assets.
- Proceeds from stock and bond sales.
- Interest earned.
- Court settlements.

14-15

How could bad debts be worked into the cash budget?

- Collections would be reduced by the amount of the bad debt losses.
- For example, if the firm had 3% bad debt losses, collections would total only 97% of sales.
- Lower collections would lead to higher borrowing requirements.

14-16

Analyze SKI's forecasted cash budget

- Cash holdings will exceed the target balance for each month, except for October and November.
- Cash budget indicates the company is holding too much cash.
- SKI could improve its EVA by either investing cash in more productive assets, or by returning cash to its shareholders.

14-17

Why might SKI want to maintain a relatively high amount of cash?

- If sales turn out to be considerably less than expected, SKI could face a cash shortfall.
- A company may choose to hold large amounts of cash if it does not have much faith in its sales forecast, or if it is very conservative.
- The cash may be used, in part, to fund future investments.

14-18

Types of inventory costs

- Carrying costs – storage and handling costs, insurance, property taxes, depreciation, and obsolescence.
- Ordering costs – cost of placing orders, shipping, and handling costs.
- Costs of running short – loss of sales or customer goodwill, and the disruption of production schedules.

  Reducing the average amount of inventory generally reduces carrying costs, increases ordering costs, and may increase the costs of running short.

14-19

Is SKI holding too much inventory?

- SKI's inventory turnover (4.82) is considerably lower than the industry average (7.00). The firm is carrying a lot of inventory per dollar of sales.
- By holding excessive inventory, the firm is increasing its costs, which reduces its ROE. Moreover, this additional working capital must be financed, so EVA is also lowered.

14-20

If SKI reduces its inventory, without adversely affecting sales, what effect will this have on the cash position?

- Short run: Cash will increase as inventory purchases decline.
- Long run: Company is likely to take steps to reduce its cash holdings and increase its EVA.

14-21

Do SKI's customers pay more or less promptly than those of its competitors?

- SKI's DSO (45.6 days) is well above the industry average (32 days).
- SKI's customers are paying less promptly.
- SKI should consider tightening its credit policy in order to reduce its DSO.

14-22

Elements of credit policy

1. Credit Period – How long to pay? Shorter period reduces DSO and average A/R, but it may discourage sales.
2. Cash Discounts – Lowers price. Attracts new customers and reduces DSO.
3. Credit Standards – Tighter standards tend to reduce sales, but reduce bad debt expense. Fewer bad debts reduce DSO.
4. Collection Policy – How tough? Tougher policy will reduce DSO but may damage customer relationships.

14-23

Does SKI face any risk if it tightens its credit policy?

- Yes, a tighter credit policy may discourage sales. Some customers may choose to go elsewhere if they are pressured to pay their bills sooner.

14-24

If SKI succeeds in reducing DSO without adversely affecting sales, what effect would this have on its cash position?

- Short run: If customers pay sooner, this increases cash holdings.
- Long run: Over time, the company would hopefully invest the cash in more productive assets, or pay it out to shareholders. Both of these actions would increase EVA.

14-25

Working capital financing policies

- Moderate – Match the maturity of the assets with the maturity of the financing.
- Aggressive – Use short-term financing to finance permanent assets.
- Conservative – Use permanent capital for permanent assets and temporary assets.

14-26

Moderate financing policy

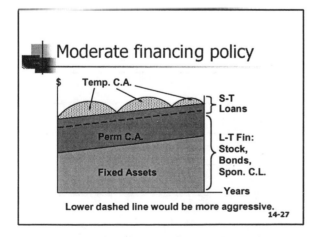

Lower dashed line would be more aggressive.
14-27

Conservative financing policy

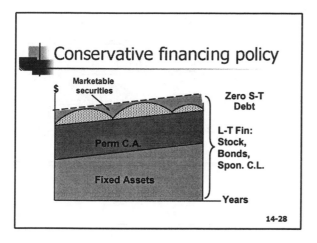

14-28

Accrued liabilities

- Continually recurring short-term liabilities, such as accrued wages or taxes.
- Is there a cost to accrued liabilities?
  - They are free in the sense that no explicit interest is charged.
  - However, firms have little control over the level of accrued liabilities.

14-29

What is trade credit?

- Trade credit is credit furnished by a firm's suppliers.
- Trade credit is often the largest source of short-term credit, especially for small firms.
- Spontaneous, easy to get, but cost can be high.

14-30

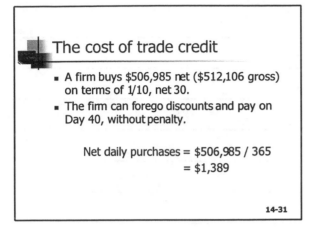

The cost of trade credit

- A firm buys $506,985 net ($512,106 gross) on terms of 1/10, net 30.
- The firm can forego discounts and pay on Day 40, without penalty.

Net daily purchases = $506,985 / 365
= $1,389

14-31

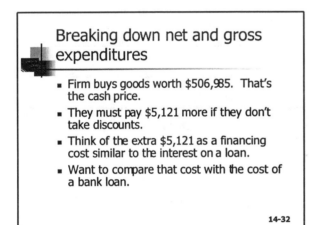

Breaking down net and gross expenditures

- Firm buys goods worth $506,985. That's the cash price.
- They must pay $5,121 more if they don't take discounts.
- Think of the extra $5,121 as a financing cost similar to the interest on a loan.
- Want to compare that cost with the cost of a bank loan.

14-32

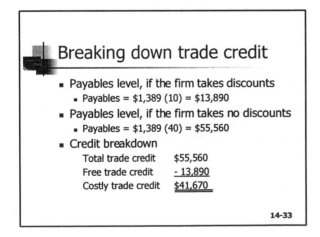

Breaking down trade credit

- Payables level, if the firm takes discounts
  - Payables = $1,389 (10) = $13,890
- Payables level, if the firm takes no discounts
  - Payables = $1,389 (40) = $55,560
- Credit breakdown

Total trade credit	$55,560
Free trade credit	- 13,890
Costly trade credit	$41,670

14-33

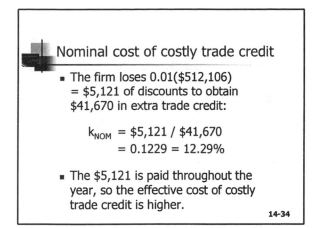

Nominal cost of costly trade credit

- The firm loses 0.01($512,106) = $5,121 of discounts to obtain $41,670 in extra trade credit:

  $$k_{NOM} = \$5,121 / \$41,670$$
  $$= 0.1229 = 12.29\%$$

- The $5,121 is paid throughout the year, so the effective cost of costly trade credit is higher.

14-34

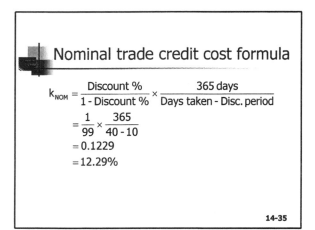

Nominal trade credit cost formula

$$k_{NOM} = \frac{\text{Discount \%}}{1 - \text{Discount \%}} \times \frac{365 \text{ days}}{\text{Days taken - Disc. period}}$$
$$= \frac{1}{99} \times \frac{365}{40 - 10}$$
$$= 0.1229$$
$$= 12.29\%$$

14-35

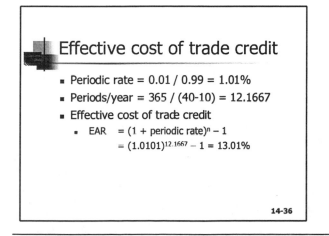

Effective cost of trade credit

- Periodic rate = 0.01 / 0.99 = 1.01%
- Periods/year = 365 / (40-10) = 12.1667
- Effective cost of trade credit
  - EAR $= (1 + \text{periodic rate})^n - 1$
    $= (1.0101)^{12.1667} - 1 = 13.01\%$

14-36

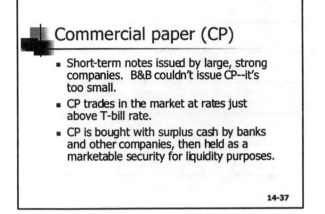

Commercial paper (CP)

- Short-term notes issued by large, strong companies. B&B couldn't issue CP--it's too small.
- CP trades in the market at rates just above T-bill rate.
- CP is bought with surplus cash by banks and other companies, then held as a marketable security for liquidity purposes.

14-37

EXAM-TYPE PROBLEMS

14-1. Ziltest Company's treasurer had $1 million of excess funds that were invested in marketable securities. At the time the investment was made, it was known that the funds would be needed in 6 months to fund an ongoing construction project. Six-month T-bills with a face value of $10,000 sold for $9,708.74 to yield a 6 percent nominal annual rate. As an alternative, the treasurer could purchase 7 percent coupon, semiannual payment, 10-year Treasury bonds at par. Seeking to earn a higher yield, he purchased the T-bonds. At the end of 6 months, when the funds were needed for construction, interest rates had risen to 9.5 percent on the T-bonds. The treasurer was forced to liquidate the T-bond holdings at a lower price. What was the absolute value of the dollar difference between the T-bond's purchase price and selling price? ($154,192.20)

14-2. Which of the following statement completions is most correct? If the yield curve is upward sloping, then a firm's marketable securities portfolio, assumed to be held for liquidity purposes, should be

a. Weighted toward long-term securities because they pay higher rates.

b. Weighted toward short-term securities because they pay higher rates.

c. Weighted toward U.S. Treasury securities to avoid interest rate risk.

d. Weighted toward short-term securities to avoid interest rate risk.

e. Balanced between long- and short-term securities to minimize the effects of either an upward or a downward shift in interest rates.

14-3. Which of the following statements is most correct?

a. If a firm's volume of credit sales declines then its DSO will also decline.

b. If a firm changes its credit terms from 1/20, net 40 days, to 2/10, net 60 days, the impact on sales can't be determined because the increase in the discount is offset by the longer net terms, which tends to reduce sales.

c. The DSO of a firm with seasonal sales can vary because while the sales per day figure is usually based on the total annual sales, the accounts receivable balance will be high or low depending on the season.

d. An aging schedule is used to determine what portion of customers pay cash and what portion buy on credit.

e. Aging schedules can be constructed from the summary data provided in the firm's financial statements.

14-4. Jarrett Enterprises is considering whether to pursue a restricted or a relaxed current asset investment policy. The firm's annual sales are $400,000; its fixed assets are

$100,000; debt and equity are each 50 percent of total assets. EBIT is $36,000, the interest rate on the firm's debt is 10 percent, and the firm's tax rate is 40 percent. With a restricted policy, current assets will be 15 percent of sales. Under a relaxed policy, current assets will be 25 percent of sales. What is the difference in the projected ROEs between the restricted and relaxed policies? (5.4%)

14-5. Porta Stadium Inc. has annual sales of $40,000,000 and keeps average inventory of $10,000,000. On average, the firm has accounts receivable of $8,000,000. The firm buys all raw materials on credit and its trade credit terms are net 30 days. It pays on time. The firm's managers are searching for ways to shorten the cash conversion cycle. If sales can be maintained at existing levels but inventory can be lowered by $2,000,000 and accounts receivable lowered by $1,000,000, what will be the net change in the cash conversion cycle? (27.375 days shorter)

14-6. The Lasser Company needs to finance an increase in its working capital for the coming year. The firm can increase its accounts payable by not taking discounts. Lasser buys on credit terms of 1/30, net 60 days. What is the effective annual cost (not the approximate cost) of trade credit? (13.01%)

14-7 Which of the following statements is most correct?

a. Under normal conditions the shape of the yield curve implies that the interest cost of short-term debt is greater than that of long-term debt, although short-term debt has other advantages that make it desirable as a financing source.

b. Flexibility is an advantage of short-term credit but this is somewhat offset by the higher flotation costs associated with the need to repeatedly renew short-term credit.

c. A short-term loan can usually be obtained more quickly than a long-term loan but the penalty for early repayment of a short-term loan is significantly higher than for a long-term loan.

d. Statements about the flexibility, cost, and riskiness of short-term versus long-term credit are dependent on the type of credit that is actually used.

e. Short-term debt is often less costly than long-term debt and the major reason for this is that short-term debt exposes the borrowing firm to much less risk than long-term debt.

14-8. A chain of lighting fixture stores, LCG Corporation, purchases inventory with a net price of $750,000 each day. The company purchases the inventory under the credit terms of 2/20, net 50. LCG always takes the discount, but takes the full 20 days to pay its bills. What is the average accounts payable for LCG? ($15,000,000)

15-19 Sue Wilson, the new financial manager of New World Chemicals (NWC), a California producer of specialized chemicals for use in fruit orchards, must prepare a financial forecast for 2003. NWC's 2002 sales were $2 billion, and the marketing department is forecasting a 25 percent increase for 2003. Wilson thinks the company was operating at full capacity in 2002, but she is not sure about this. The 2002 financial statements, plus some other data, are given in Table IC15-1.

Table IC15-1. Financial Statements and Other Data on NWC
(Millions of Dollars)

A. 2002 Balance Sheet

Cash and securities	$ 20	Accounts payable and accrued liabilities	$100
Accounts receivable	240	Notes payable	100
Inventories	240	Total current liabilities	$200
Total current assets	$ 500	Long-term debt	100
Net fixed assets	500	Common stock	500
		Retained earnings	200
Total assets	$1,000	Total liabilities and equity	$1,000

B. 2002 Income Statement

Sales	$2,000.00
Less: Variable costs	1,200.00
Fixed costs	700.00
Earnings before interest and taxes (EBIT)	$ 100.00
Interest	16.00
Earnings before taxes (EBT)	$ 84.00
Taxes (40%)	33.60
Net income	$ 50.40
Dividends (30%)	$ 15.12
Addition to retained earnings	$ 35.28

C. Key ratios

	NWC	Industry	Comment
Basic earning power	10.00%	20.00%	
Profit margin	2.52	4.00	
Return on equity	7.20	15.60	
Days sales outstanding (365 days)	43.80 days	32.00 days	
Inventory turnover	8.33×	11.00×	
Fixed assets turnover	4.00	5.00	
Total assets turnover	2.00	2.50	
Debt/assets	30.00%	36.00%	
Times interest earned	6.25×	9.40×	
Current ratio	2.50	3.00	
Payout ratio	30.00%	30.00%	

Assume that you were recently hired as Wilson's assistant, and your first major task is to help her develop the forecast. She asked you to begin by answering the following set of questions.

a. Assume (1) that NWC was operating at full capacity in 2002 with respect to all assets, (2) that all assets must grow proportionally with sales, (3) that accounts payable and accrued liabilities will also grow in proportion to sales, and (4) that the 2002 profit margin and dividend payout will be maintained. Under these conditions, what will the company's financial requirements be for the coming year? Use the AFN equation to answer this question.

b. Now estimate the 2003 financial requirements using the projected financial statement approach. Disregard the assumptions in part a, and now assume (1) that each type of asset, as well as payables, accrued liabilities, and fixed and variable costs, grow in proportion to sales; (2) that NWC was operating at full capacity; (3) that the payout ratio is held constant at 30 percent; and (4) that external funds needed are financed 50 percent by notes payable and 50 percent by long-term debt. (No new common stock will be issued.)

c. Why do the two methods produce somewhat different AFN forecasts? Which method provides the more accurate forecast?

d. Calculate NWC's forecasted ratios, and compare them with the company's 2002 ratios and with the industry averages. How does NWC compare with the average firm in its industry, and is the company expected to improve during the coming year?

e. Calculate NWC's free cash flow for 2003.

f. Suppose you now learn that NWC's 2002 receivables and inventories were in line with required levels, given the firm's credit and inventory policies, but that excess capacity existed with regard to fixed assets. Specifically, fixed assets were operated at only 75 percent of capacity.

   (1) What level of sales could have existed in 2002 with the available fixed assets? What would the fixed assets-to-sales ratio have been if NWC had been operating at full capacity?

   (2) How would the existence of excess capacity in fixed assets affect the additional funds needed during 2003?

g. Without actually working out the numbers, how would you expect the ratios to change in the situation where excess capacity in fixed assets exists? Explain your reasoning.

h. On the basis of comparisons between NWC's days sales outstanding (DSO) and inventory turnover ratios with the industry average figures, does it appear that NWC is operating efficiently with respect to its inventories and accounts receivable? If the company were able to bring these ratios into line with the industry averages, what effect would this have on its AFN and its financial ratios?

i. How would changes in these items affect the AFN? (1) The dividend payout ratio, (2) the profit margin, (3) the capital intensity ratio, and (4) if NWC begins buying from its suppliers on terms that permit it to pay after 60 days rather than after 30 days. (Consider each item separately and hold all other things constant.)

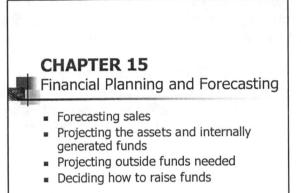

CHAPTER 15
Financial Planning and Forecasting

- Forecasting sales
- Projecting the assets and internally generated funds
- Projecting outside funds needed
- Deciding how to raise funds

15-1

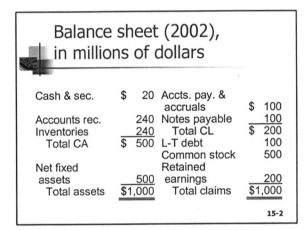

Balance sheet (2002), in millions of dollars

Cash & sec.	$ 20	Accts. pay. & accruals	$ 100
Accounts rec.	240	Notes payable	100
Inventories	240	Total CL	$ 200
Total CA	$ 500	L-T debt	100
		Common stock	500
Net fixed		Retained	
assets	500	earnings	200
Total assets	$1,000	Total claims	$1,000

15-2

Income statement (2002), in millions of dollars

Sales		$2,000.00
Less:	Var. costs (60%)	1,200.00
	Fixed costs	700.00
EBIT		$ 100.00
Interest		16.00
EBT		$ 84.00
Taxes (40%)		33.60
Net income		$ 50.40
Dividends (30%)		$15.12
Add'n to RE		$35.28

15-3

Key ratios

	NWC	Industry	Condition
BEP	10.00%	20.00%	Poor
Profit margin	2.52%	4.00%	"
ROE	7.20%	15.60%	"
DSO	43.80 days	32.00 days	"
Inv. turnover	8.33x	11.00x	"
F. A. turnover	4.00x	5.00x	"
T. A. turnover	2.00x	2.50x	"
Debt/assets	30.00%	36.00%	Good
TIE	6.25x	9.40x	Poor
Current ratio	2.50x	3.00x	"
Payout ratio	30.00%	30.00%	O. K.

15-4

Key assumptions

- Operating at full capacity in 2002.
- Each type of asset grows proportionally with sales.
- Payables and accruals grow proportionally with sales.
- 2002 profit margin (2.52%) and payout (30%) will be maintained.
- Sales are expected to increase by $500 million. (%$\Delta$S = 25%)

15-5

Determining additional funds needed, using the AFN equation

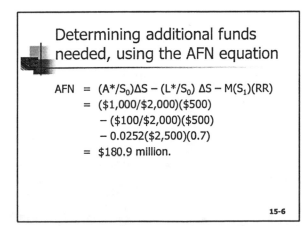

$$AFN = (A^*/S_0)\Delta S - (L^*/S_0)\,\Delta S - M(S_1)(RR)$$
$$= (\$1{,}000/\$2{,}000)(\$500)$$
$$- (\$100/\$2{,}000)(\$500)$$
$$- 0.0252(\$2{,}500)(0.7)$$
$$= \$180.9 \text{ million.}$$

15-6

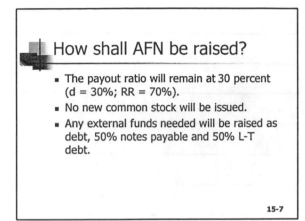

How shall AFN be raised?

- The payout ratio will remain at 30 percent (d = 30%; RR = 70%).
- No new common stock will be issued.
- Any external funds needed will be raised as debt, 50% notes payable and 50% L-T debt.

15-7

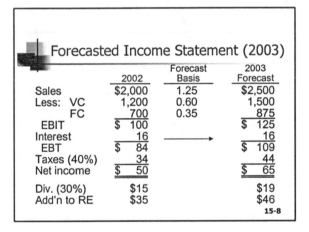

Forecasted Income Statement (2003)

	2002	Forecast Basis	2003 Forecast
Sales	$2,000	1.25	$2,500
Less: VC	1,200	0.60	1,500
FC	700	0.35	875
EBIT	$ 100		$ 125
Interest	16		16
EBT	$ 84		$ 109
Taxes (40%)	34		44
Net income	$ 50		$ 65
Div. (30%)	$15		$19
Add'n to RE	$35		$46

15-8

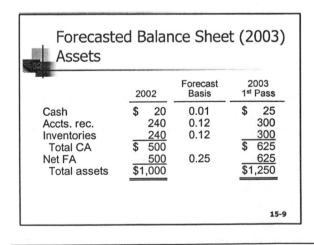

Forecasted Balance Sheet (2003) Assets

	2002	Forecast Basis	2003 1st Pass
Cash	$ 20	0.01	$ 25
Accts. rec.	240	0.12	300
Inventories	240	0.12	300
Total CA	$ 500		$ 625
Net FA	500	0.25	625
Total assets	$1,000		$1,250

15-9

Forecasted Balance Sheet (2003) Liabilities and Equity

	2002	Forecast Basis	2003 1st Pass
AP/accruals	$ 100	0.05	$ 125
Notes payable	100	→	100
Total CL	$ 200		$ 225
L-T debt	100	→	100
Common stk.	500	→	500
Ret.earnings	200	+46*	246
Total claims	$1,000		$1,071

* From income statement.

15-10

What is the additional financing needed (AFN)?

- Required increase in assets = $ 250
- Spontaneous increase in liab. = $ 25
- Increase in retained earnings = $ 46
- Total AFN = $ 179

NWC must have the assets to generate forecasted sales. The balance sheet must balance, so we must raise $179 million externally.

15-11

How will the AFN be financed?

- Additional N/P
  - 0.5 ($179) = $89.50
- Additional L-T debt
  - 0.5 ($179) = $89.50

- But this financing will add to interest expense, which will lower NI and retained earnings. We will generally ignore financing feedbacks.

15-12

Forecasted Balance Sheet (2003) Assets – 2nd pass

	2003 1st Pass	AFN	2003 2nd Pass
Cash	$ 25	-	$ 25
Accts. rec.	300	-	300
Inventories	300	-	300
Total CA	$ 625		$ 625
Net FA	625	-	625
Total assets	$1,250		$1,250

15-13

Forecasted Balance Sheet (2003) Liabilities and Equity – 2nd pass

	2003 1st Pass	AFN	2003 2nd Pass
AP/accruals	$ 125	-	$ 125
Notes payable	100	+89.5	190
Total CL	$ 225		$ 315
L-T debt	100	+89.5	189
Common stk.	500	-	500
Ret.earnings	246	-	246
Total claims	$1,071		$1,250

* From income statement.

15-14

Why do the AFN equation and financial statement method have different results?

- Equation method assumes a constant profit margin, a constant dividend payout, and a constant capital structure.
- Financial statement method is more flexible. More important, it allows different items to grow at different rates.

15-15

Forecasted ratios (2003)

	2002	2003(E)	Industry	
BEP	10.00%	10.00%	20.00%	Poor
Profit margin	2.52%	2.62%	4.00%	"
ROE	7.20%	8.77%	15.60%	"
DSO (days)	43.80	43.80	32.00	"
Inv. turnover	8.33x	8.33x	11.00x	"
F. A. turnover	4.00x	4.00x	5.00x	"
T. A. turnover	2.00x	2.00x	2.50x	"
D/A ratio	30.00%	40.34%	36.00%	"
TIE	6.25x	7.81x	9.40x	"
Current ratio	2.50x	1.99x	3.00x	"
Payout ratio	30.00%	30.00%	30.00%	O. K.

15-16

What was the net investment in operating capital?

- OC_{2003} = NOWC + Net FA
  = $625 - $125 + $625
  = $1,125

- OC_{2002} = $900

- Net investment in OC = $1,125 - $900
  = $225

15-17

How much free cash flow is expected to be generated in 2003?

FCF = NOPAT − Net inv. in OC
= EBIT (1 − T) − Net inv. in OC
= $125 (0.6) − $225
= $75 − $225
= -$150.

15-18

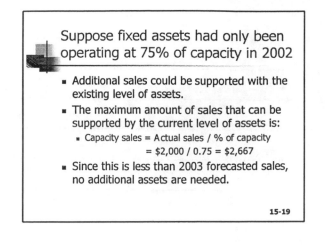

Suppose fixed assets had only been operating at 75% of capacity in 2002

- Additional sales could be supported with the existing level of assets.
- The maximum amount of sales that can be supported by the current level of assets is:
  - Capacity sales = Actual sales / % of capacity
    = $2,000 / 0.75 = $2,667
- Since this is less than 2003 forecasted sales, no additional assets are needed.

15-19

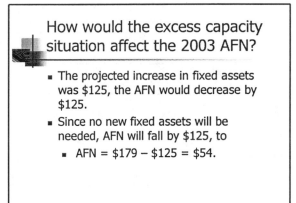

How would the excess capacity situation affect the 2003 AFN?

- The projected increase in fixed assets was $125, the AFN would decrease by $125.
- Since no new fixed assets will be needed, AFN will fall by $125, to
  - AFN = $179 – $125 = $54.

15-20

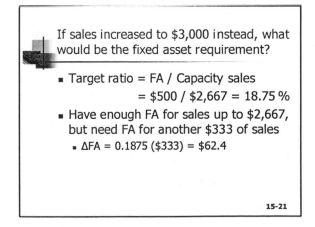

If sales increased to $3,000 instead, what would be the fixed asset requirement?

- Target ratio = FA / Capacity sales
  = $500 / $2,667 = 18.75 %
- Have enough FA for sales up to $2,667, but need FA for another $333 of sales
  - ΔFA = 0.1875 ($333) = $62.4

15-21

How would excess capacity affect the forecasted ratios?

- Sales wouldn't change but assets would be lower, so turnovers would be better.
- Less new debt, hence lower interest, so higher profits, EPS, ROE (when financing feedbacks were considered).
- Debt ratio, TIE would improve.

15-22

Forecasted ratios (2003) with projected 2003 sales of $2,500

| | % of 2002 Capacity | | |
	100%	75%	Industry
BEP	10.00%	11.11%	20.00%
Profit margin	2.62%	2.62%	4.00%
ROE	8.77%	8.77%	15.60%
DSO (days)	43.80	43.80	32.00
Inv. turnover	8.33x	8.33x	11.00x
F. A. turnover	4.00x	5.00x	5.00x
T. A. turnover	2.00x	2.22x	2.50x
D/A ratio	40.34%	33.71%	36.00%
TIE	7.81x	7.81x	9.40x
Current ratio	1.99x	2.48x	3.00x

15-23

How is NWC managing its receivables and inventories?

- DSO is higher than the industry average, and inventory turnover is lower than the industry average.
- Improvements here would lower current assets, reduce capital requirements, and further improve profitability and other ratios.

15-24

How would the following items affect the AFN?

- Higher dividend payout ratio?
  - Increase AFN: Less retained earnings.
- Higher profit margin?
  - Decrease AFN: Higher profits, more retained earnings.
- Higher capital intensity ratio?
  - Increase AFN: Need more assets for given sales.
- Pay suppliers in 60 days, rather than 30 days?
  - Decrease AFN: Trade creditors supply more capital (i.e., L^*/S_0 increases).

15-25

EXAM-TYPE PROBLEMS

15-1. Snowball & Company has the following balance sheet:

Current assets	$ 7,000	A/P & accrued liabilities	$ 1,500
Fixed assets	3,000	S-T (3-month) loans	2,000
		Common stock	1,500
		Retained earnings	5,000
Total assets	$10,000	Total claims	$10,000

Snowball's after-tax profit margin is 11 percent, and the company pays out 60 percent of its earnings as dividends. Its sales last year were $10,000; its assets were used to full capacity; no economies of scale exist in the use of assets; and the profit margin and payout ratio are expected to remain constant. The company uses the AFN equation to estimate funds requirements, and it plans to raise any required external capital as short-term bank loans. If sales grow by 50 percent, what will Snowball's current ratio be after it has raised the necessary funds? (1.34)

15-2. Hogan Inc. generated EBIT of $240,000 this past year on $750,000 of sales and using assets of $1,100,000. The interest rate on its existing long-term debt of $640,000 is 12.5 percent and the firm's tax rate is 40 percent. The firm paid a dividend of $1.27 on each of its 37,800 shares outstanding from net income of $96,000. The total book value of equity is $446,364 of which the common stock account equals $335,000. The firm's shares sell for $28.00 per share. The firm forecasts a 10 percent increase in sales, assets, and EBIT next year, and a dividend of $1.40 per share. If the firm needs additional capital funds, it will raise 60 percent with debt and 40 percent with equity. The spontaneous liabilities balance is $13,636. Except for spontaneous liabilities, the firm uses no other sources of current liabilities and will continue this policy in the future. What will be the AFN Hogan will need to balance its projected balance sheet using the projected financial statement method? Do not include any financing feedbacks. ($51,156)

16-19 Citrus Products Inc. is a medium-sized producer of citrus juice drinks with groves in Indian River County, Florida. Until now, the company has confined its operations and sales to the United States, but its CEO, George Gaynor, wants to expand into the Pacific Rim. The first step would be to set up sales subsidiaries in Japan and Australia, then to set up a production plant in Japan, and, finally, to distribute the product throughout the Pacific Rim. The firm's financial manager, Ruth Schmidt, is enthusiastic about the plan, but she is worried about the implications of the foreign expansion on the firm's financial management process. She has asked you, the firm's most recently hired financial analyst, to develop a 1-hour tutorial package that explains the basics of multinational financial management. The tutorial will be presented at the next board of directors meeting. To get you started, Schmidt has supplied you with the following list of questions.

a. What is a multinational corporation? Why do firms expand into other countries?

b. What are the six major factors that distinguish multinational financial management from financial management as practiced by a purely domestic firm?

c. Consider the following illustrative exchange rates.

	U.S. Dollars Required to Buy One Unit of Foreign Currency
Japanese yen	0.009
Australian dollar	0.650

(1) Are these currency prices direct quotations or indirect quotations?

(2) Calculate the indirect quotations for yen and Australian dollars.

(3) What is a cross rate? Calculate the two cross rates between yen and Australian dollars.

(4) Assume Citrus Products can produce a liter of orange juice and ship it to Japan for $1.75. If the firm wants a 50 percent markup on the product, what should the orange juice sell for in Japan?

(5) Now, assume Citrus Products begins producing the same liter of orange juice in Japan. The product costs 250 yen to produce and ship to Australia, where it can be sold for 6 Australian dollars. What is the U.S. dollar profit on the sale?

(6) What is exchange rate risk?

d. Briefly describe the current international monetary system.

e. What is a convertible currency? What problems arise when a multinational company operates in a country whose currency is not convertible?

f. What is the difference between spot rates and forward rates? When is the forward rate at a premium to the spot rate? At a discount?

g. What is interest rate parity? Currently, you can exchange 1 yen for 0.0095 U.S. dollar in the 30-day forward market, and the risk-free rate on 30-day securities is 4 percent in both Japan and the United States. Does interest rate parity hold? If not, which securities offer the highest expected return?

h. What is purchasing power parity (PPP)? If grapefruit juice costs $2.00 a liter in the United States and purchasing power parity holds, what should be the price of grapefruit juice in Australia?

i. What impact does relative inflation have on interest rates and exchange rates?

j. Briefly discuss the international capital markets.

k. To what extent do average capital structures vary across different countries?

l. What is the impact of multinational operations on each of the following financial management topics?

(1) Cash management.

(2) Capital budgeting decisions.

(3) Credit management.

(4) Inventory management.

CHAPTER 16
Multinational Financial Management

- Multinational vs. domestic financial management
- Exchange rates and trading in foreign exchange
- International money and capital markets

16-1

What is a multinational corporation?

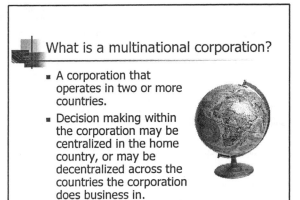

- A corporation that operates in two or more countries.
- Decision making within the corporation may be centralized in the home country, or may be decentralized across the countries the corporation does business in.

16-2

Why do firms expand into other countries?

1. To seek new markets.
2. To seek raw materials.
3. To seek new technology.
4. To seek production efficiency.
5. To avoid political and regulatory hurdles.
6. To diversify.

16-3

What factors distinguish multinational financial management from domestic financial management?

1. Different currency denominations.
2. Economic and legal ramifications.
3. Language differences.
4. Cultural differences.
5. Role of governments.
6. Political risk.

16-4

Consider the following exchange rates

	US $ to buy 1 unit
Japanese yen	0.009
Australian dollar	0.650

- Are these currency prices direct or indirect quotations?
    - Since they are prices of foreign currencies expressed in dollars, they are direct quotations.

16-5

What is an indirect quotation?

- The number of units of a foreign currency needed to purchase one U.S. dollar, or the reciprocal of a direct quotation.
- Are you more likely to observe direct or indirect quotations?
    - Most exchange rates are stated in terms of an indirect quotation.
    - Except the British pound, which is usually in terms of a direct quotation.

16-6

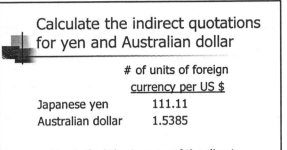

Calculate the indirect quotations for yen and Australian dollar

	# of units of foreign currency per US $
Japanese yen	111.11
Australian dollar	1.5385

- Simply find the inverse of the direct quotations.

16-7

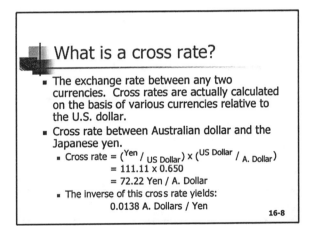

What is a cross rate?

- The exchange rate between any two currencies. Cross rates are actually calculated on the basis of various currencies relative to the U.S. dollar.
- Cross rate between Australian dollar and the Japanese yen.
  - Cross rate = $(^{Yen}/_{US\ Dollar}) \times (^{US\ Dollar}/_{A.\ Dollar})$
    = 111.11 x 0.650
    = 72.22 Yen / A. Dollar
  - The inverse of this cross rate yields:
    0.0138 A. Dollars / Yen

16-8

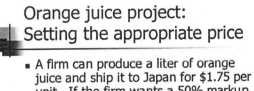

Orange juice project: Setting the appropriate price

- A firm can produce a liter of orange juice and ship it to Japan for $1.75 per unit. If the firm wants a 50% markup on the project, what should the juice sell for in Japan?

  Price = (1.75)(1.50)(111.11)
       = 291.66 yen

16-9

Orange juice project: Determining profitability

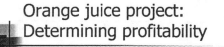

- The product will cost 250 yen to produce and ship to Australia, where it can be sold for 6 Australian dollars. What is the U.S. dollar profit on the sale?
  - Cost in A. dollars = 250 yen (0.0138)
    = 3.45 A. dollars
  - A. dollar profit = 6 − 3.45 = 2.55 A. dollars
  - U.S. dollar profit = 2.55 / 1.5385 = $1.66

16-10

What is exchange rate risk?

- The risk that the value of a cash flow in one currency translated to another currency will decline due to a change in exchange rates.
- For example, in the last slide, a weakening Australian dollar (strengthening dollar) would lower the dollar profit.
- The current international monetary system is a floating rate system.

16-11

European Monetary Union

- In 2002, the full implementation of the "euro" was completed. The national currencies of the 12 participating countries were phased out in favor of the "euro." The newly formed European Central Bank controls the monetary policy of the EMU.

16-12

Member nations of the EMU

- Austria
- Belgium
- Finland
- France
- Germany
- Greece

- Ireland
- Italy
- Luxembourg
- Netherlands
- Portugal
- Spain

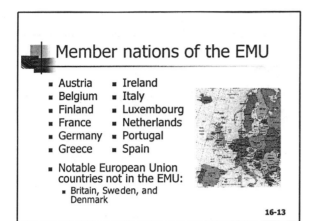

- Notable European Union countries not in the EMU:
  - Britain, Sweden, and Denmark

16-13

What is a convertible currency?

- A currency is convertible when the issuing country promises to redeem the currency at current market rates.
- Convertible currencies are traded in world currency markets.

16-14

What problems may arise when a firm operates in a country whose currency is not convertible?

- It becomes very difficult for multi-national companies to conduct business because there is no easy way to take profits out of the country.
- Often, firms will barter for goods to export to their home countries.

16-15

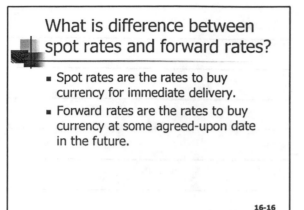

What is difference between spot rates and forward rates?

- Spot rates are the rates to buy currency for immediate delivery.
- Forward rates are the rates to buy currency at some agreed-upon date in the future.

16-16

When is the forward rate at a premium to the spot rate?

- If the U.S. dollar buys fewer units of a foreign currency in the forward than in the spot market, the foreign currency is selling at a premium.
- In the opposite situation, the foreign currency is selling at a discount.
- The primary determinant of the spot/forward rate relationship is relative interest rates.

16-17

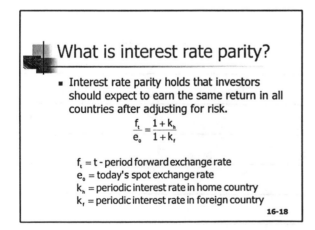

What is interest rate parity?

- Interest rate parity holds that investors should expect to earn the same return in all countries after adjusting for risk.

$$\frac{f_t}{e_0} = \frac{1 + k_h}{1 + k_f}$$

f_t = t - period forward exchange rate
e_0 = today's spot exchange rate
k_h = periodic interest rate in home country
k_f = periodic interest rate in foreign country

16-18

Evaluating interest rate parity

- Suppose one yen buys $0.0095 in the 30-day forward exchange market and k_{NOM} for a 30-day risk-free security in Japan and in the U.S. is 4%.
  - $f_t = 0.0095$
  - $k_h = 4\% / 12 = 0.333\%$
  - $k_f = 4\% / 12 = 0.333\%$

16-19

Does interest rate parity hold?

$$\frac{0.0095}{e_0} = \frac{1.0033}{1.0033}$$

$$\frac{0.0095}{e_0} = 1$$

- Therefore, for interest rate parity to hold, e_0 must equal $0.0095, but we were given earlier that $e_0 = \$0.0090$.

16-20

Which security offers the highest return?

- The Japanese security.
  - Convert $1,000 to yen in the spot market. $1,000 x 111.111 = 111,111 yen.
  - Invest 111,111 yen in 30-day Japanese security. In 30 days receive 111,111 yen x 1.00333 = 111,481 yen.
  - Agree today to exchange 111,481 yen 30 days from now at forward rate, 111,481/105.2632 = $1,059.07.
  - 30-day return = $59.07/$1,000 = 5.907%, nominal annual return = 12 x 5.907% = 70.88%.

16-21

What is purchasing power parity (PPP)?

- Purchasing power parity implies that the level of exchange rates adjusts so that identical goods cost the same amount in different countries.

$$P_h = P_f(e_0)$$
-OR-
$$e_0 = P_h/P_f$$

16-22

If grapefruit juice costs $2.00 per liter in the U.S. and PPP holds, what is the price of grapefruit juice in Australia?

$$e_0 = P_h/P_f$$
$$\$0.6500 = \$2.00/P_f$$
$$P_f = \$2.00/\$0.6500$$
$$= 3.0769 \text{ Australian dollars.}$$

16-23

What impact does relative inflation have on interest rates and exchange rates?

- Lower inflation leads to lower interest rates, so borrowing in low-interest countries may appear attractive to multinational firms.
- However, currencies in low-inflation countries tend to appreciate against those in high-inflation rate countries, so the effective interest cost increases over the life of the loan.

16-24

International money and capital markets

- Eurodollar markets
    - a source of dollars outside the U.S.
- International bonds
    - Foreign bonds – sold by foreign borrower, but denominated in the currency of the country of issue.
    - Eurobonds – sold in country other than the one in whose currency the bonds are denominated.

16-25

To what extent do average capital structures vary across different countries?

- Previous studies suggested that average capital structures vary among the large industrial countries.
- However, a recent study, which controlled for differences in accounting practices, suggests that capital structures are more similar across different countries than previously thought.

16-26

Impact of multinational operations

- Cash management
    - Distances are greater.
    - Access to more markets for loans and for temporary investments.
    - Cash is often denominated in different currencies.

16-27

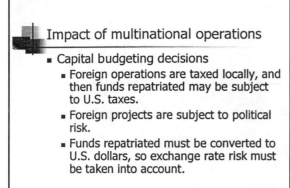

Impact of multinational operations

- Capital budgeting decisions
  - Foreign operations are taxed locally, and then funds repatriated may be subject to U.S. taxes.
  - Foreign projects are subject to political risk.
  - Funds repatriated must be converted to U.S. dollars, so exchange rate risk must be taken into account.

16-28

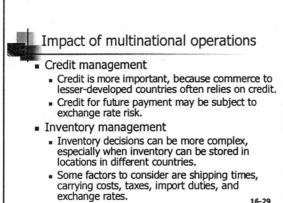

Impact of multinational operations

- Credit management
  - Credit is more important, because commerce to lesser-developed countries often relies on credit.
  - Credit for future payment may be subject to exchange rate risk.
- Inventory management
  - Inventory decisions can be more complex, especially when inventory can be stored in locations in different countries.
  - Some factors to consider are shipping times, carrying costs, taxes, import duties, and exchange rates.

16-29

EXAM-TYPE PROBLEMS

16-1. In 1985, a particular Japanese imported automobile sold for 1,476,000 yen or $8,200. If the car still sells for the same amount of yen today but the current exchange rate is 105 yen per dollar, what is the car selling for today in U.S. dollars? ($14,057.14)

16-2. Sunware Corporation, a U.S.-based importer, makes a purchase of crystal glassware from a firm in Germany for 24,830 euros or $24,000, at the spot rate of 1.0346 euros per dollar. The terms of the purchase are net 90 days, and the U.S. firm wants to cover this trade payable with a forward market hedge to eliminate its exchange rate risk. Suppose the firm completes a forward hedge at the 90-day forward rate of 1.0546 euros. If the spot rate in 90 days is actually 1.005 euros, how much will the U.S. firm have saved in U.S. dollars by hedging its exchange rate exposure? ($1,162.00)

16-3. Six months ago, a Swiss investor bought a 6-month U.S. Treasury bill at a price of $9,708.74, with a maturity value of $10,000. The exchange rate at that time was 1.420 Swiss Francs per dollar. Today, at maturity, the exchange rate is 1.324 for Swiss Francs. What is the nominal annual rate of return to the Swiss investor? (-7.93%)

16-4. A refrigerator costs $899 in the United States. The same set costs 856 euros in France. If purchasing power parity holds, what is the spot exchange rate between the euro and the dollar? ($1.0502 per euro or 0.9522 euro per U.S. dollar)

16-5. 3-month T-bills have a nominal rate of 5 percent, while default-free Swiss bonds that mature in 3 months have a nominal rate of 3.5 percent. In the spot exchange market, one Swiss Franc equals $0.6935. If interest rate parity holds, what is the 3-month forward exchange rate? ($0.6961)

SOLUTIONS TO EXAM-TYPE PROBLEMS

CHAPTER 1

1-1. d.

1-2. e.

CHAPTER 2

2-1. a.

EBIT	$1,250,000
Interest	0
EBT	$1,250,000
Taxes (40%)	500,000
Net income	$ 750,000

b. Net cash flow = Net income + Depreciation
$$= \$750,000 + \$300,000$$
$$= \$1,050,000.$$

c. Operating cash flow = EBIT(1 – T) + Depreciation
$$= \$1,250,000(0.6) + \$300,000$$
$$= \$1,050,000.$$

d. NOPAT = EBIT(1 – T)
$$= \$1,250,000(1 – 0.4)$$
$$= \$750,000.$$

e. FCF = NOPAT – Net investment in operating capital
$$= \$750,000 – \$500,000$$
$$= \$250,000.$$

CHAPTER 3

3-1. ROE = Profit margin × Total assets turnover × Equity multiplier
= NI/Sales × Sales/TA × TA/Equity.

Now we need to determine the inputs for the equation from the data that were given. On the left we set up an income statement, and we put numbers in it on the right:

Sales (given)	$20,000
Cost	NA
EBIT (given)	$ 2,000
Interest (given)	500
EBT	$ 1,500
Taxes (30%)	450
Net income	$ 1,050

Now we can use some ratios to get some more data:

Total assets turnover = S/TA = 2.5 (given).

D/A = 70%, so E/A = 30%, and therefore A/E = 1/(E/A) = 1/0.3 = 3.3333.

Now we can complete the Du Pont equation to determine ROE:
ROE = $1,050/$20,000 × 2.5 × 3.3333 = 43.75%.

3-2.   a.   Current NI = 0.05 × $5,000,000 = $250,000.

      Current ROE = NI/Equity = $250,000/$4,000,000 = 6.25%.

      Current DSO = Receivables/(Sales/365)
                   = $2,250,000/($5,000,000/365) = 164.25 days.

      Reduce DSO to 60 days.

      Freed up cash = 104.25 × $5,000,000/365 = $1,428,082.

      Alternatively,

      Accounts receivable/($5,000,000/365) = 60
                       Accounts receivable = $821,918.

      Δ in A/R = $2,250,000 − $821,918 = $1,428,082.

      Reduce Common Equity: $4,000,000 − $1,428,082 = $2,571,918.

      New ROE = $250,000/$2,571,918 = 9.72%.

      Change in ROE = 9.72% − 6.25% = +3.47%.

   b.   (1) Doubling the dollar amounts would not affect the answer; it would still be +3.47%.

(2) Target DSO = 70 days.

Freed up cash = 94.25 × $5,000,000/365 = $1,291,096.

Reduce Common Equity: $4,000,000 − $1,291,096 = $2,708,904.

New ROE = $250,000/$2,708,904 = 9.23%.

Change in ROE = 9.23% − 6.25% = +2.98%.

(3)   Sales/Receivables = 6

$5,000,000/Receivables = 6

Receivables = $5,000,000/6 = $833,333.

Δ in AR = $2,250,000 − $833,333 = $1,416,667.

Reduce Common Equity: $4,000,000 − $1,416,667 = $2,583,333.

New ROE = $250,000/$2,583,333 = 9.68%.

Change in ROE = 9.68% − 6.25% = +3.43%.

(4) Original EPS = NI/Shares = $250,000/250,000 = $1.00.

New EPS calculation: Assume Book value = Market value. (M/B = 1.)

Price = $4,000,000/250,000 shares = $16. Stock is selling for $16 per share.

Thus, must buy back $\dfrac{\$1,428,082}{\$16}$ = 89,255 shares.

Number of shares outstanding = 250,000 − 89,255
= 160,745 shares.

New EPS = $\dfrac{\$250,000}{160,745}$ = $1.56.

Δ in EPS = $1.56 − $1.00 = +$0.56 per share.

(5) From Part 4, Book value = $16 per share. Market value = 2 × $16 = $32.

Thus, firm must buy back $1,428,082/$32 = 44,628 shares.

Number of shares outstanding = 250,000 − 44,628 = 205,372 shares.

New EPS = $250,000/205,372 = $1.22.

Δ in EPS = $1.22 – $1.00 = +$0.22 per share.

c. We could have started with lower receivables and higher fixed assets or inventory, then had you calculate the fixed assets or inventory turnover ratios. Then, we could have the company move to lower fixed assets or inventory turnover reducing equity by like amounts, and then had you determine the effects on ROE and EPS under different conditions. In any of these cases, we could have used the funds generated to retire debt, which would have lowered interest charges, and consequently, increased net income and EPS. (Note that information would have had to be given on interest and EBIT too.)

If we had to increase assets, then we would have had to finance this increase by adding either debt or equity, which would have lowered ROE and EPS, other things held constant.

3-3. a.

3-4. TIE = EBIT/I, so find EBIT and I.
Interest = $800,000 × 0.1 = $80,000.
Net income = $3,200,000 × 0.06 = $192,000.
Pre-tax income = $192,000/(1 – T) = $192,000/0.6 = $320,000.
EBIT = $320,000 + $80,000 = $400,000.
TIE = $400,000/$80,000 = 5.0×.

3-5. Before:
Equity multiplier = 1/(1 – D/A) = 1/(1 – 0.5) = 2.0.
ROE = (PM)(Assets turnover)(EM) = (10%)(0.25)(2.0) = 5%.

After:
ROE = 2(5%) = 10%
10% = (12%)(0.25)(EM)
EM = 3.33.

$$\frac{A}{E} = \frac{3.33}{1.00}$$
A = D + E
3.33 = D + 1.00
D = 2.33.

D/A = 2.33/3.33 = 0.70 = 70%.

3-6. a. $ROA = \dfrac{NI}{S} \times \dfrac{S}{A}$

$12.5\% = 3\% \times \dfrac{S}{A}$

$\dfrac{S}{A} = 4.167$.

b. $ROE = \dfrac{NI}{S} \times \dfrac{S}{A} \times \dfrac{A}{E}$

$16\% = 3\% \times 4.167 \times EM$

$EM = 1.28$.

c. From Part b, we know that A/E = 1.28; therefore, the firm's ratio of equity to assets is 1/1.28 = 0.78125 ≈ 78%. Consequently, the firm's debt ratio = D/A = 1 − E/A = 1 − 0.78 = 0.22 = 22%.

CHAPTER 4

4-1. b.

4-2. First, note that we will use the equation $k_t = 4\% + IP_t + MRP_t$. We have the data needed to find the IPs:

$IP_5 = (9\% + 6\% + 4\% + 4\% + 4\%)/5 = 27\%/5 = 5.4\%$.

$IP_2 = (9\% + 6\%)/2 = 7.5\%$.

Now we can substitute into the equation:

$k_5 = 4\% + 5.4\% + MRP_5 = 12\%$.

$k_2 = 4\% + 7.5\% + MRP_2 = 12\%$.

Now we can solve for the MRPs, and find the difference between them:

$MRP_5 = 12\% - 9.4\% = 2.6\%$.

$MRP_2 = 12\% - 11.5\% = 0.5\%$.

Difference = 2.6% − 0.5% = +2.1%.

4-3. $k_{T8} = 6.6\%$; $k_{C8} = 9.3\%$; $LP_{C8} = 0.6\%$.

$k = k^* + IP + DRP + LP + MRP$.

$k_{T8} = 6.6\% = k^* + IP + MRP$; $DRP = LP = 0$.

$k_{C8} = 9.3\% = k^* + IP + MRP + 0.6\% + DRP$.

Because both bonds are 8-year bonds the inflation premium and maturity risk premium on both bonds are equal. The only difference between them is the liquidity and default risk premiums.

$k_{C8} = 9.3\% = k^* + IP + MRP + 0.6\% + DRP$.

But we know from above that $k^* + IP + MRP = 6.6\%$; therefore,

$k_{C8} = 9.3\% = 6.6\% + 0.6\% + DRP$
$\quad\quad DRP = 2.1\%$.

CHAPTER 5

5-1.   a.

5-2.   c.

5-3.   Before: $1.15 = 0.95(b_R) + 0.05(1.0)$
$\quad\quad\quad 0.95(b_R) = 1.10$
$\quad\quad\quad\quad\quad b_R = 1.15789$.

After: $b_p = 0.95(b_R) + 0.05(2.0) = 1.10 + 0.10 = 1.20$.

5-4.   Electro b = 1.7; Flowers Galore b = 0.6; $k_M = 14\%$; $k_{RF} = 7.8\%$.

$\begin{aligned} \text{Electro } k &= k_{RF} + (k_M - k_{RF})b \\ &= 7.8\% + (14\% - 7.8\%)1.7 \\ &= 18.34\%. \end{aligned}$

$\begin{aligned} \text{Flowers Galore } k &= k_{RF} + (k_M - k_{RF})b \\ &= 7.8\% + (14\% - 7.8\%)0.6 \\ &= 11.52\%. \end{aligned}$

$\begin{aligned} \Delta k &= 18.34\% - 11.52\% \\ &= +6.82\%. \end{aligned}$

CHAPTER 6

6-1. d.

6-2. **Time line:**

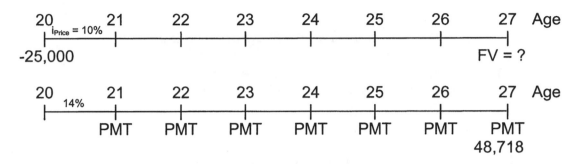

Financial calculator solution:

Price of car on 27th birthday.

Inputs: N = 7; I = 10; PV = -25000; PMT = 0.
Output: FV = $48,717.93 ≈ $48,718.

Annual investment required.

Inputs: N = 7; I = 14; PV = 0; FV = 48718.
Output: PMT = -$4,540.15.

6-3. **Time line:**

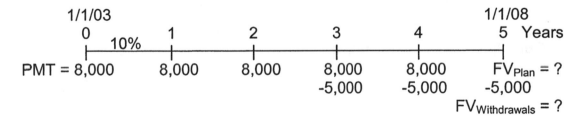

Financial calculator solution:

Calculate the FV of the withdrawals, which is how much her actual account fell short of her plan.

END mode Inputs: N = 3; I = 10; PV = 0; PMT = -5000.
          Output: FV = $16,550.

Alternative solution:

Calculate FV of original plan.

BEGIN mode   Inputs: N = 5; I = 10; PV = 0; PMT = -8000.
               Output: FV = $53,724.88.

Calculate FV of actual deposit less withdrawals, take the difference.

Step 1:   Calculate PV of actual deposit less withdrawals.
          Inputs: CF_0 = 8000; CF_1 = 8000; N_j = 2; CF_2 = 3000; N_j = 2; CF_3 = -5000;
          I = 10.
          Output: NPV = $23,082.68.

Step 2:   Calculate FV of PV found in Step 1.
          Inputs: N = 5; I = 10; PV = -23082.68; PMT = 0.
          Output: FV = $37,174.88.

Difference: $53,724.88 – $37,174.88 = $16,550.

6-4.   **Time line:**

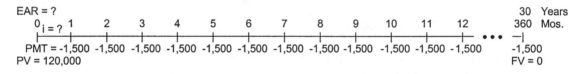

Financial calculator solution:

Calculate periodic rate.

Inputs: N = 360; PV = 120000; PMT = -1500; FV = 0.
Output: I = 1.235% per period.

Use interest rate conversion feature to calculate the mortgage's EAR.

Inputs: NOM% = 1.235 × 12 = 14.82; P/YR = 12.
Output: EFF% = 15.868% ≈ 15.87%.

6-5.   Steps:

1. He will save for 10 years, then receive payments for 25 years.

2. He wants a payment of $40,000 per year in today's dollars for the first payment only. Real income will decline. Inflation will be 5%. Enter N = 10, I = 5, PV = -40000, PMT = 0, and press FV to get FV = $65,155.79.

3. He now has $100,000 in an account that pays 8%, annual compounding. We need to find the FV of the $100,000 after 10 years. Enter N = 10, I = 8, PV = -100000, PMT = 0, and press FV to get FV = $215,892.50.

4. He wants to withdraw, or have payments of, $65,155.79 per year for 25 years, with the first payment made at the beginning of the first retirement year. So, we have a 25-year annuity due with PMT = $65,155.79, at an interest rate of 8%. (The interest rate is 8% annually, so no adjustment is required.) Set the calculator to BEGIN MODE, then enter N = 25, I = 8, PMT = 65155.79, FV = 0, and press PV to get PV = $751,165.35. This amount must be on hand to make the 25 payments.

5. Since the original $100,000, which grows to $215,892.50, will be available, we must save enough to accumulate $751,165.35 − $215,892.50 = $535,272.85.

6. The $535,272.85 is the FV of a 10-year ordinary annuity. The payments will be deposited in the bank and earn 8% interest. Therefore, set the calculator to END MODE and enter N = 10, I = 8, PV = 0, FV = 535272.85, and press PMT to find PMT = $36,949.61 ≈ $36,950.

6-6.   a. $i_{PER} = \dfrac{i_{Nom}}{m}$

   $= \dfrac{0.10}{4} = 0.025 = 2.5\%.$

b. i_{Nom} = stated interest = 10%.

c. $EAR = \left(1 + \dfrac{i_{Nom}}{m}\right)^{m} - 1$

   $= \left(1 + \dfrac{0.10}{4}\right)^{4} - 1$

   $= 0.1038 = 10.38\%.$

CHAPTER 7

7-1. Time line:

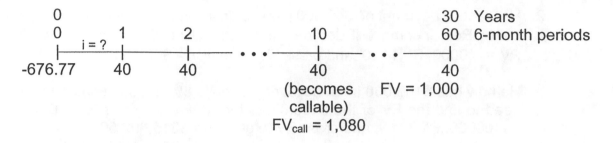

Investors would expect to earn either the YTM or the YTC, and the expected return on the old bonds is the cost GSU would have to pay in order to sell new bonds.

Financial calculator solution:

Calculate the YTM on the old bonds.

Inputs: N = 2(30) = 60; PV = -676.77; PMT = 80/2 = 40; FV = 1000.
Output: I = 6% = $k_d/2$. 6% is the semiannual or periodic rate.

YTM = 2(6%) = 12%.

Calculate the YTC for comparison.

Inputs: N = 2(5) = 10; PV = -676.77; PMT = 80/2 = 40; FV = 1080.
Output: I = 9.70% = $k_d/2$.

YTC = 2(9.70%) = 19.40%.

Would investors expect the company to call the bonds? No. The company currently pays interest of only 8% on its debt. New debt would cost GSU at least 12%. It would be foolish for the company to call the bonds, because investors would logically expect to earn the current YTM of 12% on new bonds. So k_d = 12% is the best estimate of the nominal annual interest rate GSU would have to pay on the new bonds.

7-2. **Time line:**

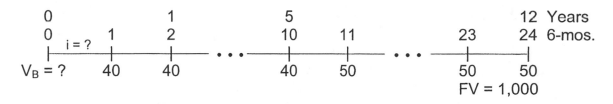

Financial calculator solution:

We are comparing securities with different payment patterns, semiannual and quarterly. To properly value the student loan securities, we must match the opportunity cost rate on the bonds with the payment period on the student loan securities, which is semiannual. Thus, convert the quarterly (periodic) rate on the bonds to a semiannual effective rate.

    Since the bonds are selling at par value, the 9% coupon rate is also the market rate. The semiannual periodic rate is then 9%/2 = 4.5%. There are 2 compounding periods (quarters) in a half year.

Calculate the opportunity cost semiannual EAR of the quarterly payment bonds (using the interest rate conversion feature).

Inputs: P/YR = 2; NOM% = 9/2 = 4.5.
Output: EFF% = 4.55% = semiannual effective rate.

Calculate the present value of the student loan package, V_B, using the semiannual effective rate (using cash flow register).

Inputs: CF_0 = 0; CF_1 = 40; N_j = 10; CF_2 = 50; N_j = 13; CF_3 = 1050; I = 4.55.
Output: NPV = V_B = $985.97.

7-3. **Time line:**

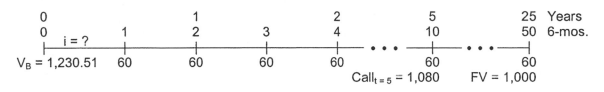

Calculate the nominal yield to call.

The bonds are selling at a premium because the coupon interest rate is above the market rate. Under the expectation of a flat yield curve, the bonds will most likely be called so that the firm can issue new, cheaper bonds. The FV is the call price and the period is 5 years or 10 semiannual periods.

Financial calculator solution:

Calculate the semiannual interest rate and convert to a nominal annual rate.

Inputs: N = 10; PV = -1230.51; PMT = 60; FV = 1080.
Output: I = 3.85% periodic rate (semiannual).

The nominal annual rate equals 2 × 3.85% = 7.70%. Thus, the before-tax cost of debt is 7.70%.

7-4. **Time line:**

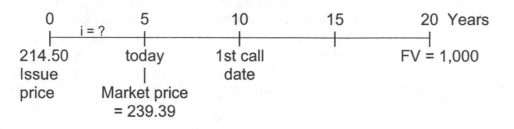

Financial calculator solution:

Calculate the original YTM when the bonds were issued.

Inputs: N = 20; PV = -214.50; PMT = 0; FV = 1000.
Output: I = 8.0%.

Calculate the current market rate using the current market price of $239.39.

Inputs: N = 15; PV = -239.39; PMT = 0; FV = 1000.
Output: I = 10.0%.

At a current market price of $239.39, market rates are 10%. Since market rates have risen, the bond will not likely be called. So today, at Year 5, the YTM of 10% is the most likely annual rate of return an investor who purchases the bonds today will earn.

7-5. e.

7-6. d.

7-7.   **Time line:**

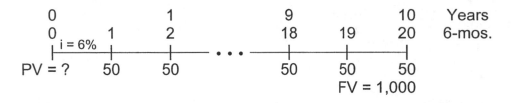

Financial calculator solution:

Calculate the PV of the bond so the current yield can then be calculated.

Inputs: N = 2 × 10 = 20; I = 12/2 = 6; PMT = 100/2 = 50; FV = 1000.
Output: PV = $885.30.

Calculate the current yield.

$$\text{Current yield} = \frac{\text{Interest}}{\text{Bond value}} = \frac{\$100}{\$885.30} = 11.30\%.$$

CHAPTER 8

8-1.   Step 1:   *Calculate required rate of return.*

$$k_s = \frac{\$2}{\$20} + 6\% = 10\% + 6\% = 16\%.$$

Step 2:   *Calculate risk-free rate.*

$$16\% = k_{RF} + (15\% - k_{RF})1.2$$
$$16\% = k_{RF} + 18\% - 1.2k_{RF}$$
$$0.2k_{RF} = 2\%$$
$$k_{RF} = 10\%.$$

Step 3:   *Calculate capital gain.*

New k_s = 10% + (15% − 10%)0.6 = 13%.

$$\hat{P}_{New} = \frac{\$2}{0.13 - 0.06} = \$28.57.$$

Therefore, the percentage capital gain is approximately 43%, as calculated below:

$$\text{Capital gain} = \frac{\$28.57 - \$20.00}{\$20.00} = \frac{\$8.57}{\$20.00} = 0.4285 \approx 43\%.$$

8-2.   **Time line**:

$$\hat{P}_0 = \underline{\$71.538} \approx \$71.54.$$

Financial calculator solution:

Inputs: $CF_0 = 0$; $CF_1 = 0.48$; $CF_2 = 0.576$; $CF_3 = 94.001$; $I = 10$.
Output: NPV = $\hat{P}_0 = \$71.54$.

8-3.   e.

8-4. $\hat{k}_p = \dfrac{D_p}{P_p}$

$0.125 = \dfrac{\$8.75}{P_p}$

$P_p = \$70.$

8-5. $FCF_1 = EBIT(1 - T) + \text{Depreciation} - \underset{\text{expenditures}}{\text{Capital}} - \Delta\left(\begin{array}{c}\text{Net operating}\\\text{working capital}\end{array}\right)$

   $= \$800,000,000 + \$160,000,000 - \$320,000,000 - \$0$
   $= \$640,000,000.$

$$\text{Firm value} = \frac{FCF_1}{WACC - g}$$

$$= \frac{\$640,000,000}{0.09 - 0.04}$$

$$= \frac{\$640,000,000}{0.05}$$

$$= \$12,800,000,000.$$

This is the total firm value. Now find the market value of its equity.

$$MV_{Total} = MV_{Equity} + MV_{Debt}$$
$$\$12,800,000,000 = MV_{Equity} + \$4,800,000,000$$
$$MV_{Equity} = \$8,000,000,000.$$

This is the market value of all the equity. Divide by the number of shares to find the price per share. $8,000,000,000/320,000,000 = $25.00.

CHAPTER 9

9-1. Time line:

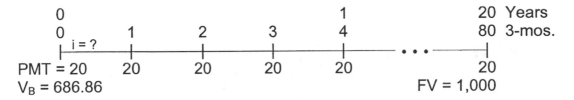

Financial calculator solution:

Calculate the <u>nominal</u> YTM of the bond.

Inputs: N = 4 × 20 = 80; PV = -686.86; PMT = 80/4 = 20; FV = 1000.
Output: I = 3.05% periodic rate = quarterly rate.

Nominal annual rate = 3.05% × 4 = 12.20%.

Calculate k_d after-tax.

$k_{d,\,AT}$ = 12.20%(1 − T) = 12.20%(1 − 0.4) = 7.32%.

9-2. Information given:

Debt = 0.4; Equity = 0.6; P_0 = $28; D_0 = $2.20; g = 6%; F = 15%.

Use the dividend growth model to calculate k_e.

$$k_e = \frac{D_0(1+g)}{P_0(1-F)} + g = \frac{\$2.20(1.06)}{\$28(1-0.15)} + 0.06 = \frac{\$2.33}{\$23.80} + 0.06$$
$$= 0.0980 + 0.06 = 0.1580 = 15.8\%.$$

9-3.   Step 1:   *Calculate the cost of common stock, k_s.*

$$k_s = \frac{D_1}{P_0} + g = \frac{\$3.00(1.10)}{\$42.50} + 0.10$$

$$= \frac{\$3.30}{\$42.50} + 0.10 = 0.0776 + 0.10 = 0.1776 = 17.76\%.$$

Step 2:   *Use the target capital structure weights to calculate WACC.*

WACC = 0.55(0.10)(1 - 0.35) + 0.45(17.76%) = 11.57%.

9-4.   Debt = 42%; Equity = 58%; YTM = 11%; T = 40%; WACC = 10.53%.
k_s = ?

k_d (1 – T) = 11%(1 – 0.4) = 6.6%.

WACC $= w_d k_d(1 - T) + w_c k_s$
10.53% = 0.42(6.6%) + (0.58)k_s
7.758% = (0.58)k_s
     k_s = 13.38%.

CHAPTER 10

10-1. **Time line:**

	0		1	2	3	4	Years
		12%					
Cash flows: S	-1,100		900	350	50	10	
	NPV_s = ? IRR_s = ?						
Cash flows: L	-1,100		0	300	500	850	
	NPV_L = ? IRR_L = ?						

Financial calculator solution:

Calculate the NPV and IRR of each project, and then select the IRR of the higher NPV project.

Project S: Inputs: $CF_0 = -1100$; $CF_1 = 900$; $CF_2 = 350$; $CF_3 = 50$; $CF_4 = 10$; $I = 12$.
　　　　　Outputs: $NPV_S = \$24.53$; $IRR_S = 13.88\%$.

Project L: Inputs: $CF_0 = -1100$; $CF_1 = 0$; $CF_2 = 300$; $CF_3 = 500$; $CF_4 = 850$; $I = 12$.
　　　　　Outputs: $NPV_L = \$35.24$; $IRR_L = 13.09\%$.

Project L has the higher NPV and its IRR = 13.09%.

10-2. Time line:

	0	1	2	3	4 Years
$IRR_X = ?$ $IRR_Z = ?$					
CF_X	-100	50	40	30	10
CF_Z	-100	10	30	40	60
CF_{X-Z}	0	40	10	-10	-50

Financial calculator solution:

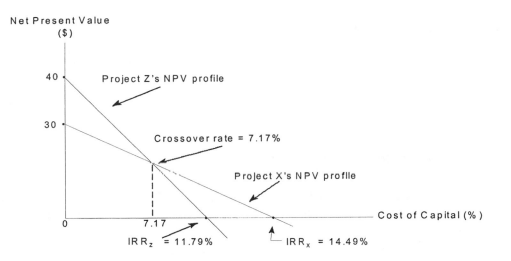

Calculate the IRR of each project.

Project X:

Inputs: $CF_0 = -100$; $CF_1 = 50$; $CF_2 = 40$; $CF_3 = 30$; $CF_4 = 10$.
Output: IRR = 14.489% ≈ 14.49%.

Project Z:

Inputs: $CF_0 = -100$; $CF_1 = 10$; $CF_2 = 30$; $CF_3 = 40$; $CF_4 = 60$.
Output: IRR = 11.79%.

Calculate the NPVs of the projects at k = 0 discount rate.

$NPV_{X,k = 0\%}$ = -$100 + $50 + $40 + $30 + $10 = $30.

$NPV_{Z,k = 0\%}$ = -$100 + $10 + $30 + $40 + $60 = $40.

Calculate the IRR of the residual project cash flows, i.e., Project$_{X-Z}$.

IRR_{X-Z}: Inputs: $CF_0 = 0$; $CF_1 = 40$; $CF_2 = 10$; $CF_3 = -10$; $CF_4 = -50$.
Output: IRR = 7.167% $\approx$ 7.17%.

Using the calculator we can determine that the two NPV profiles cross in the relevant part of the NPV profile graph. Project X has the higher IRR. Project Z has the higher NPV at k = 0. The crossover rate is 7.17%.

10-3. Time line:

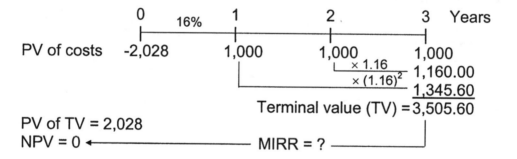

Step 1: *Calculate the historical beta.*

> **Regression method; Financial calculator:** Different calculators have different list entry procedures and key stroke sequences.
>
> Enter Nulook returns as the y-list:
> Inputs: Item(1) = 9 INPUT; Item(2) = 15 INPUT; Item(3) = 36 INPUT.
>
> Enter market returns as the x-list:
> Inputs: Item(1) = 6 INPUT; Item(2) = 10 INPUT; Item(3) = 24 INPUT; use linear model.
> Output: m or slope = 1.50 = historical beta.

Graphical/numerical method: Note that this method works precisely in this problem because the data points lie in a straight line. If the plotted data points don't lie in a straight line, regression is a better method.

Slope = Rise/Run = $(36 - 9)/(24 - 6) = 27/18 = 1.5$. Beta = 1.5.

Step 2: *Calculate the cost of equity using CAPM and beta, given inputs.*

$k_s = k_{RF} + (RP_M)b = 7.0\% + (6.0\%)1.5 = 16.0\%$.

Step 3: *Calculate MIRR.*

Financial calculator solution:

Terminal value using TVM:
Inputs: N = 3; I = 16; PV = 0; PMT = -1000.
Output: FV = $3,505.60.

Terminal value using cash flows:
Inputs: $CF_0 = 0$; $CF_1 = 1000$; $N_j = 3$; I = 16.
Output: NFV = $3,505.60.

Note: Some calculators do not have the Net Future Value (NFV) function. You can still calculate the NFV or terminal value using cash flows to calculate NPV, then TVM to calculate NFV or TV from the NPV.

Calculate *NPV of cash inflows.*

Inputs: $CF_0 = 0$; $CF_1 = 1000$; $N_j = 3$; I = 16.
Output: NPV = -$2,245.89.

Now take the NPV of $2,245.89 and bring it forward at 16% for three periods to get the FV or terminal value.

Inputs: N = 3; I = 16; PV = -2245.89; PMT = 0.
Output: FV = $3,505.60.

MIRR using TVM:
Inputs: N = 3; PV = -2028; PMT = 0; FV = 3505.60.
Output: I = 20.01% = MIRR ≈ 20%.

CHAPTER 11

11-1. $E(NPV) = 0.20(-\$9,000) + 0.45(\$20,500) + 0.35(\$45,675)$
$= -\$1,800 + \$9,225 + \$15,986.25$
$= \$23,411.25.$

Since the NPV numbers are in thousands of dollars, $E(NPV) = \$23,411,250.$

$\sigma_{NPV} = [0.20(-\$9,000 - \$23,411.25)^2 + 0.45(\$20,500 - \$23,411.25)^2$
$+ 0.35(\$45,675 - \$23,411.25)^2]^{\frac{1}{2}}$
$= [\$210,097,825.31 + \$3,813,919.45 + \$173,486,097.42]^{\frac{1}{2}}$
$= \$19,682.42.$

Since the NPV numbers are in thousands of dollars, $\sigma_{NPV} = \$19,682,424.70.$

$CV_{NPV} = \dfrac{\$19,682,424.70}{\$23,411,250} = 0.8407.$

11-2. The net cost is $630,000:

Price	($540,000)
Modification	(62,500)
Increase in NOWC	(27,500)
Cash outlay for new machine	($630,000)

The operating cash flows follow:

	Year 1	Year 2	Year 3
After-tax savings[1]	$143,000	$143,000	$143,000
Depreciation tax savings[2]	69,589	94,894	31,631
Net cash flow	$212,589	$237,894	$174,631

Notes:

[1]The after-tax cost savings is $220,000(1 – T) = $220,000(0.65)
$= \$143,000.$

[2]The depreciation expense in each year is the depreciable basis, $602,500, times the MACRS allowance percentages of 0.33, 0.45, and 0.15 for Years 1, 2, and 3, respectively. Depreciation expense in Years 1, 2, and 3 is $198,825, $271,125, and $90,375. The depreciation tax savings is calculated as the tax rate (35 percent) times the depreciation expense in each year.

The terminal cash flow is $253,511:

Salvage value	$325,000
Tax on SV*	(98,989)
Return of NOWC	27,500
	$253,511

BV in Year 4 = $602,500(0.07) = $42,175.

*Tax on SV = ($325,000 – $42,175)(0.35) = $98,989.

The project has an NPV of $54,202; thus, it should be accepted.

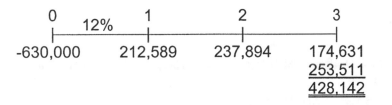

With a financial calculator, input the appropriate cash flows into the cash flow register, input I = 12, and then solve for NPV = $54,202.

11-3. a.

0	1	2	3	4	Years
10%					
-13.6	6.8	6.8	6.8	6.8	

NPV = $7.9551 million.

b. Wait 2 years:

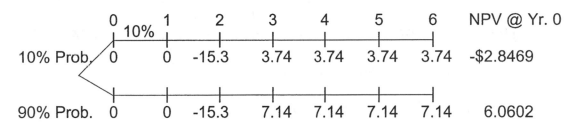

If the cash flows are only $3.74 million, the NPV of the project is negative and, thus, would not be undertaken. The value of the option of waiting two years is evaluated as 0.10($0) + 0.90($6.0602) = $5.4542 million.
    Since the NPV of waiting two years is less than going ahead and proceeding with the project today, it makes sense to drill today.

CHAPTER 12

12-1. b.

12-2. $EPS_1 = \left[\left(Sales - \dfrac{Variable}{costs} - \dfrac{Fixed}{costs} - Interest\right)(1-T)\right]/$Shares outstanding.

Step 1: *Calculate the amount of debt and interest expense.*

Debt = $0.60 \times \$400,000 = \$240,000$.

Interest = $0.12 \times \$240,000 = \$28,800$.

Step 2: *Solve for sales using the forecasted EPS.*

$\$4.00 = [(S - 0.40S - \$80,000 - \$28,800)(1 - 0.40)]/10,000$
$\$4.00 = [(0.60S - \$108,800)(0.6)]/10,000$
$\$4.00 = (0.36S - \$65,280)/10,000$
$\$105,280 = 0.36S$
Sales $= \$292,444.44 \approx \$292,445$.

Alternative method:

Note that Sales – VC – FC = EBIT. Calculate net income from EPS and shares outstanding and work back up the income statement.

$EPS_1 = [(EBIT - Interest)(1 - T)]/$Shares outstanding.

Solve for net income, then EBT, interest (step 1 above), and EBIT.

Net Income = EPS $\times$ Shares outstanding = $\$4.00 \times 10,000 = \$40,000$.

EBT = NI/(1 – T) = $\$40,000/0.6 = \$66,667$.

Interest (from above) = $\$28,800$.

EBIT = EBT + Interest = $\$66,667 + \$28,800 = \$95,467$.

Solve for sales using VC percentage, EBIT, and FC.

$S = 0.40S + \$95,467 + \$80,000$
$0.6S = \$175,467$
$S = \$175,467/0.6 = \$292,445$.

12-3. $F = \$900{,}000$; $VC = \$3.25$/unit; $P = \$4.75$; $Q_{BE} = ?$

$$Q_{BE} = \frac{F}{P - V}$$
$$= \frac{\$900{,}000}{\$4.75 - \$3.25}$$
$$= 600{,}000 \text{ units.}$$

12-4. Facts as given: Current capital structure: 30% D; 70% E; $k_{RF} = 6\%$; $k_M - k_{RF} = 5\%$; $T = 40\%$; $k_s = 12\%$.

Step 1: Determine the firm's current beta.

$$k_s = k_{RF} + (k_M - k_{RF})b$$
$$12\% = 6\% + (5\%)b$$
$$6\% = 5\%b$$
$$1.2 = b.$$

Step 2: Determine the firm's unlevered beta, b_U.

$$b_U = b_L/[1 + (1 - T)(D/E)]$$
$$b_U = 1.2/[1 + (1 - 0.4)(0.30/0.70)]$$
$$b_U = 1.2/1.2571$$
$$b_U = 0.9545.$$

Step 3: Determine the firm's beta under the new capital structure.

$$b_{L, 45\%D} = b_U[1 + (1 - T)(D/E)]$$
$$b_{L, 45\%D} = 0.9545[1 + (1 - 0.4)(0.45/0.55)]$$
$$b_{L, 45\%D} = 0.9545(1.4909)$$
$$b_{L, 45\%D} = 1.4231.$$

Step 4: Determine the firm's new cost of equity under the changed capital structure.

$$k_s = k_{RF} + (k_M - k_{RF})b$$
$$k_s = 6\% + (5\%)1.4231$$
$$k_s = 13.1157\% \approx 13.12\%.$$

CHAPTER 13

13-1. b.

12-2. d. The dividend irrelevance theory is MM's theory. The tax preference theory says that capital gains are preferred to dividends, while the bird-in-the-hand (G-L) theory says that dividends are preferred to capital gains. The clientele effect assumes that investors are attracted to a firm's particular dividend payout policy.

12-3. *Calculate the amount of debt and interest expense (in millions).*

Total assets = $200; 40% debt × $200 = $80 debt.

Interest expense = $80 × 0.10 = $8.

Calculate net income (in millions).

EBIT	$98.0
Less: Interest	8.0
EBT	$90.0
Less: Taxes (34%)	30.6
Net income	$59.4

Calculate portion of projects financed with retained earnings.

Capital budget consists of $60 million in positive NPV projects.

Retained earnings portion: $60M × 0.60 = $36 million.
Debt portion: $60M × 0.40 = $24 million.

Calculate residual of earnings available for dividends.

$59.4 – $36.0 = $23.4 million in dividends.

CHAPTER 14

14-1. **Time line:**

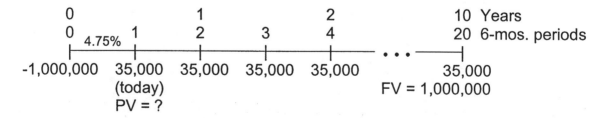

Financial calculator solution:

Calculate the market value of the bonds, V_{B1}, today, at t = 1, on the time line above using the new market interest rate.

Inputs: N = 19; I = 9.5/2 = 4.75; PMT = 35000; FV = 1000000.
Output: PV = -$845,807.80; V_{B1} = $845,807.80.

Calculate the capital loss on the bonds.

The bonds were purchased at par for $1,000,000, but are resold 6 months later for considerably less.

Capital loss on bonds = $1,000,000 − $845,807.80 = $154,192.20.

14-2. d.

14-3. c.

14-4. Construct a simplified comparative balance sheet and income statement for the restricted and relaxed policies (in thousands):

	15% of Sales Restricted	25% of Sales Relaxed
Balance sheet accounts:		
Current assets	$ 60	$ 100
Fixed assets	100	100
Total assets	$ 160	$ 200
Debt	$ 80	$ 100
Equity and retained earnings	80	100
Total liabilities and equity	$ 160	$ 200
Income statement accounts:		
EBIT	$ 36.0	$ 36.0
Less: Interest (10%)	8.0	10.0
EBT	$ 28.0	$ 26.0
Less: Taxes (40%)	11.2	10.4
Net income	$ 16.8	$ 15.6

Calculate ROEs under each policy.

ROE = NI/Equity.
ROE (Restricted policy) = $16.8/$80 = 21.0%.
ROE (Relaxed policy) = $15.6/$100 = 15.6%.
Difference in ROEs = 0.21 − 0.156 = 0.054 = 5.4%.

14-5. (Account balances stated in millions)

Old	With Change

Inventory conversion period:

$$ICP = \frac{365}{\frac{40}{10}} = \frac{365}{4} = 91.25 \text{ days.} \qquad ICP = \frac{365}{\frac{40}{8}} = \frac{365}{5} = 73 \text{ days.}$$

Receivables conversion period (or days sales outstanding):

$$DSO = \frac{8}{\frac{40}{365}} = 73 \text{ days.} \qquad DSO = \frac{7}{\frac{40}{365}} = 63.875 \text{ days.}$$

Payables deferral period:

PDP = 30 days.   PDP = 30 days.

CCC = 91.25 + 73 – 30 = 134.25 days.   CCC = 73 + 63.875 – 30 = 106.875 days.
Change in CCC = 134.25 – 106.875 = 27.375 days.
Net change is -27.375 days (CCC is 27.375 days shorter).

14-6. **Financial calculator solution:**

Trade credit: Terms 1/30, net 60.

Note that the approximate rate is really the rate per period multiplied by the number of periods, or a nominal annual rate.

1/99 × 365/(60 – 30) = 0.0101 × 12.1667 = 12.29% approximate rate.

Calculate the EAR.

$$EAR = (1 + 1/99)^{365/30} - 1$$
$$= (1.0101)^{12.1667} - 1$$
$$= 0.13007 = 13.007\% \approx 13.01\%.$$

14-7. d.

14-8. 20 × $750,000 = $15,000,000.

CHAPTER 15

15-1. Formula solution:

Step 1: *Use the AFN formula to calculate AFN.*

$$AFN = A^*/S_0(\Delta S) - L^*/S_0(\Delta S) - M(S_1)(RR)$$

$$= \frac{\$10,000}{\$10,000}(\$5,000) - \frac{\$1,500}{\$10,000}(\$5,000) - 0.11(\$15,000)(0.4)$$

$$= 1(\$5,000) - 0.15(\$5,000) - 0.11(\$15,000)(0.4)$$

$$= \$5,000 - \$750 - \$660 = \$3,590.$$

Step 2: *Calculate the new account levels for current assets and current liabilities.*

Current assets will increase by ($7,000/$10,000)($15,000) = $10,500.

The AFN will be funded using short-term debt.

Current liabilities will increase to:

A/P + Accrued liabilities = ($1,500/$10,000)($15,000)	= $2,250
S-T Debt = $2,000 + $3,590	= _5,590_
Total C.L.	= $7,840

Step 3: *Calculate the new current ratio.*

New current ratio = $10,500/$7,840 = 1.34.

15-2. Construct a partial projected income statement and balance sheet:

	Last Year	Forecast Basis[a]	First Pass	AFN	Second Pass
EBIT	$ 240,000	×1.10	$ 264,000		
Interest	80,000		80,000		
EBT	$ 160,000		$ 184,000		
Taxes (40%)	64,000		73,600		
NI	$ 96,000		$ 110,400		$ 110,400
NI avail. to common	$ 96,000		$ 110,400		
Divs. to common					
(37,800 × $1.27)	48,006	37,800 × $1.40	52,920		
Addition to RE	$ 47,994		$ 57,480		$ 57,480

	Last Year	Forecast Basis[a]	First Pass	AFN	Second Pass
Total assets	$1,100,000	×1.10	$1,210,000		$1,210,000
Accrued liabilities	$ 13,636	0.0182	$ 15,000		$ 15,000
Long-term debt	640,000		640,000	+30,694	670,694
Equity	335,000		335,000	+20,462	355,462
RE	111,364	+57,480[b]	168,844		168,844
Total liab & equity	$1,100,000		$1,158,844		$1,210,000
AFN[c]			$ 51,156		

Notes:
[a]Operating income and assets are increased by 10%. Accrued liabilities are divided by last year's sales to determine the appropriate ratio to apply to next year's sales to calculate next year's account balances.
[b]See income statement.
[c]AFN financing:
   The shortfall will be financed in accordance with the target capital structure.
   Long-term debt $0.60 \times \$51,156 = \$30,694$
   Common stock $0.40 \times \$51,156 = \underline{\ \ 20,462}$
                                    $\underline{\$51,156}$

CHAPTER 16

16-1. Today's price = 1,476,000/105 = $14,057.14.

16-2. **Time line:**

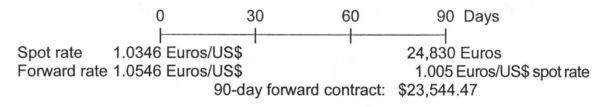

Spot rate   1.0346 Euros/US$ 24,830 Euros
Forward rate 1.0546 Euros/US$ 1.005 Euros/US$ spot rate
            90-day forward contract: $23,544.47

Calculate the cost of the forward contract at the forward rate.

24,830 Euros/(1.0546 Euros/US$) = $23,544.47.

Calculate the cost of purchasing exchange currency at the spot rate in 90 days to satisfy the payable.

24,830 Euros/1.005 Euros/US$ = $24,706.47.

Calculate the savings from the forward market hedge.

$24,706.47 – $23,544.47 = $1,162.00.

16-3. **Time line:**

```
     0                                              6 months
        i = ?
     ├──────────────────────────────────────────────┤
US$:      -9,708.74                    FV = 10,000
Spot rate: 1.42 SWF/US$                Spot rate = 1.324 SWF/US$
SWF:      -13,786.41 SWF               FV = 13,240 SWF
```

PV of T-Bill in SWF is calculated as 9,708.74 × 1.42 = 13,786.41 SWF.

FV of T-Bill in SWF is calculated as 10,000 × 1.324 = 13,240 SWF.

Financial calculator solution:

Calculate the 6-month return to the Swiss investor after she has exchanged US$ for Swiss Francs.

Inputs: N = 1; PV = -13786.41; PMT = 0; FV = 13240.
Output: I = -3.963%. This is a 6-month periodic rate.

Annualized nominal rate of return = -3.963%(2) = -7.93%.

16-4. Spot rate = $\dfrac{P_h}{P_f}$

$= \dfrac{\$899}{856}$ = $1.0502 per euro or $\dfrac{1}{1.0502}$ = 0.9522 euro per U.S. dollar.

16-5. *Convert the annual yields to quarterly yields.*

k_h = U.S. T-Bill (90-day): 5%/4 = 1.25%.
k_f = Swiss: 3.5%/4 = 0.875%.

Calculate the 3-month forward exchange rate.

$\dfrac{\text{Forward rate}}{\text{Spot rate}} = \dfrac{1+k_h}{1+k_f}$

$\dfrac{\text{Forward rate}}{\$0.6935} = \dfrac{1.0125}{1.00875}$

$\dfrac{\text{Forward rate}}{\$0.6935} = 1.003717$

Forward rate = $0.6961.